TOM DOUGLAS'
Seattle Kitchen

TOM DOUGLAS'

Seattle Kitchen

TOM DOUGLAS

WITH DENIS KELLY,
SHELLEY LANCE,
AND DUSKIE ESTES

FOREWORD BY ED LEVINE

WM
WILLIAM MORROW
An Imprint of HarperCollinsPublishers

HarperCollins books may be purchased for educational, business, or sales promotional use. For information please write: Special Markets Department, HarperCollins Publishers Inc., 10 East 53rd Street, New York, NY 10022.

FIRST EDITION

Designed by Leah Carlson-Stanisic

Photographs by Jane Armstrong and Craig Harrold

Printed on acid-free paper

Library of Congress Cataloging-in-Publication Data

Douglas, Tom, 1958–
    Tom Douglas' Seattle kitchen / Tom Douglas with Denis Kelly, Shelley Lance, and Duskie Estes. Foreword by Ed Levine.
        p. cm.
      ISBN 0-688-17242-3
      1. Cookery, American—Pacific Northwest style. 2. Cookery—Washington(State)—Seattle. I. Title.
TX715.2.P32 D68 2000
641.59795—dc21   00-025212

00 01 02 03 04 / QW 10 9 8 7 6 5 4 3 2 1

To all of my family, especially Jackie and Loretta,
for whom traveling and eating are life's choicest cuts

Contents

Acknowledgments

WHO SAYS TOO many cooks spoil the broth? There wouldn't be a book without the dedication and hard work of all the chefs, dining room managers, sous-chefs, bookkeepers, cooks, waiters, bakers, dishwashers, janitors, preppers, bussers, bartenders, and butchers.

All of us do what we do because some talented individuals have dedicated themselves to farm, grow, fish, ferment, distill, or just plain forage the best products. And, equally important, our customers have decided that the way *we* cook these products is worth paying for. For all these folks, I am most thankful and appreciative.

I have surrounded myself with many people I consider tops in the business. People like Pam Leydon, Colleen Kennelley, Steven Steinbock, Shelley Lance, Eric Tanaka, Maureen Miller, Matt Costello, Chris Hunter, Duskie Estes, R. E. Mason, and Gretchen Geisness.

Still others, mentors, have helped form and shape my cooking style: Kenny Raider, Jim Cross, Clarence Cross, Debbie Girts, and Gigi Steinbock.

Even through all the torture of new menu tastings and young vintage selections, Pam Hinckley, Michael Teer, and Peter, Peggy, Molly, and Maddy Dow have rarely complained.

To those whose job it was to get this book off the ground—my agent, Judith Riven, and my editors, Pam Hoenig and Harriet Bell. In addition, Kate Stark, Carrie Weinberg, Leah Carlson-Stanisic, Karen Lumley, Ann Cahn, Ed Levine, Vicky Bijur, Denis Kelly, Jane Armstrong, Craig Harold, Carol Phillips, and Patty Whittman—thanks to you all!

- Gather a group of ten to twelve friends and take the First Thursday Gallery Walk through Pioneer Square. Move on to the Sea Garden in the International District and sit around one of their big tables for a crab feast.

- Visit Macrina Bakery in Belltown and pick up a picnic to take to a summer concert at the pier. Finish with a nightcap at the Virginia Inn.

- Take a round-trip ferry ride from Coleman Dock to Bainbridge Island, sit upstairs with a discreet bottle of wine, and by the time you return to Seattle you'll be ready for the satay bar at Wild Ginger.

- Take in an afternoon baseball game at Safeco Field. Before you go, stop by the nearby Pecos Pit for a sliced brisket BBQ sandwich.

- Reserve a room at the Inn at the Market. Start the day with a brioche and café latte at the Café Campagne. Stroll the cobblestone alleys of the Pike Place Market as you watch it come to life. Have lunch on the sun deck of the Pink Door.

- Stroll the piers at Fishermen's Terminal in the Magnolia neighborhood. When you get hungry, head to Red Mill Burgers on Dravus for a BBQ bacon burger, killer onion rings, and a mocha malt shake.

- Go to the Harvest Vine in the Madison Valley neighborhood for tapas and Rioja.

- Browse the hip shops on Pike and Pine streets (east of the Convention Center). From retro clothes to cool antiques, this unique Seattle neighborhood is also home to the Petroleum Museum. Get your hair cut at Rudy's. Try the margaritas at Bimbo's.

- Rent a kayak and paddle around Lake Union; dodge the seaplanes as you cruise by houseboats, Gasworks Park, and Dale Chihuly's glass studio. Stop for pupus at any of the dozens of waterfront restaurants that ring the lake.

- Work your way through Uwajimaya and stock up on sushi to go for a picnic at Volunteer Park, where the fabulous Seattle Asian Art Museum and Conservatory is located.

Foreword

Tom Douglas loves to eat as much as I do. That's saying (and eating) a lot. He says it's "R and D" (research and development) when he orders half a menu's worth of food for the two of us, and while it might be, I think the man just likes to chow down. And though you might think that all famous chefs love to eat, as someone who's done more than his fair share of hanging out with well-known chefs, I can report that this is not necessarily so.

How passionate is Tom about food? The first time I hung out with Tom was five years ago in Boston, where we were both attending a Northwest Airlines consulting chefs meeting. Tom and I set off for Biba, Lydia Shire and Susan Regis's famed Back Bay gastronomic temple. Though there were only two of us, Tom did not hesitate to order at least eight appetizers and eight main courses. When I opined that perhaps this was excessive (it was, I think, the first and only time I have ever accused someone of being excessive when it came to ordering in a restaurant), he waved me off with that trademark Douglas smile and laugh. "R and D, Ed. R and D. How else am I going to find out what Lydia and Susan's food is all about? Who knows when I'll get back to Boston next?" I actually don't even remember much of what we ate that night (except for a lobster pizza), but I do remember thinking I had met a kindred spirit, a food soul mate, a passionate, unpretentious *fresser* who, like me, spends his life in endless pursuit of the good stuff.

His pursuit of the good stuff, his never-ending "R and D" excursions, are reflected in Tom's earthy, deeply flavored cooking. His excursions into the Asian communities of Seattle inspired his lobster and shiitake mushroom potstickers and one of my favorite Tom Douglas dishes of all time, his kasu cod marinated in sake lees. Yet his respect for Thai, Vietnamese, and Japanese food means his fusion cooking never veers into "confusion" food territory.

Tom reveres the seafood plucked from the frigid waters in and around Seattle, and shows his reverence in the irresistible yet simple ways he cooks with it. Sitting in his restaurant the Palace Kitchen one gorgeous summer evening, I found myself devouring a huge platter of Dungeness crabs with ginger and lemongrass. My dining companions that night included bread baker and pastry chef Nancy Silverton of La Brea Bakery and Campanile fame. We just kept eating and eating, even though we were both full from the ten other dishes Tom had already sent out. Finally Nancy turned to me and said, "This is one of the best things I have ever tasted." And so it was.

Tom and I have eaten our way through quite a number of cities together. And though I pride myself on my eating stamina, I have never figured out a way to keep up with Tom. The man is a veritable foodie marathoner. We once met in San Francisco to attend the Fancy Food show together. We started our gastronomic journey that night at Roti, Cindy Pawlcyn's rotisserie palace near the financial district. We ate lightly (for us, that is), four appetizers and four main courses. We chatted about the kind of rotisseries the restaurant was utilizing, the duck and chicken we were eating, and about where else we might eat that night.

We hit Boulevard next and once again had a light repast of three or four appetizers and a half-dozen main courses. We both love Nancy Oakes's Wolfgang Puck-meets-Betty Crocker cooking, so although I knew we were not even at the midpoint of our gastronomic journey that night, I found myself eating more of the food than I should have. Tom urged me to go lightly on the dishes in front of us, as he wanted me to save room for the pizza in North Beach he planned to eat next. I realized about halfway through our meal at Boulevard that I was probably not going to be able to accompany Tom to North Beach (not to mention the two or three other places he planned to hit that night). I was simply too full and too tired, given the fact that I had just flown in from New York that day, so my body clock thought it was midnight instead of nine P.M. "I know you're going to punk out on me, you wuss," said Tom with a twinkle in his eye. He was right. I headed for the hotel, and he headed off to North Beach.

After eating our way through San Francisco (and many other cities, for that matter) together, it has become clear that Tom and I share many food passions: steak, short ribs, barbecue, and pork in its many and varied forms. We have eaten all of these things in copious portions at haute cuisine restaurants and barbecue joints all over the country. Tom is no food snob, as any reader of *Tom Douglas' Seattle Kitchen* will find out. He loves to cook with foie gras and dumplings and ribs equally. So you won't have to look too hard in this book to find elemental things like maple-cured pork roast and long-bone short ribs. And that tells you everything you need to know about Tom Douglas' food.

Tom Douglas is blessed many times over. He has a wife who is talented, beautiful, and a soul mate to boot; a daughter who absolutely floors me and my wife with her presence, poise, and beauty every time we see her; three wonderful restaurants where I have eaten very well indeed; a talent and a passion for eating, cooking, and living that I marvel at; and now, a book that will enable readers to get to know the Tom Douglas I am privileged already to know. Reading the book won't be quite as much fun as consuming a ten-course feast at one of his restaurants or going on an eating adventure with Tom, but it will have to do until we meet up again for another 10,000-calorie "R and D" excursion.

—*Ed Levine*

Introduction

WHAT ATTRACTS PEOPLE to Seattle is what drew me here in the first place: the Seattle Spirit—a free-wheeling attitude that celebrates life and good times and borrows, absorbs, transforms, and enjoys whatever flows our way. We in Seattle are perched on the edge of the continent and are a booming seaport for Asia and Alaska, with Puget Sound teeming with fish and seafood at our doorstep and fertile valleys at our backs. Sure, it rains a lot up here, but who cares? That rain and the warm Japanese current that sweeps in close to the shore give us our year-round greenery and wonderful natural resources. All that water just means more fish on the plate and greens to garnish it with. And besides, it makes my hair curly.

Seattle's always been a boom town, from the days of Henry Yesler's Skid Road, which slid logs down to the docks, to the Alaska Gold Rush fueled by Seattle merchants, to Boeing and Microsoft and Starbucks today. It boasts the surreal and downright goofy Space Needle and breathtaking vistas of the Olympic Mountains across the Sound. We have museums that honor Jimi Hendrix and Leonardo Da Vinci, millionaires in T-shirts and jeans, and an espresso stand on every corner. And with its economic and cultural boom, Seattle has become the center of a new style of cooking—eclectic, lively, and constantly changing.

I've lived here for close to twenty-five years and I was lucky to get here when I did. It was a time when young West Coast chefs were breaking free of the "fine dining" tradition of tired Continental classics and looking to local resources to create a new style of cooking. I started cooking using the fresh fish and seafood we have in abundance, our beautiful ripe fruits and berries, local lamb and beef, wine from the Yakima Valley, ale from Redhook in the Ballard district, and all the great fresh produce and mushrooms and cheese and eggs and olives and honey from the lush countryside that surrounds Seattle.

I was especially lucky early on to discover and develop a love and respect for the cooking of the Asian communities that make up much of Seattle's population. The International District is home to great chefs and food merchants. At the market Uwajimaya, "exotic" ingredients become ordinary—you can walk down the aisles and find virtually any product, from live eels and still-swimming spot prawns to togarishi pepper, shiso leaves, and fresh young ginger. Vietnamese and other Southeast Asian immigrants arrived in Seattle in droves just about when I did and their spicy, clean-flavored cooking is a constant inspiration. To this day, my favorite lunch is the impeccably pure and delicious *phò*—beef noodle soup—made at the tiny Saigon Restaurant in Pike Place Market.

I get all of my fish and many of my best ideas from friends like Harry Yoshimura of the Mutual Fish Company. When you stand in the cutting room at Mutual Fish among glistening, perfectly fresh salmon, grouper, black cod, and halibut, you cannot help but be awed by the reverence and respect with which the fish is handled and shipped. When Harry says buy, I buy. When Harry says cook it this way, we argue a bit, and then I cook it his way. At Dahlia Lounge, every day we feature a Harry Yoshimura's Fish Selection.

Seattle is a place where opposites come together: land and sea, mountains and valleys, East and West. I think I've been permanently altered by this as a person and as a cook—the Pacific Ocean and Puget Sound, the towering Olympics and the Cascades, the eastern Washington desert, the far-reaching tentacles of Asia and Alaska—they all come together here and in my cooking, along with traditions from my own and my Spokane-born wife Jackie's family. Our Seattle-native daughter Loretta's heritage combines Delaware, Washington, Scotland, Ireland, Idaho, Italy, and Greece—Grandma D'Amico's fennel sausages drying in her attic, and her pasta making all Sunday afternoon, along with Grandma Fogarty's corned beef and cabbage and my neighbor Mr. Joe's tomato and bacon gravy. They are all in the food I cook.

COOKING IN SEATTLE

I came to Seattle with a love of food and the sea, a six-month apprenticeship as a line cook at the Hotel Dupont in Delaware, and not much else. I was eighteen years old, fresh from the Chesapeake Bay region where I'd grown up on Southern home cooking—roast chicken and dumplings, Mom's pot roast, fresh greens from the garden, country ham with grits, sweet peach cobbler with fresh cream. And, of course, there was seafood: blue crab cooked every which way, from crabcakes to she-crab soup, from boiled shrimp flavored with Old Bay Seasoning to tender steamed clams and succulent chowders. My first morning in town I headed down the hill toward the waterfront to see this Pike Place Market I'd been hearing so much about.

It was early morning. I could see farmers unloading their trucks and setting up tables, piling up lettuce and kale, collards and kohlrabi, stacking carrots and beets alongside heaps of green beans, wax beans, and yellow onions. I was beginning my Seattle education: The fertile volcanic soil and the long, temperate growing season and (yes) all that rain make the valleys to the east, north, and south of the city some of the best regions for growing great fruit and vegetables virtually year-round.

As I walked farther into the market, I got my first glimpse of the sea harvest that makes Seattle such a wonderful food city: Heaps of fresh-caught silver salmon and fat chinooks were piled up everywhere. The countermen were hawking their fish, holding them up for shoppers to see, tossing them back to the guys behind the fish case to slice and fillet. And it wasn't just salmon that caught my eye: two-hundred-pound halibut with flat, pale bellies and bulging eyes, sea bass and grouper, ling cod and black cod, neat stacks of pink steamed shrimp, bins of clams, from tiny steamers to huge geoducks, and rough-shelled oysters of every size and kind.

And then there were the crabs: These plump, claw-waving Dungeness weighing two or three pounds each were nothing like the five-to-a-pound blue crabs I grew up on. They were monsters. I wondered how they tasted—and soon found out. An Italian counterman was handing out hunks of steamed cracked crab to shoppers, chumming the crowd. I got in line and tasted my first Dungeness: sweet and succulent with the briny taste of the sea.

Over the next few years I worked in restaurants in downtown Seattle and out on Bainbridge Island. I started to eat my way through Seattle's neighborhoods, assisted by some good friends and fellow chefs, many of them still working with me today. We had a great time, cooking up a storm all day and half the night. After work we set out for the International District to feast at Chinese seafood houses or for late-night pasta dinners at Italian trattorias. I once figured that some nights I was spending more money in restaurants than I paid for a month's rent. But, I thought, what the hell, it's better to live in a hovel and eat rich, than to have a palace and eat poor.

I want food to taste good, above all, and I'm happy to borrow from anybody or any tradition to achieve it. In my opinion, this is what the Seattle style is all about. American cooking is the cooking of immigrants, wherever they're from. The first immigrants to Seattle were Native Americans who took advantage of the region's rich resources to live well and create a great culture based on the sea. Then came the first settlers, Doc Maynard and Henry Yesler and the Terrys—early entrepreneurs who founded the city on logging, salmon, and trade. They brought with them the English tradition of meat and potatoes and apple pie that some think defines American food. Later waves of immigrants from Scandinavia, Italy, Latin America, and, especially, Asia gave us here in Seattle the opportunity to create our own distinctive style of cooking.

In 1989, I opened the Dahlia Lounge in downtown Seattle. The décor is right out of the 1940s or '50s, with a neon café sign in the middle of the room, Chinese-red walls and ceiling, brocade banquettes, and fish-shaped shades over the lights. The Dahlia Lounge has been going strong since day one and has become a destination for diners who want flavor and originality. A Seattle institution, the Dahlia Lounge has won wide acclaim regionally and nationally, including the James Beard Association Award for Best Northwest Chef in 1994. In 1995, with my wife and business partner, Jackie Cross, I opened our second restaurant, Etta's Seafood, near the Pike Place Market in the location once occupied by Café Sport (where I used to be chef). Etta's, named after our daughter, Loretta, showcases the best and freshest local seafood and continues the creative amalgam of traditions and flavors that is the signature of Seattle cooking. What we wanted at Etta's was a good, old-fashioned neighborhood joint where you could have brunch or lunch or dinner in a relaxed atmosphere with the drink of your choice. Pike Place Market is not just a market—it's a neighborhood all its own, with condos and hardware stores, gardening shops, senior centers, and food banks. We wanted Etta's to fit in; so we kept the décor simple, with big windows opening out onto the market, sturdy wood tables and booths, and a hefty full bar with plenty of stools.

In 1996, Jackie and I opened our third restaurant, Palace Kitchen, to satisfy my craving for roast meat and hearty food. At the Palace diners can sit at large tables surrounding our huge grill, or at the massive tiled bar, and watch whole maple-cured pork loins or prime rib roasts, crusted with rosemary and garlic, turn on the spit over an apple-wood fire.

And the Palace Kitchen really *is* a huge open kitchen where we bake all the bread and pastry for our restaurants. We also prepare our own pasta, sausage, fresh chèvre, and ice cream there. Staff from all three restaurants hang out in the kitchen and try out new recipes and ideas. We taste and argue and cook together at the Palace all day long (it's only open for dinner), all the while giving thanks to the goddess of prep and our super prepsters for the huge kitchen. It's a cook's dream and our own research laboratory and playground.

With this book, we hope to communicate our experience of Seattle, to know why it is that Seattle consistently ranks in the top ten most livable cities year after year. We want to share our thriving food scene with you—you can get on a plane and come see us or you can use this book to create your own "Seattle" in your kitchen. All of the recipes are easy to use and many Chinese, Japanese, and Southeast Asian ingredients, such as soy, fresh ginger, *panko* (Japanese bread crumbs), Japanese *togarashi* pepper, fish sauce, etc., are available in markets all over the country. If you can't find an ingredient locally, we provide you with mail-order sources at the end of the book.

Shoppin'

SEATTLE HAS PLENTY of great neighborhoods for food, but the heart and soul of food in Seattle is the Pike Place Market, where all the fresh products of the region seem to gather every morning. Pike Place Market is a neighborhood in itself; it's where I started out eating and learning about and loving the food of Seattle. I don't do much buying there anymore—I usually buy direct from farmers and other suppliers—but the market still acts as my encyclopedia of food. It's where I can find out what's ripe, what's in season, what the prices are; and where I get many of my ideas for dishes to put on my menus. I talk to farmers every morning to find out how their crops are doing, and I make contact with sources for the restaurant kitchens. Most of the farmers I buy from, I talk to first at Pike Place Market.

The market is where I start my day. I love walking the newly hosed-down streets at seven or eight A.M. when the stalls are still setting up. I've been looking at the same faces for twenty-five years now and talking about what's fresh today with the same growers and suppliers. I always stop at the original Starbucks for my first shot of espresso. I pick up a couple of almond croissants at Le Panier and say hello to Christy, who has the best smile in the market.

I usually walk through the high stalls first, permanent produce stands all along the main arcade, and check in with Frank Gonzales at Frank's produce stand. Frank comes from generations of farmers down in Kent Valley, southeast of Seattle, and offers the freshest produce around and plenty of sound advice about what's good in the market.

Then I check out the low stalls on the main floor of the open market that are rented for the day by local farmers, most with only a specialty item like cherries or honey or pea

Picture-perfect produce at the Pike Place Market

until our own asparagus arrive in the farmers' low stalls and then pig out until they're gone, eating them every which way but in ice cream. So, as the spring progresses, I look for asparagus from Ellensburg, fresh new hop shoots from Yakima, baby turnips, and tiny fresh greens from the Lombricis in Skagit Valley.

The stone fruits that the Yakima and Wenatchee valleys are justly famous for arrive in late spring and early summer: cherries—Bings, Rainiers, sour cherries, Lamberts. And God knows how many varieties of plums: deep purple damsons, blue-skinned Italian plums, yellow friar plums, dark, plump Santa Rosas. We turn these ripe, colorful fruits into cobblers, pies, tarts, and in many chutneys and savory relishes.

In midsummer the squash arrive—zucchini and its relative, zuchetta, summer squash and pattypans—and tons of peppers. Beans of every color show up: green, yellow, cranberry. Heirloom squash—butternut, sugarpie pumpkins, kabochas—are cooked up into sautés, soups, fritters, and pies all season long. When the first berries come out each summer, I have friends at the market who show up once a year with raspberries or blackberries or blueberries, marionberries or gooseberries. I taste their berries, talk with them, and find out the season's news and how the year's been going. Market friendships carry over season to season, like an old pal you have on the other coast who you only see once in a while.

Late summer brings ripe tomatoes—finally—and we gorge on them. We don't use tomatoes much the rest of the year, but wait for their brief period of ripeness here in the Northwest. As a result of growing up in Delaware, though, with its tradition of tasty fried green tomatoes, a lot of green

vines. I've discovered many unusual ethnic ingredients here.

In the spring I start looking for young Walla Walla spring or salad onions. Walla Wallas are the sweetest onions grown, and I (chauvinistically) think they are superior to Vidalia, Maui, or other designer onions. During the season, shoppers can buy dried Walla Wallas and ship them home. When they're at their peak, we use Walla Walla onions every way we can think of: in salads, grilled, or made into confits and relishes.

Frankly, I don't believe in trying to extend the season. For example, in the spring, when the first California asparagus show up in the high-stall produce stands, some chefs want to jump into them right away. I'd rather wait

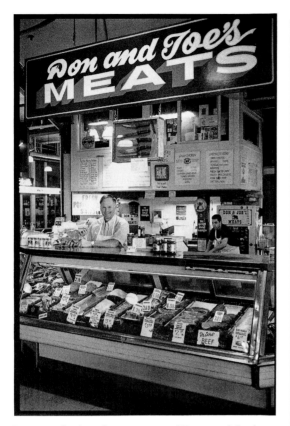

Donny, the butcher-owner of Don and Joe's Meats

Market fishmongers with a crate of wild Pacific salmon

tomatoes go into sautés, grills, and relishes.

I feel the same way about corn in September. My philosophy is: eat it when you've got it, enjoy the harvest when it's here. Eat local produce when it's at its best and ripest.

I usually say hello to Donnie, the butcher, at Don and Joe's Meats, and, if I have guests coming, I pick up a dry-aged steak or lamb leg for a backyard barbecue. These guys get whole carcasses from local feedlots, cut them up, and age the meat themselves. If you want to eat great meat at home, always get to know the meat man. There's a premium butcher shop in just about any city or town, and it pays to find it. At Don and Joe's, I also like to check on sales of my Rub

with Love Spice Rubs: Donnie carries them and gives plenty of advice on how to use them to season and cook the premium meats he offers.

I always enjoy stopping by Nancy Nipples Creamery for the highest-butterfat cream and silky sweet butter. Just about all the regional cheesemakers can be found here: I use many of their cheeses in my restaurants, and we make our own chevre from Bainbridge Island goat's milk just across the Sound from Pike Place Market.

Even though Harry Yoshimura at Mutual Fish provides all our fish, I still browse other fish markets to see who's got what, to see which fish or shellfish are looking good, and to check on what's in season—whether the

Michael Teer carries the city's largest selection of Northwest wines at Pike and Western Wine Shop

Dungeness crab is the smaller, two-pound Washington crab, or the bigger, meatier Alaskan Dungeness, which grows up to four pounds. The razor clam season lasts only a day or two a year, and local singing scallops are delicious but hard to find and very perishable. Checking the fishmongers also tells me which salmon types are available and which river is running—the Quinault River on the Olympic Peninsula, the Campbell River, in Vancouver Island, the Columbia River, or the Copper River in Alaska, from which is fished the most prized, fattiest, and richest salmon of all. I can also see which species are in the market: kings and sockeyes, chum and silvers, or dog salmon. I often pick up some squaw candy—heavily smoked, brown sugar—cured salmon belly—to nibble on while walking.

I poke my head in the door of Bavarian Smoked Meats to check on what's in the deli case: sauerkraut, *landjaeger* sausage, the tastiest bacon I've ever eaten. They smoke their own ham and *kassler* (smoked pork loin), and make all their sausages and prepared meats, which I use at home and in my restaurants. And I don't throw out any bacon fat, ham fat, duck fat, or chicken fat. I use it to cook fried potatoes for extra flavor and usually end up with less cholesterol than butter. At Palace Kitchen we often spit-roast lamb or duck over a pan full of potatoes to catch the juices and fat. And at Etta's we use a little bacon fat in our hash browns, eggs, or pasta dishes.

After looking at all that food, I'm usually ready for a bowl of steaming *phò* or braised tofu at the Saigon Restaurant lunch counter. Many folks, hungry and staggering under the weight of the bags of goodies they have bought, come to Etta's Seafood for one of our famous Bloody Marys with fresh-grated horseradish and house-pickled Yakima Valley asparagus, and, on the side, some fried calamari with smoky paprika sauce.

Shoppers can find the best current releases of Northwest wines at Pike and Western Wine Shop. It's a great place to finish your shopping. Mike Teer, the proprietor, will look in your bag, check out your meat or fish or produce, and match the food up with Northwest wine choices. Often you can taste wines to see if you agree with him.

Classic barbecued duck at King's BBQ in Chinatown

Much of our food is influenced by Asian and Pacific cooking. After my visit to Pike Place Market, I usually take a quick tour of the International District to see what's in the Chinese markets. Most of the time I pick up some lacquered roast duck or *char su*—barbecued marinated pork—for the kitchen crew to nibble on while while we work out new dishes. These roasted and barbecued Chinese meats and poultry, along with the sweet and savory sausage *lup chong*, provide great flavor to soups, vegetables, and other dishes. They are a good example of the Chinese philosophy of treating meat as a condiment, not as a main course. Try some char su sliced into a spicy clam soup with a few thin slices of pickled ginger. My favorite place for Chinese barbecue is King's BBQ, just across from my next stop, the Uwajimaya Market in the center of the International District.

This is the largest Asian market in the United States. Uwajimaya Market draws customers from all over the state and does a large mail-order business (see Sources, page 260). Entering the huge, teeming supermarket is like walking into a living museum of Asian culture. The market is swarming with people speaking Japanese, Chinese, Vietnamese, Thai, Tagalog. Everybody's there, from grandmas to tiny tots, all ages, everybody mixing together, everybody busy and headed somewhere.

Once through the door, you fall right into the pickle section, with its pickled daikon, salted plums, kim chi, preserved seaweed, pickled quail eggs, dried squid and shrimp and radish and eggplant, and even *bêches-de-mer,* or dried sea slugs. Virtually anything organic that can be salted, pickled, dried, or otherwise preserved can be found on the crowded shelves.

The produce department has every kind of produce imaginable: fresh daikon, lotus root, burdock root, taro. There are different kinds of eggplants: little white Thai eggplants, which we like to pickle; fat black globe eggplants that are great when grilled; long purple Chinese eggplants that are wonderful sautéed. You can find all sorts of greens: Chinese mustard, bok choy, *choy sum, yow choy,* Chinese broccoli, and Napa cabbage. Fresh water chestnuts are piled up next to chrysan-

Live crawfish straight from Lake Washington

PHÒ BAC

It's pink, crowded, greasy, it smells funky, it's fast, cheap, hot, fresh, delicious, it's Seattle's (and perhaps the world's) best bowl of soup, it's $4.95. Vietnamese fast food at Phò Bac, a tiny restaurant in Seattle's International District, is perhaps the greatest food for the price you'll ever find. Order the king-size beef-brisket noodles for the main course and Vietnamese coffee for dessert and you'll be back on the street in only fifteen minutes, stuffed, happy, and only five bucks poorer.

1314 S. Jackson Street, Seattle
(206) 323-4387

themum leaves, luffa squash with fuzzy melons, kabocha squash beside heaps of bean, radish, kiware, pea, and alfalfa sprouts.

Mushrooms and fungi of every sort, fresh and dried, are piled up in boxes or arranged on shelves and racks: shiitakes, of course, but also cloud-ear fungus and oyster mushrooms alongside fragrant matsutakes, monkey-head fungus, and enokis.

I love to wander around Uwajimaya to get ideas for new dishes. Once I found myself staring at a huge pile of fresh sugar cane. The next day I served customers what has become a favorite seasonal dish: tangy shrimp sausage wrapped around pieces of the sweet cane and grilled.

Then there are the noodles. There are four noodlemakers in Seattle's International District. You can find just about any variety at Uwajimaya—fresh or dried wheat noodles, rice noodles, mung-bean-flour noodles, buckwheat noodles, thin noodles, fat noodles, wide noodles, and narrow noodles, along with dim sum wrappers, wonton skins, dumplings, pancakes, spring rolls, and bean curd sheets. You can even find *cha soba*, buckwheat noodles made with green tea.

The shelves are stacked with every kind of soy sauce from light and delicate to dark and heavy. My favorite is a dark, rich Japanese soy made on the slopes of Mount Fuji. Another sauce we use often is mushroom soy sauce flavored with enoki (straw mushrooms).

In my basket one summer day I had spicy fried peas with wasabi, which Jackie and I like to eat with cold beer on the deck; rice crackers for Loretta, who loves them anytime; *nori*-wrapped rice crackers; rice candies in ten different shapes and forms for a birthday party; three types of fermented black beans;

COMPOSED SOUPS—THEY'RE PHO ME

Acomposed soup is one in which the bite-size parts are prepared separately, then arranged and put together to order. It is more than a good broth, with a lot of garnishes or condiments that add texture or serve as filler. The components are integral to the flavor, just like seasoning. They pull the entire dish together and add depth. The *lup chong* and seaweed salad in the Tiny Clam and Seaweed Soup (page 36) serve this purpose.

Phò is a Vietnamese composed soup that is a meal in a bowl, often served with a fresh salad of bean sprouts and Thai basil on top. The meat is sliced thin and arranged in a bowl with the other elements, then a hot flavorful broth is poured over. The hot broth cooks the raw meat. Udon with Sea Scallops in Miso Broth (page 70) uses a similar technique.

a couple of thousand-year-old eggs (not really a thousand years old, but funky enough to try on a squeamish friend); two bottles of Asian fish sauce, a sampling of kim chis—Napa cabbage, lotus root, garlic, eggplant, carrot, and potato—and piles of Asian greens to braise with some country-style pork ribs.

Not very far from Uwajimaya and the International District is Harry Yoshimura's Mutual Fish. In the restaurant business and at home, too, it's important to develop a relationship with your food purveyors. That means that you won't always be shopping for the best price, but that you'll shop for quality. There's always a better price somewhere, but when you develop a relationship with someone you can be sure he's going to be selling you his best stuff. This is especially true for fish and seafood, where freshness and quality are paramount.

We buy all of our seafood and fish from Harry Yoshimura. Over the last twenty years, we've spent well over $5 million at Mutual Fish and have never had to send back one piece of fish. This is the kind of relationship you want to establish, hopefully for less than millions of dollars. But spending money is worth it if you can be guaranteed quality.

When you walk into Mutual Fish, the first thing you smell is the ocean, clean and fresh. There is no fishy smell. The live tanks are teeming with lively pink spot prawns, brooding crabs, and green Maine lobsters clacking their claws. Instead of oysters being stored in a burlap bag somewhere, here they are kept in fresh salt water so that they stay clean, plump, and fresh. Clams and mussels also stay in clean, circulating salt water; most fish shops just pack them in ice.

I love to walk into Mutual's immense reefers (refrigerators). You see piles of huge halibut from Alaska; salmon of every type, size, and shape, packed in shaved ice; deep red 30-pound loins from 150-pound tunas ready to slice into sushi and sashimi; beautiful deep-sea yellow-eyed rockfish from the Bering Sea; piles of tiny steamed octopus from the Sea of Japan; glistening black cod from the Washington coast, marinating in *kasu zuke* (sake lees); and mountains of silvery smelt from Puget Sound.

Harry sells *tobiko* (flying fish roe), which is a natural golden orange in color, but he also sells Japanese tobiko blended with wasabi (green) or red chile (red) or squid ink (black). These varied tobikos provide a perfect crunchy texture to a dish and are beauti-

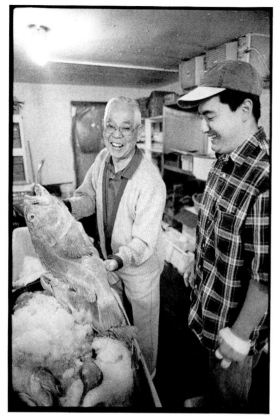

Dick and Kevin Yoshimura at Mutual Fish

Harry's dad, or Kevin, Harry's son, or Lisa, Harry's sister, or Harry himself. They'll tell you how to get the best seafood you'll ever find (they'll package it and ship it anywhere in the world). And don't forget to grab a box of strawberry-ice-cream *mochi* sweet rice balls for the trip home, like I do.

Another influence on Seattle cooking, and one that's really big in my neighborhood, the Ballard section across the canal from downtown, is Scandinavian food. Logging and fishing were big industries in early Seattle, and many Swedes, Norwegians, and Danes came to the Northwest area. Their almost constant need for coffee is most likely the source of our coffee mania. Olsen's Scandinavian Foods is one of my favorite stops for *lefsa* (homemade potato flatbread), tasty dried lamb legs, spiced lamb sausages, and pickled herring. Olsen's is great for snacks and a good source for menu ideas.

And so my shopping day continues. I move around the city, looking at what's in the markets, tasting old favorites and finding new ones, talking to the people who can supply me with the fresh, authentic food I want to serve in my restaurants.

Seattle cooking is based on the great resources—natural and human—of our region. And you should be able to find similar high-quality ingredients and the people who sell them in your own hometown. In our recipes we'll give suggestions that will enable you to make the dish using local ingredients. If you can't find Dungeness crab or black cod, we'll tell you how to substitute regional products. The key here is to go shopping the way I do: look and taste and talk to purveyors of good, honest food. It's up to you to find suppliers of the best bread and cheese, to seek out the finest butchers, fishmongers, and farmers in your city or town. A good place to start is in

ful to see atop a mound of sliced raw tuna or grilled halibut. We use them often in all our restaurants; they really liven up any fish or seafood dish.

Harry carries just about any seafood that's available on a given day in Seattle. If it's out there, you can buy it: long-necked geoducks; lobsters from Maine or Mexico; clams and oysters and mussels of all types; tilapia, or farm perch; salmon; sea bass; eels in season; periwinkles; spot prawns; tiger prawns; sushi-grade tuna, whole or presliced.

Harry's my fish guru: When there are no crabs around, he tells me why, and when there are tons of crabs around, he gets me the best he can find. So when you're in Seattle, stop by Mutual Fish and talk to Dick, ethnic neighborhoods—Chinese, Japanese, Italian, Latino—where customers demand the freshest and tastiest food every day. Farmer's markets are excellent places to find high-quality produce, homemade cheese, and hand-baked bread, and even fresh fish, sausages, and meats. In the Seattle area (and in many parts of the country), a short drive from the city there are farmers who sell their products to the public on a seasonal basis.

So, while we'd love to see you here in Seattle and will be glad to greet you at our restaurants, you don't have to visit our city to use this book. It's best to seek out purveyors of high-quality food, but, if you can't find what you want, check the Sources section in the back of the book (page 260) and order by mail.

SEATTLE'S ETHNIC MARKETS

Ethnic markets are the soul of any great city. The steady increase in the immigrant population of Seattle has blessed us with plenty of soul. Here are some of our favorite markets.

MEXICAN
The Mexican Grocery
1914 Pike Place, Seattle
(206) 441-1147

SOUTH AND CENTRAL AMERICAN
El Mercado Latino
1514 Pike Place, Seattle
(206) 623-3240

Salvadoran Bakery
1719 S.W. Roxbury Street, Seattle
(206) 762-4046

SPANISH
The Spanish Table
1427 Western Avenue, Seattle
(206) 682-2827
Fax: (206) 682-2814

GERMAN
Bavarian Meats
1920 Pike Place, Seattle
(206) 441-0942

SCANDINAVIAN
Olsen's Scandinavian Foods
2248 N.W. Market Street, Seattle
(206) 783-8288

VIETNAMESE
Viet Wah Supermarket
1032 S. Jackson Street, Seattle
(206) 329-1399 and (206) 328-3557
Fax: (206) 328-6334

JAPANESE/PAN-ASIAN
Uwajimaya
519 6th Street at King Street, Seattle
(206) 624-6248

Maruta Shoten
1024 S. Bailey Street, Seattle
(206) 767-5002

ITALIAN
De Laurenti
1435 First Avenue, Seattle
(206) 622-0141

KOREAN

Center Oriental Foods
9641 15th Avenue S.W., Seattle
(206) 762-5620

RUSSIAN

Ukraine International Foods
10410-C Greenwood Avenue N., Seattle
(206) 781-0619

AFRICAN

Amy's Mercado
2922 E. Cherry Street, Seattle
(206) 324-2527

SPICES FROM AROUND THE WORLD

World Spice
1509 Western Avenue, Seattle
(206) 682-7274
Fax: (206) 622-7564

Sacks of rice in the International District

Vinh Pham elegantly stir-fries your
lunch at the Saigon Restaurant.

Ingredients

GOOD FOOD BEGINS at the supermarket, farmstand, or warehouse club. If you don't buy high-quality ingredients, it's pretty darn hard to make a good meal. Be very picky. Taste the butter. Does it have good farm flavor, or does it just have a funny commer-

cial on TV? Taste your favorite olive oil against a few others. Is it the cheapest or does it taste the best? Smell the spices on your shelf. Are they robust and bursting with aromas or are they flat and listless from sitting on the shelves year after year? These are the basics, the complements to the very expensive cuts of meat and fish you shop for so carefully. Reevaluate your pantry. If you're going to take the time to cook soul-satisfying food, give yourself a fighting chance to make the best of your talents.

Butter: I use unsalted butter. It's usually fresher, and it lets you control the seasoning of your dish. You can adjust the amount of salt to your taste.

Bread: We use rustic, European-style bread with a dense crumb and a good heavy crust on the table in our restaurants and in most of our dishes (such as Tuscan Bread Salad with Fresh Mozzarella and Basil, page 178). A light French loaf is perfect for a poorboy-style Cornmeal-Fried Oyster Sandwich with Lemon Tartar Sauce (page 64).

Cheese: Cheese is integral to our cooking. We make our own fresh chèvre and buy handcrafted cheeses from Northwestern and other regional cheesemakers. Try some cheeses made in your area. The king in my book, though, is still Parmigiano-Reggiano; freshly cut from the center of the round, it makes great eating and, of course, it's the perfect dry cheese for grating. A delicious American grating cheese is the Vella Cheese Company's Dry Jack from Sonoma, California: a nutty cheese whose surface is rubbed with cocoa and pepper.

Chiles: The heat may vary in chiles, even of the same type, so taste them first. Most of the heat is in the seeds, so remove them if you want to tone down the effect. Be careful when handling hot chiles: Wear rubber gloves or wash your hands immediately after working with them. Above all, don't touch your eyes after handling hot chiles. Chiles range from very hot habaneros and piquins to pretty hot serranos, jalapeños, and dried and smoked chipotles, to mild (sometimes) poblanos and Anaheims.

Chocolate/Cocoa: Semisweet chocolate and cocoa are slightly sweeter than bittersweet, and either can be used in the recipes in this book. Valrhona, Sharffen-Berger, and Callebaut chocolates are all good brands. Buy the best white chocolate you can find; we use Callebaut. I like premium unsweetened cocoas, like Valrhona, which are very dark and flavorful.

Herbs: We prefer to use fresh herbs in our recipes. Most herbs are available fresh in supermarkets and produce stands. You can sometimes use a smaller quantity of dried herbs, such as rosemary or thyme. But there is no dried substitute for fresh parsley, mint, cilantro, or basil.

Mushrooms: Make sure you buy wild mushrooms from somebody you trust. Don't take any chances and don't experiment with anything that is not familiar. Farmed "wild" mushrooms, like shiitake and oyster mushrooms, and others that people think are wild, such as portobello, are widely available and give excellent results. I prefer these to common white mushrooms, but use them if others are not available. To prepare mushrooms, wipe them with a damp cloth and trim away tough stems.

Olive oil: There are so many to choose from. I like Italian oils, but there are also excellent ones from California, Spain, Morocco, and other regions of the world. I use estate-bottled, vintage-dated, extra virgin olive oils for seasoning salads, meats, and soups, and a pure olive oil with mild olive flavor for searing or panfrying.

Salt: We use kosher salt in our kitchens and our recipes for two reasons: It has a less harsh and salty taste than table salt and it is

---

FINISHING SALTS

A finishing salt brightens the flavor of a dish at the last moment before it is served. It is especially effective sprinkled on grilled or roasted meat or poultry. Slice the meat, fan the slices out, and sprinkle them lightly with a finishing salt. You'll get seasoning in every bite. (The interior of a piece of meat would otherwise be unseasoned.)

We use sea salt as a finishing salt, sometimes mixed with a little bit of spice, such as toasted and crushed fennel seeds or toasted and ground star anise pods. Use only a little spice, though; subtlety is key here; a generous pinch in ¼ cup of salt is enough. Instead of spice, add a bit of chopped herb that complements your meat or poultry. One-half teaspoon finely chopped fresh tarragon mixed into ¼ cup of salt would be nice with roasted chicken, for example.

easier to add by hand (because it is coarser and you can feel its texture better), just as professional cooks do. Kosher salt is about half as salty as regular salt, so if you decide to use table salt in our recipes, use less and taste carefully. I also like to sprinkle "finishing salts" right on the meat or fish just before it is served. These salts are mixed with a complementary herb or spice (see page 12).

Spices: If possible, buy whole fresh aromatic spices at a specialty spice store. And don't keep them forever: Toss spices after a year. Toast and grind them yourself, for maximum flavor.

Vegetable oil: for frying, we recommend canola, peanut, or grapeseed oils.

We use many Japanese, Chinese, Korean, Indonesian, Vietnamese, and Thai products in our restaurants. If these are not available in your area, check Sources, page 260. Uwajimaya Market in Seattle and in Portland, Oregon, does an extensive mail-order business.

Chile oil: This is an oil—often sesame oil—infused with red chile pepper. Fiery hot, chile oil is used as a seasoning or condiment, not as a cooking oil.

Chinese chile paste with garlic: There are many bottled Asian chile pastes on the market. We like the flavor of the Lan Chi brand, which is made of chile peppers and oil, with a nice kick of garlic. Use this spicy paste as a seasoning and as a condiment at the table.

Chinese wheat noodles (mein): These noodles are available fresh and dried in most markets. Thin Chinese rice noodles and delicate cellophane noodles made from mung bean flour are also popular. *Udon* (thick white flour noodles), *soba* (made from buckwheat), *cha soba* (made from green tea and buckwheat), and *somen* (a delicate, thin wheat noodle) are used extensively in Japanese cooking and are usually served in a fragrant broth.

Dashi: Made from dried bonito flakes and *konbu*, a seaweed, dashi is the standard stock or soup base in Japanese cooking. We use instant *dashi-no-moto*, like many Japanese cooks, because it's so convenient and the flavor is good. Instant *dashi-no-moto* is available in several sizes and types of packaging.

Dried shiitake mushrooms: The oldest cultivated mushrooms, skiitakes are sold both fresh and dried. Dried shiitakes add a nutty flavor to many dishes and are widely available. Remove and discard the tough stems (or save them for stock); soak the caps in hot water for a few minutes before using.

Enoki mushrooms: Also called straw mushrooms, these tiny mushrooms are great in soups, salads, and as a garnish. Cut off the roots and rinse before using.

Fermented Chinese black beans: These fermented and salted soybeans flavor many classic Chinese dishes. Use them whenever you want a winey, salty taste—black beans are especially good with seafood (see Wok-Fried Crab with Ginger and Lemongrass, page 90) and go nicely with asparagus. Rinse before using.

Fish sauce: *Nuoc mam* is the Vietnamese version, *nam pla* the Thai. Made from salted and fermented fish, these sauces add a

A glorious display of local berries

pleasant, pungent, and lightly salty undertone to many Asian dishes or dipping sauces.

Gyoza or wonton wrappers: These are used to make Japanese *gyoza* (dumplings), or for wontons and potstickers.

Kaffir lime leaves: These dried leaves from a Southeast Asian tree add a lemon/lime flavor to soups and sauces.

Kiware radish sprouts, mung bean sprouts, soybean sprouts, pea sprouts: Sprouted seeds, beans, or peas add crunch and flavor to many dishes. They also make a handsome garnish.

Lemongrass: This is a lemon-flavored grass popular in Southeast Asia. Use only the inner stalk and cut it in big enough pieces for easy removal from the dish.

Lup chong: Also called *lop cheong*, this dry Chinese pork sausage is available in China-town pork stores. Its slightly sweet and pleasantly pungent flavors add a lot to stews, soups, and rice dishes.

Mirin: This sweetened sake intended for cooking is an ingredient in many Japanese sauces.

Miso: This fermented soybean paste is made by injecting a fungus (*koji*) into cooked soybeans. There are many types of miso, whose differences depend on three factors: (1) the kind of koji used (the funguses are cultivated in barley, rice, or soybeans); (2) the balance of soybeans, koji, and salt; and (3) the length of fermentation (from six months to three years). There are two basic types of miso: light and dark. Among these are *shinshu* (golden brown, mellow, and high in salt), *sendai* (reddish brown, from northern Japan), *hatcho* (dark brown, from central Japan), and *saikyo* (mild and light). We generally use light misos in our recipes. Wrapped well, miso will keep for two months in the refrigerator. The proportion of miso paste to liquid is usually 1 tablespoon miso paste to 1 cup stock.

Nori: Also called laver, these sheets of dried seaweed are used to wrap sushi and as a flavoring or garnish. Nori is often toasted over an open flame to increase its flavor and make it more flexible.

Ocean salad or seaweed salad: This prepared salad is sold in Japanese fish markets and specialty stores. It is composed of various types of seaweed, dressed with sesame oil and rice vinegar.

Pickled ginger: Japanese pickled ginger can be found in small glass jars or plastic containers in the refrigerator case of large supermarkets or specialty markets. The thin, pale, pink slices of gingerroot are pickled in a mixture of rice wine vinegar, sugar, and salt. Pickled ginger makes a slightly sweet and tangy garnish for a bento or for fresh tuna or broiled black cod.

Rice: The only rice we use in this book is the Japanese short-grain (California grown) variety. We like its flavor, texture, and the slightly sticky quality it takes on while cooking.

Rice wine vinegar: White rice vinegars from Japan and China are delicate and often lightly sweet. If you can find some Chinese black vinegar made from sorghum and other grains that grow in northern China, give it a try. Bruce Cost, in his fine book *Bruce Cost's Asian Ingredients*, describes this vinegar as "reminiscent of Italy's balsamic vinegar . . . aged for years."

Sake: We love sake, Japan's national drink, made from fermented rice. There are many different kinds, from light to full-bodied, dry to sweet.

Sambal badjak: A chile paste condiment with onion often used in Indonesian dishes, its name translates as "pirate's sauce." You can also use *sambal olek*. Both pastes are quite hot.

Shiso leaves: A member of the mint family, these flavorful leaves are used in many Japanese dishes and make a nice garnish.

Sour shrimp paste (tom yum): a fragrant paste made from dried shrimp and spices.

Star anise: This star-shaped spice is the flower head of a Chinese evergreen tree. Each point of the star contains a seed. The sweet and aromatic quality of star anise can be released by steeping the pods in hot liquid, or the pods can be crushed with a rolling pin or ground in a spice mill. Star anise is one of the components of Chinese five-spice powder.

Szechuan peppercorns: This popular Chinese spice is not related to black pepper, but it adds a slightly hot undertone to meat and poultry dishes. Toast the peppercorns and grind them just before using.

Thai curry pastes: Thai curry pastes are sold in small cans, jars, and plastic tubs. We like the Mae Ploy brand. Thai curry pastes are classified by color: red, green, and yellow. These are complex mixtures containing chile peppers, lemongrass, shallots, garlic, galangal, coriander roots and seeds, shrimp paste, and other ingredients. Red curry paste is probably the most versatile, with good flavor and medium heat. (Medium heat for a Thai curry paste is still plenty hot!) Green curry paste is truly incendiary—use it with care. Yellow curry paste is the mildest and contains curry powder and turmeric.

Tobiko: flying fish roe, often used in sushi. The tiny golden eggs of the flying fish add a delicious, salty crunch to many sushi preparations. Tobiko is sold by Japanese fishmongers, such as Harry Yoshimura at Mutual Fish (see Sources, page 260), and can be flavored with wasabi (green), squid ink (black), and chile paste (red). These colorful tobikos make interesting garnishes for seafood dishes.

Tofu: This soybean curd, made by cooking crushed dry soybeans, extracting the soy milk, and then curdling, draining, and pressing it, is popular all over Asia. It is available in different forms: firm, silken, soft, pressed, and dried. The texture is determined by how much whey is pressed out in the forming process. We like to use firm tofu in the restaurants because it holds up best to cooking. Its bland, nutty taste takes on whatever flavors you add to it. Stored in water that is changed daily, it will keep for less than a week in the refrigerator. Dried bean curd is sold in flat sheets that do not need to be refrigerated, but need to be soaked in water before using.

Wasabi: The hot green paste you get with your sushi is a pungent and powerful root from Japan. The roots are also now being farmed commercially in Oregon. Available dried and powdered (just add water and stir) and as a premixed paste. Use it sparingly, mixed with soy for a spicy dipping sauce.

Pike Place Market

Starters

APPETIZERS PLAY A large role in my cooking style. I like to provide small bites of really intense flavors that wake up the palate and excite the imagination. Some of our best appetizers evolved from employee meals and tasting sessions in the kitchen. For

example, we used to make Tabasco chicken wings for the staff lunches. The wings were cheap and plentiful, and we made them really hot, crusty with red chiles. The spicy wings soon became an in-house favorite. Today Hot Pepper Wings (page 30) are a fixture on the menu at Palace Kitchen.

Many of our recipes are based on foods brought in by the lively, diverse, and ever-changing group of kitchen workers we call our "prepsters." These are the folks that do the most important but unacknowledged work in any kitchen: chopping and peeling and cutting, and generally all the preparations that enable cooks to cook and chefs to chef. In Seattle many of our prepsters like to

eat the food they grew up with for lunch: Mexican, Honduran or Nicaraguan, Thai, Laotian, or Vietnamese, just to name a few.

Other recipes begin as dishes we have tasted at a friend's house or a street fair or another restaurant. We come up with a recipe and offer the dish as a special in one or another of the restaurants. We expect the dish to last a week or two on the menu, but some become favorites with our diners, so we make them again and again. For example, the black bean soup we serve at Etta's is just a simple, hearty soup, but our customers love its robust flavors. It became an instant classic, and the regulars would hang us if we ever tried to take it off the menu.

OTHER APPETIZERS

❋

Other recipes that would make tasty appetizers are:

TOGARASHI PRAWNS (PAGE 45)

GRILLED CHICKEN SKEWERS WITH TANGERINE GINGER GLAZE (PAGE 46)

SAKE-CURED HOT-SMOKED SALMON (PAGE 47)

OCTOPUS WITH GREEN PAPAYA SLAW AND GREEN CURRY VINAIGRETTE (PAGE 48)

MATSUTAKE DASHI (PAGE 49)

SHIITAKE THAI STICKS (PAGE 50)

SWEET POTATO TEMPURA (PAGE 52)

WASHINGTON OYSTERS ON THE HALF SHELL WITH THREE MIGNONETTES (PAGE 63)

FIRE-ROASTED OYSTERS WITH GINGER THREADS AND WASABI BUTTER (PAGE 66)

SINGING SCALLOPS WITH MUSCAT SABAYON (PAGE 68)

OVEN-ROASTED CLAMS WITH CHANTERELLES, BACON, AND TOMATOES (PAGE 74)

WOK-FRIED MUSSELS WITH SAKE-GINGER BUTTER (PAGE 75)

KING CRAB LEGS WITH THREE DIPPING SAUCES (PAGE 79)

BLUE CRAB RÉMOULADE WITH FRIED GREEN TOMATOES (PAGE 85)

DUNGENESS CRABCAKES WITH GREEN COCKTAIL SAUCE (PAGE 87)

KASU ZUKE BLACK COD (PAGE 99)

Seattle is blessed with an abundance of sushi joints. I've had some of the oddest food I've ever eaten in my life, from salmon-nose salad to fermented mountain potato paste, in these places, and some of the most delicious food, from grilled *hamachi*, or yellowtail collar, to succulent fatty *maguro no toro*, or tuna belly.

When you are in town, you should sample some of my favorite places:

Nishino: This place has some of the most original sushi combinations in Seattle.
3130 E. Madison
(206) 322-5800

Shiro's: traditional, but fabulous. Great sushi and sashimi. Also try the sole kurage and house-cured saba.
2401 Second Avenue
(206) 433-9844

Sanmi: Sample the seared albacore tuna and sweet onion salad as well as the whole roasted daikon radish.
2601 W. Marina Place
(206) 283-9978

Tom's Tasty Sashimi Tuna Salad with Green Onion Pancakes

{ Makes 4 servings }

Cool, rosy ribbons of raw sashimi-grade tuna and bright green radish sprouts make this salad a perfect lunch, along with a glass of cool sake on a hot and lazy summer day. Better yet, start lunch with an icy Thai Basil and Lime Kamikaze (page 22).

The success of this dish depends on the quality of the tuna. Be sure it is fresh, from a purveyor you trust, who has a high turnover of fish. If you buy it from a Japanese market, ask for sashimi-grade tuna, the best available. Use the tuna immediately or store it in the refrigerator, wrapped tightly in plastic on a tray of ice for up to a day. Kiware radish sprouts are delicate, beautiful, and flavorful. You can substitute mung or soybean sprouts, found in most supermarkets.

---

12 ounces sashimi-grade tuna

⅓ cup thinly sliced green onions or scallions, white and green parts, cut on the bias

One 2½-ounce package kiware radish sprouts or ⅓ cup fresh bean sprouts

⅓ cup loosely packed cilantro

2 teaspoons sesame seeds, toasted (page 39)

¾ cup Sake Sauce (page 28), chilled

4 teaspoons peanut oil

1 teaspoon sesame oil

½ teaspoon Asian chile oil

2 Green Onion Pancakes (recipe follows)

Slice the tuna into strips about ⅛ inch thick. Place the sliced tuna in a bowl with the green onions, half the kiware radish sprouts or bean sprouts, the cilantro, and sesame seeds. Add the sake sauce (the sauce must be cold, so as not to cook the raw tuna). Toss gently. Drizzle with the peanut, sesame, and chile oils and toss gently again. This salad is best served right away; it is not something you want to marinate for long because this will "cook" the fish.

ON THE PLATE Place equal amounts of the tuna salad on each of 4 plates. Drizzle extra dressing from the bowl around the plates. Cut each warm green onion pancake into 6 wedges and divide them among the plates. Garnish with the remaining kiware radish or bean sprouts. We also like to add a lime wedge, wasabi or wasabi tobiko, and pickled ginger (see page 15) as a garnish.

IN THE GLASS Have an icy Kamikaze or try Momokawa sake from Oregon.

Green Onion Pancakes

{ Makes 4 servings; 2 pancakes }

These green pancakes are Loretta's favorite part of the tasty sashimi tuna salad. Flour tortillas make this dish easy, and they work perfectly when filled with green onions and sesame seeds, then panfried in peanut oil.

1 large egg
2 teaspoons sesame oil
Four 8-inch flour tortillas
2 teaspoons sesame seeds, toasted (page 39)
⅓ cup finely chopped green onions or scallions, white and green parts
1 tablespoon peanut or vegetable oil, or more as needed

In a small bowl, lightly beat the egg with the sesame oil. Brush each tortilla with the egg mixture and then sprinkle two of the tortillas with the sesame seeds and green onions. Place one of the plain tortillas over each of the sprinkled tortillas and sandwich them together, pressing down to seal, forming two whole pancakes. Heat the peanut or vegetable oil in a sauté pan over medium heat. When hot, add a pancake to the pan and cook until lightly browned on both sides, about 2 minutes per side. Repeat with the remaining pancake, using more oil if needed.

A STEP AHEAD The uncooked green onion pancakes will hold a day in the refrigerator, wrapped well in plastic. Or panfry them an hour ahead. Keep them at room temperature and rewarm them in a preheated 350°F oven for 5 minutes before serving.

HOW TO TOAST AND GRIND SPICES

The flavor of some spices, such as cumin, coriander, and Szechuan peppercorns, is heightened by toasting them briefly before grinding. It may seem like extra trouble to grind your own spices, but we think you'll find the flavor difference worthwhile. To toast spices, place them in a heavy skillet over medium heat for a few minutes, shaking or stirring constantly until they are very lightly browned and aromatic. Don't overcrowd the pan. The spices should be in a single layer. Spices burn very quickly, so watch them carefully while you are toasting them.

You can grind a small amount of spices using a mortar and pestle. Some spices, such as star anise, need only be crushed. Just press on them with a heavy knife or roll a heavy rolling pin over them. If you decide to grind your own spices, buy an electric coffee grinder that you set aside specifically for this purpose.

THAI BASIL AND LIME KAMIKAZE

{ Makes 1 serving }

My wife, Jackie, grows all kinds of basil in her herb garden, and sometimes we put a few leaves in a glass of sparkling water. A little Thai basil also perks up an icy Kamikaze on a hot summer day.

1 small sprig fresh Thai basil or regular basil
¾ ounce vodka
½ ounce Triple Sec
½ lime, cut into 4 wedges

Pick the basil leaves from the stem and set 1 leaf aside for garnish. Chill a martini glass. In a mixing glass, half filled with crushed ice or broken-up ice cubes, muddle the vodka, Triple Sec, and lime with a bar stick. Add the basil leaves and bruise them. Strain into the chilled martini glass, garnish with the remaining basil leaf, and serve.

Local farmers bringing freshly cut sunflowers
to the market

Flash-Fried Squid with
Horseradish Gremolata and Parsley Aioli

{ Makes 6 to 8 servings }

I never thought we would ever eat this dish again after serving four thousand pounds of it, or some twelve thousand orders, in three days at Seattle's favorite food festival, "The Bite of Seattle." We were sick of the smell of frying squid, but it is still my favorite lunch at Etta's, matched with cool Spinach, Pear, and Frisée Salad with Smoked Bacon and Curried Cashews (page 176).

The secret to great fried squid is "flash-frying" it for only a few minutes in hot oil to keep it tender. Also read How to Deep-Fry (page 51).

FOR THE HORSERADISH GREMOLATA
2 tablespoons chopped fresh flat-leaf parsley
1 tablespoon peeled and grated fresh horseradish root
1½ teaspoons minced lemon zest

FOR THE FRIED SQUID
2 cups all-purpose flour
1 tablespoon paprika
1 teaspoon kosher salt
1 teaspoon freshly ground black pepper
Pinch of cayenne
Peanut oil for frying
1½ pounds cleaned squid, tubes cut into
  ¼-inch-wide rings

TO SERVE
Kosher salt and freshly ground black pepper
Lemon wedges
Parsley Aioli (recipe follows)

1. To make the gremolata, combine the parsley, horseradish, and lemon zest in a small bowl. Set aside.

2. Combine the flour, paprika, salt, black pepper, and cayenne in a medium bowl. Set aside.

3. To cook the squid, heat 2 inches of oil to 375°F in a straight-sided pot, but be sure to not fill your pot more than halfway up the side with oil because it will foam during frying. Check the temperature with a deep-fry thermometer.

4. Pat the squid dry and toss in the seasoned flour to coat. Let it sit a minute and toss it again to recoat. Shake the floured squid in a sieve to remove excess flour. Fry in batches without crowding until golden brown, 1 to 3 minutes. Drain the squid on paper towels. (Frying a batch of squid will bring the temperature of the oil down. Be sure to reheat the oil in between batches and check the temperature again with the thermometer before adding the squid.)

ON THE PLATE Divide the fried squid among the plates. Season to taste with salt and pepper. Sprinkle the gremolata over each serving, garnish with lemon wedges, and place ramekins of the aioli beside each plate. Serve immediately.

IN THE GLASS A fresh young Sauvignon Blanc

Parsley Aioli

{ Makes 1 cup }

This herb-and-garlic-flavored mayonnaise makes a good dipping sauce with fried squid. You can also serve it with poached prawns, or grilled salmon or tuna. Or use it on sandwiches and with artichokes or asparagus.

1 large egg yolk (see Note)
1 tablespoon fresh lemon juice
1 tablespoon Dijon mustard
1 tablespoon red wine vinegar
1½ teaspoons chopped garlic
1 cup olive oil
1 tablespoon finely chopped fresh flat-leaf parsley
½ teaspoon finely chopped fresh sage
½ teaspoon finely chopped fresh rosemary
½ teaspoon finely chopped fresh thyme
Kosher salt and freshly ground black pepper

In a food processor or blender, combine the egg yolk, lemon juice, mustard, vinegar, and garlic. With the machine running, slowly pour the olive oil in a steady stream through the feed tube. The mixture will emulsify into a mayonnaise. Add the herbs and process to combine. Season to taste with salt and pepper. Remove the aioli to a small bowl, cover, and keep refrigerated.

NOTE: It's important to be aware of the potential dangers of salmonella and other harmful bacteria and take precautions. Use very fresh grade A or grade AA eggs (check the expiration date on the cartons before buying), and always keep your eggs well refrigerated. Don't keep eggs at room temperature for more than 1 hour, and *always* wash your hands, work surface, and equipment thoroughly before and after using raw eggs. Use products that have been made with raw eggs within one day.

HOW TO CLEAN SQUID

If you buy whole squid, they will need to be cleaned. Place the squid on a cutting board and grasp the head and tentacles with one hand and the body with the other. Pull your hands apart; the head and tentacles will separate from the body.

Take the head and tentacle piece and, with a knife, slice off the tentacles just past the eyes. Squeeze out the hard beak and discard. Reserve the tentacles. Holding the body piece, pull out and discard the transparent quill. Use your finger to reach inside the body and pull out any remaining guts. Peel off the skin and rinse the inside of the body under running water. Slice the body into rings and set aside.

LOBSTER AND SHIITAKE POTSTICKERS WITH SAKE SAUCE

{ Makes 24 potstickers; 6 servings }

These potstickers were the silver lining of a New Year's Eve gone bust. One year a huge number of no-shows left us with cartons of lobsters and no one to eat them. I came up with the notion to combine the lobster meat with shrimp and shiitake mushrooms in the recipe here. Not only did the potstickers save us a loss, they took the spot as our top-selling appetizer, a signature dish you can always find on our menu.

The filling is a sausage-style mixture, done in a food processor. We use lobster and shrimp meat, but all lobster or all shrimp are fine, if you prefer. One 12-ounce frozen lobster tail was just right for this recipe. Defrost it, remove the meat from the shell, and chop.

The casing is a basic wonton or gyoza wrapper (the regular thick wrapper, not the thin one), just like the kind you'd find in any Chinese or Japanese grocery (if you can't find them in your area, see Sources on page 260). We are fortunate enough to have a Laotian potsticker specialist, Fahm, on staff. One day she came to the back door to pick up her husband, and we asked her if she knew how to fold a wonton. Five years and thousands of potstickers later, she's still with us, sitting quietly on two milk crates, in her black fur hat, still folding.

½ pound shelled raw lobster, coarsely chopped
⅓ pound peeled raw shrimp
1 tablespoon peanut oil
1½ cups thinly sliced fresh shiitake mushroom caps
⅓ cup finely diced carrots

2 tablespoons finely chopped green onions or
*   scallions, white and green parts*
2 tablespoons finely chopped cilantro
1 tablespoon sesame seeds, toasted (page 39)
2 teaspoons peeled and grated fresh ginger
2 teaspoons Chinese chile paste with garlic
1 teaspoon minced garlic
1 teaspoon kosher salt

2 dozen wonton or gyoza wrappers
Cornstarch for dusting
2 tablespoons vegetable or peanut oil for panfrying,
*   or more as needed*

1. Place the lobster and shrimp in a food processor and process until coarsely pureed. (If the shrimp is wet, it is important to squeeze out as much liquid as possible before pureeing.) Heat the peanut oil in a skillet over medium heat, then cook the shiitake mushrooms and carrots until soft, stirring about 10 minutes, then allow to cool. In a large bowl, combine the pureed lobster and shrimp, sautéed shiitakes and carrots, green onions, cilantro, sesame seeds, ginger, chile paste, garlic, and salt. Mix thoroughly.

2. To form potstickers, lay a wrapper down on your work surface. Wet the edges of the wrapper with an index finger dipped in water. (It is important to use your finger rather than a brush, because a brush will make the wrapper too wet.) Place 1 slightly rounded tablespoon of the filling in the cen-

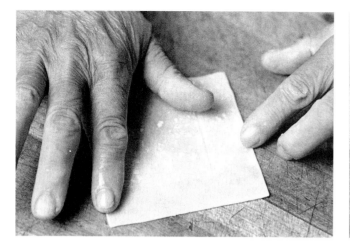

Lay a wonton wrapper down on your work surface and wet the edges of the wrapper with an index finger dipped in water.

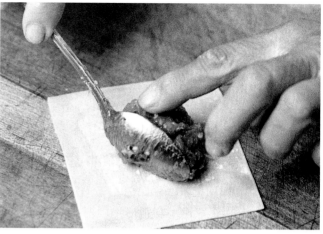

Place a slightly rounded tablespoon of filling in the center of the wrapper.

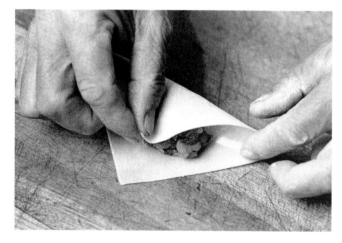

Bring the two opposing points of the wrapper together to form a triangle and press the edges together to seal.

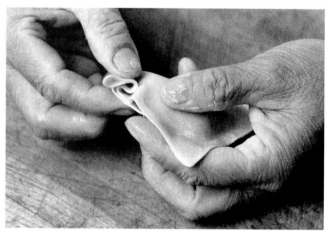

Lightly wet the surface of the two straight sides of the triangle and begin to seal by making a small crease.

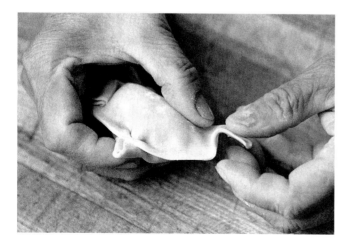

Finish each potsticker by pressing the edges together and making a series of small creases.

ter of the wrapper, and bring the two opposing points of the wrapper together to form a triangle. Press the edges together to seal. Lightly wet the surface of the two straight sides of the triangle, making a series of small creases. Place the potstickers on a baking sheet lined with parchment or wax paper, lightly dusted with cornstarch.

3. Fill a large pot with water and bring to a boil. Add the potstickers in batches (do not overcrowd them) and cook until they float to the surface, about 5 minutes. Using a small sieve or slotted spoon, gently scoop the potstickers out of the water. Put them on a baking sheet as they are cooked. If they seem to be sticking, toss them with a little oil. Before you fry them, be sure to drain or pat off any excess water that may have collected around them. Heat the oil in a nonstick sauté pan over medium-high heat. Panfry the potstickers in batches, using more oil as needed, until lightly golden brown on both sides, about 5 minutes. Keep warm on a baking sheet in a 200°F oven until all the potstickers have been panfried.

ON THE PLATE We use black Asian-style plates to serve these crispy golden potstickers, nestled up against a mound of bean sprouts, cilantro sprigs, and julienned carrots. Sprinkle with toasted sesame seeds and put a ramekin of Sake Sauce (page 28) and a lime wedge on each plate.

A STEP AHEAD The potstickers can be formed up to 2 weeks ahead and stored in the freezer. To freeze, place the potstickers, without allowing them to touch each other, on a parchment or wax paper–lined baking sheet dusted with cornstarch. Put them in the freezer. When they are frozen hard, the potstickers can be removed from the baking sheet, sealed in a plastic bag, and stored in the freezer. When you are ready to cook, do not thaw them, but poach them while still frozen, as directed above. Frozen potstickers will take a minute or two longer to cook through. Potstickers can also be poached early in the day and kept chilled on a lightly oiled tray, covered with plastic wrap, until you are ready to panfry them.

IN THE GLASS Momokawa sake from Oregon, or a good dry sake from Japan, like Bishonen, served chilled

Sake Sauce

{ Makes 1 cup }

This makes a wonderful dipping sauce for potstickers or grilled seafood, fish, or chicken. Try it with lobster and shiitake potstickers or Togarashi Prawns (page 45).

½ cup sake
¼ cup soy sauce
¼ cup rice wine vinegar
1 tablespoon sugar
1 small serrano chile, seeded and finely chopped
¼ teaspoon minced garlic
1 tablespoon finely chopped green onions or scallions, white part only

In a small saucepan, combine the sake, soy sauce, vinegar, sugar, chile, and garlic. Warm over medium heat until the sugar dissolves. Remove from the heat and allow to cool. Add the green onions. The sauce will keep, covered in the refrigerator, for up to 2 weeks.

SAKE

Sake is one of the most underrated drinks in America. Most people only drink it warm in tiny cups with sushi or other Japanese dishes, but sake is also delicious cool and can be drunk with a range of foods. In fact, Japanese sake fanciers and professional sake tasters say the highest-quality sake should be drunk cool or at room temperature. Sake can also be served over ice and used as a base for mixed drinks.

Sake, Japan's national drink, is often referred to as rice wine, but it is technically a beer since it is based on a grain, not on fruit. A special type of short-grain pearled rice (*shinpaku-mai*) is highly polished, with up to 50 percent of the germ, proteins, and oils removed, leaving almost pure starch. As with all beers, the starch must be converted to fermentable sugars before brewing can begin.

The rice is washed, cooked, and then cooled; a special rice inoculated with a fungus called *koji* is added along with fresh spring water to create the *moto*, the brewing liquid, or wort. The starches are converted to sugar through the action of koji and then alcoholic fermentation takes place, with the alcohol content getting as high 18 percent. Most sakes are then filtered and pasteurized before bottling, although some specialty sakes are sold unfiltered or unpasteurized.

Quality in sake is determined by the amount and type of rice used and the degree of polishing, the purity of the water, and the care taken during starch conversion and fermentation. In modern times sake brewers in Japan are allowed to add pure alcohol or sugar to the rice, koji, and water mixture, and

95 percent of today's sake is made this way. The best sakes will be labeled *junmai* sake (*junmaishu*), indicating that they are made from pure rice only. Most American sakes are junmai, or pure rice, since the higher alcohol of the inferior fortified (*yakoman*) sakes would result in increased U.S. taxes.

Sake, like most beers, should be drunk while it is young and fresh. The color should be pale and, except for the unfiltered sake called *nigorizake*, clear. When tasting sake, as with wine and high-quality beer, savor the aroma (Japanese tasters have over ninety different terms to describe sake aromas). And just like in wine tasting, the sake should be slurped around in the mouth, drawing in some air to allow aromas to reach the olfactory nerve through the back of the mouth and nose. When you swallow, pay attention to the finish, or aftertaste (in Japanese, *nodokoshi*—how the sake slides down the throat).

High-quality Japanese sakes are widely available in U.S. markets, and sake breweries in California, Oregon, Hawaii, and other states are making superior sakes in increasing quantities. Markets like Uwajimaya in Seattle and Portland have shelf after shelf of every type of American and Japanese sake. Check any grocery store in a Japanese or Chinese neighborhood and you are likely to find the same range.

Here are the terms to look for on sake labels, Japanese or American: *junmai*—indicating pure rice only; *ginjo*—top quality, made only from the best highly polished rice; *nigori*—sake bottled unfiltered and at maximum strength, cloudy, flavorful, and powerful. *Mirin* is a sweetened (and often salted) sake used in cooking and for making sauces such as teriyaki. *Shochu* is a rice spirit made by distilling the rice left over after fermentation, much like grappa, which is made from wine pressings. *Kasu* is the sediment or lees that settle out during the sake-making process, and is often used as a marinade for fish (Kasu Zuke Black Cod, page 99).

My favorite sake, one that we serve in our restaurants, is Momokawa, from Portland. Their premium sake is Diamond (*junmai ginjo*), smooth and crisp and especially good with seafood. Momokawa also offers a Pearl (*nigori genshu*), cloudy and unfiltered, which goes well with spicy dishes; and a very dry, full-bodied Silver (*tokubetsu junmai*), which is delicious chilled. Momokawa also makes sweeter sakes and sakes flavored with Asian pears, raspberries, Japanese citrons, and hazelnuts that are well suited for many of our desserts.

There's a whole ritual for sake drinking: The sake is poured from a small porcelain decanter (*tokkuri*) into tiny cups (*sakazuki*); you should always pour sake for someone else, never for yourself; always toast the person who filled your cup. Or you can do what we do when we eat bento at Dahlia Lounge: Fill up a wineglass (or sake cup) with the finest cool *junmai ginjo* sake in the house and enjoy the subtle and delicious mix of flavors.

Amazing array of sake at Uwajimaya, Seattle's largest Japanese supermarket

HOT PEPPER WINGS WITH CILANTRO SOUR CREAM

{ Makes 6 servings }

What started out as one of our favorite employee meals is now one of the most popular Palace Kitchen appetizers. At Palace we grill these chicken wings over an apple-wood fire, but you can either grill or broil them. These spicy tidbits seem to cry out for a cold beer, maybe a hearty Hefe-Weizen from Redhook Brewery right here in Seattle.

What really makes these wings is their time in the marinade. You need to marinate them at least a day ahead, and two days is even better than one, so plan accordingly.

2 cups soy sauce
1 cup Dijon mustard
1 cup water
¾ cup Tabasco sauce
¼ cup chopped garlic
2 tablespoons chopped fresh flat-leaf parsley
2 teaspoons chopped fresh thyme
2 teaspoons chopped fresh sage
2 teaspoons chopped fresh rosemary
18 chicken wings
Cilantro Sour Cream (recipe follows)

I. Whisk the soy sauce, mustard, water, Tabasco, garlic, and herbs together in a large bowl. Reserve ½ cup of the marinade to be used for basting and sauce. Add the chicken wings to the remaining marinade, coat them well, cover with plastic wrap, and refrigerate overnight. Turn the wings occasionally to make sure they are well marinated.

2. Fire up your grill or preheat your broiler. Remove the chicken wings from the marinade, then discard this marinade. If grilling, grill the wings over medium-low coals, turning often, until cooked through, about 15 minutes. You want the wings to cook slowly, cooking thoroughly before the glaze burns. If broiling, place the wings in a broiling pan and broil 4 inches from the heat source, 10 minutes per side. If your broiler has a low setting, use that, otherwise, watch carefully so the glaze doesn't burn. While grilling or broiling, heat the reserved marinade in a saucepan and use some of it to baste the wings a few times while cooking. Cut into one of the wings to make sure no pink remains near the bone and serve.

ON THE PLATE   Spoon the cilantro sour cream on 6 appetizer plates. Pile 3 wings on each plate and drizzle with a teaspoon of the warm reserved marinade. Don't use more than a drizzle, though—it's really strong. Serve whatever is left of the reserved marinade on the side for hearty heat lovers.

A STEP AHEAD   You can make the marinade a few days ahead. It will keep, covered in the refrigerator, for up to a week.

IN THE GLASS   An ice-cold beer

Cilantro Sour Cream

{ Makes ½ cup }

You can also use this flavorful sour cream in burritos or on tacos. It is also delicious on our Palace Olive Poppers (page 32). The chicken wings are quite salty and hot, so we don't add salt or pepper here. For other dishes add salt and pepper to taste.

½ cup sour cream
2 tablespoons heavy cream
2 teaspoons chopped cilantro
Kosher salt and freshly ground black pepper to taste
   (optional)

In a small bowl, mix together the sour cream, heavy cream, and chopped cilantro. If not using with Hot Pepper Chicken Wings or Palace Olive Poppers, taste for salt and pepper.

PALACE OLIVE POPPERS

{ Makes 6 to 8 servings }

This slightly "retro" appetizer has been served at Palace Kitchen since the day we opened. Executive Chef Eric Tanaka was inspired by a recipe in a fifties cookbook he found in a used-bookstore—he updated it by using Kalamata olives instead of pimiento-stuffed green olives. The poppers make a great appetizer or party snack, especially when accompanied by a full-bodied ale like Redhook ESB.

If you want to make a lot of poppers for a party, double or triple the recipe and use a pastry bag with a plain ¼-inch round tip to fill the olives. Soften the cream cheese first by beating it lightly with an electric mixer.

---

24 "colossal size" Kalamata olives
3 tablespoons cream cheese
1½ cups grated sharp Cheddar cheese
9 tablespoons all-purpose flour
¾ teaspoon Tabasco sauce
½ teaspoon kosher salt
3 tablespoons unsalted butter, melted
1 to 2 tablespoons milk, as needed
Herb Sour Cream Dressing (recipe follows)

1. Pit the olives with an olive pitter, keeping them as whole and unbroken as possible. Place the cream cheese in a small bowl and beat it with a spoon to soften it slightly. Using your fingers, stuff the olives with the softened cream cheese. Set aside.

2. Combine the Cheddar cheese, flour, Tabasco, and salt in a bowl, using a wooden spoon or rubber spatula. Add the melted butter and mix. Add the milk, starting with 1 tablespoon and using more as needed, and mix. Use your hands to knead the dough for a minute until a soft dough is formed.

3. Preheat the oven to 375°F. Pinch off small balls of dough about the same size as the olives. Flatten each ball of dough with your fingers and wrap each olive with it. Place the dough-wrapped olives on a parchment paper–lined baking sheet about an inch apart. Bake until golden brown, about 25 minutes.

ON THE PLATE Drizzle herb sour cream dressing on appetizer plates and serve the warm olive poppers hot from the oven, on top of the cream.

A STEP AHEAD Unbaked, these dough-wrapped olives will keep refrigerated, covered with plastic wrap, for a day or two.

IN THE GLASS Redhook ESB or a Bombay Sapphire martini, with olives of course

Herb Sour Cream Dressing

{ Makes ¾ cup }

This also makes a delicious dip or dressing for raw vegetables. We leave salt out because the olives can be salty, but you will probably want to add some to taste if you use the dressing in other dishes.

½ cup sour cream
3 tablespoons heavy cream
1 teaspoon chopped fresh flat-leaf parsley
½ teaspoon chopped fresh thyme
½ teaspoon chopped fresh rosemary
Pinch of freshly ground black pepper
Kosher salt (optional)

In a small bowl, combine the sour cream, heavy cream, chopped herbs, and pepper. Add salt to taste if not using with olives.

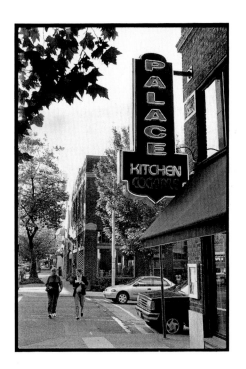

SMOKY EGGPLANT WITH SEED BREAD

{ Makes 6 to 8 servings }

One of Seattle's best chefs is Saleh Joudeh, a transplanted Syrian trained in Italy. His baba ganoush is a silky, smoky, garlicky, lemony masterpiece. He wouldn't give me the recipe, so I made up my own version.

We serve this appetizer as part of a Greek meze plate with Kalamata olives and feta cheese, but it is also a delicious side dish, especially with lamb. Use seed bread to scoop it up. If you don't want to go to the trouble of making your own flat-bread, serve the eggplant with warm pita bread.

The smokiness of the eggplant depends on the cooking method you use. It will have the best smoky taste if you grill it, preferably over charcoal or wood coals, charring the skin well. You can also get a lot of smoke flavor by cooking the eggplant directly over the flame of a gas burner, turning it with a tongs, so that it chars on all sides. You can also broil the eggplant on the highest heat. The eggplant skin should end up blackened all over and the inside should be soft and collapsed.

2 globe eggplants (weighing about
  1½ pounds each)
½ onion, sliced into ⅓-inch-thick rings
⅓ cup extra virgin olive oil, plus more for grilling
Kosher salt and freshly ground black pepper
1 tablespoon chopped garlic
3 tablespoons tahini
2 tablespoons fresh lemon juice
1 tablespoon chopped fresh flat-leaf parsley
Seed Bread (recipe follows)

1. Fire up the grill or preheat the broiler. Poke the eggplants with a fork (to keep them from exploding) and grill or broil on a baking sheet until blackened on all sides and very soft, 20 to 30 minutes. Brush the onions lightly with olive oil, sprinkle with salt and pepper, and grill (or broil) them until softened, 7 to 10 minutes. Allow the eggplants to cool enough to handle them, then cut them in half lengthwise and scoop out the pulp with a large spoon. Discard the skins. Chop the pulp and place in a bowl (you should have about 2½ cups chopped eggplant). Finely chop the grilled onions and add to the eggplant. Set aside.

2. Heat the ⅓ cup olive oil in a small skillet over medium heat. Add the chopped garlic and cook gently, stirring, for a few minutes. Remove the skillet from the heat and allow to cool slightly, then add the garlic to the eggplant-onion mixture. In a small bowl, mix the tahini and lemon juice together, then add to the eggplant-onion mixture. Add the chopped parsley and mix well. Season to taste with salt and pepper.

ON THE PLATE   Serve the eggplant in a wide, shallow bowl drizzled with extra virgin olive oil and accompanied by olives and warm seed bread or pita.

IN THE GLASS   Try a Demestica red from Greece or a light Zinfandel.

Seed Bread

These tender flatbreads are perfect with dips like our smoky eggplant. You can also serve them with hummus or tapenade.

4 cups all-purpose flour
2 tablespoons sesame seeds
1 tablespoon poppy seeds
2 teaspoons fennel seeds
2 teaspoons kosher salt
1½ teaspoons baking powder
½ teaspoon freshly ground black pepper
1⅓ cups water
¾ cup olive oil

1. In a bowl, combine the flour, seeds, salt, baking powder, and pepper. Add the water and ¼ cup of the olive oil and mix by hand until a dough is formed. Knead the dough for 3 to 4 minutes. Place the dough in a bowl, cover with plastic wrap, and allow to rest for half an hour.

2. Preheat the oven to 400°F. Remove the dough from the bowl and divide it into 8 pieces. With a lightly floured rolling pin, roll each piece into a 6-inch round about ⅛ inch thick on a lightly floured work surface.

3. For each flatbread, heat 1 tablespoon of the remaining olive oil in a skillet over medium-high heat, then panfry the flatbread until golden brown, about 1 minute, flip, and place in the oven until the other side is golden and the bread is cooked through, about 2 more minutes. Repeat for the remaining flatbreads.

TINY CLAM AND SEAWEED SOUP

{ Makes 4 servings }

The seaweed salad used in this dish is a popular Japanese appetizer, a mixture of dark green kelp and clear agar-agar (which is made from seaweed gelatin) dressed with sesame oil. Seaweed salad is available fresh or frozen in Japanese markets. A good substitution is mizuna or mustard greens dressed with a little sesame oil, sesame seeds, and *mirin*. Small or steamer-size clams are best for this dish, but if you can find really tiny clams, just use more of them.

Lup chong is a sausage available in Chinese markets. These firm, red, 6-inch-long sausages have a sweet, slightly fatty taste. There is no exact substitute, but a good alternative would be to use a little julienned Chinese barbecued pork or duck.

---

6 cups chicken stock (page 253)

4 teaspoons soy sauce

4 teaspoons Asian fish sauce

¼ cup peeled and finely julienned (see How to Julienne, below) fresh ginger

2 teaspoons chopped garlic

Pinch of red pepper flakes, or more to taste

20 Manila or steamer-sized clams, scrubbed and rinsed

⅓ cup peeled and julienned carrots

¼ cup seaweed salad

¼ cup julienned lup chong (sweet Chinese sausage)

¼ cup julienned green onions or scallions

20 fresh basil leaves (preferably Thai basil)

½ bunch (¼ cup) loosely packed cilantro

1 lime, cut into wedges

1. In a saucepan over medium-high heat, combine the chicken stock, soy sauce, fish sauce, ginger, garlic, and pepper flakes. Bring to a boil. Add the clams to the saucepan, cover, and cook until they open, 2 to 3 minutes.

2. In 4 soup bowls, arrange equal amounts of the carrots, seaweed salad, lup chong, and green onions. Divide the hot stock and clams among the bowls. Scatter the basil and cilantro leaves over the soup and season with a squeeze of lime.

ON THE PLATE   Serve this soup in big bowls along with ramekins of Asian chile paste with garlic and extra lime wedges.

IN THE GLASS   A Chinese beer like Tsing Tao

HOW TO JULIENNE

Several recipes call for fine julienne. The easiest way to do this is to cut the ingredient into thin slices, either with a knife or with a slicer or mandoline. Then cut the thin slices into thin strips. If the slices are very thin, you can stack a few at a time before you cut the strips.

Black Bean and Ham Hock Soup
with Roasted Tomatillo Salsa

{ Makes 8 to 12 servings }

This soup has been on the menu at Etta's every day, lunch and dinner, since we opened. We don't soak our beans before cooking because we think we get better color that way. But if you prefer, just cover the beans with cold water, let them sit overnight, drain, and continue with the recipe. This will lower the initial cooking time from 2 hours to 1.

2 cups dried black beans, picked over and rinsed

12 cups (3 quarts) chicken stock (page 253), or more if needed

1 smoked ham hock

2 tablespoons olive oil

1½ cups coarsely chopped onions

½ cup coarsely chopped carrots

½ cup coarsely chopped celery

1 tablespoon chopped garlic

2 cups drained canned tomatoes, chopped

2 teaspoons tomato paste

2 teaspoons coriander seeds, toasted and ground (page 21)

2 teaspoons cumin seeds, toasted and ground (page 21)

2 teaspoons paprika

¾ teaspoon cayenne, or to taste

3 to 4 tablespoons fresh lime juice, or to taste

Kosher salt and freshly ground black pepper

¼ cup chopped cilantro

Roasted Tomatillo Salsa (recipe follows)

I. Place the beans in a large pot with the chicken stock and ham hock. Bring to a simmer and cook until the beans are soft, about 2 hours (1 hour if the beans have been presoaked).

2. Meanwhile, heat the olive oil in a sauté pan over medium-low heat and slowly cook the onions, carrots, and celery, stirring occasionally, until the onions are golden and caramelized, 10 to 15 minutes. Stir in the garlic for the last few minutes of cooking. Add the onion mixture, tomatoes, tomato paste, and ground spices to the simmering beans. Continue to simmer until everything is very soft, about another hour. Pull out the ham hock and remove the fat and skin. Pull all the lean meat off the bone, finely chop the meat, and set aside. In a food processor or blender, coarsely puree the beans in batches just enough to leave a little texture. Return the soup to the pot and add the chopped meat. Season with the paprika, cayenne, lime juice, salt, and black pepper. Just before serving, stir in the chopped cilantro.

ON THE PLATE Ladle the soup into the bowls and serve with dollops of the salsa, sour cream, and a few cilantro leaves. We also serve warm cornbread (page 156) with this soup.

A STEP AHEAD You can make this soup a few days ahead and store it in the refrigerator. To serve, reheat and stir in the cilantro.

IN THE GLASS A sturdy Zinfandel or, if you're lucky enough to live in the Northwest, try Thurston Wolfe Lemberger

Roasted Tomatillo Salsa

{ Makes ¾ cup }

This tangy salsa is delicious when swirled in soups or in burritos and tacos. It also makes a great sauce for grilled pork chops or chicken breasts. Fresh tomatillos are available in Latino groceries and many supermarkets. Chipotles are dried ripe jalapeño chiles. You can find them canned in adobo sauce in Latino groceries and in many supermarkets.

8 ounces (2½ cups) tomatillos, husked, rinsed, and dried

2 teaspoons plus 1 tablespoon olive oil

1 poblano chile or other mild green chile such as Anaheim, roasted (page 127), peeled, seeded, and finely chopped

1 tablespoon finely chopped red onion

2 tablespoons chopped fresh cilantro

1 teaspoon chopped garlic

1 tablespoon fresh lime juice

1 teaspoon seeded and minced canned chipotle in adobo, or more to taste

Kosher salt and freshly ground black pepper

Preheat the oven to 400°F. Toss the tomatillos with 2 teaspoons of the olive oil in a sauté pan or small metal pan (like a pie plate) and place in the oven, tossing them around a couple times until softened and lightly browned here and there, about 10 minutes. Allow the tomatillos to cool slightly, then put them on a cutting board and chop coarsely. Put the tomatillos in a sieve and drain off all the liquid. Combine the drained tomatillos, roasted chile, onions, cilantro, garlic, lime juice, chipotle, and the remaining 1 tablespoon olive oil. Season to taste with salt and pepper. It's best to use the salsa the same day, but it can be kept, covered, in the refrigerator for 2 days.

HOW TO TOAST SEEDS AND NUTS

Toast seeds and nuts by placing them in a heavy skillet over medium heat for a few minutes, tossing and stirring constantly until they brown lightly and give off a toasted aroma. You can also place seeds and nuts on a baking sheet in a preheated 350° to 375°F oven for 5 to 10 minutes (sesame seeds and pine nuts brown quickly, while large nuts like pecan halves take a bit longer). Stir the seeds or nuts occasionally and watch them carefully so they don't burn. Don't overcrowd the nuts. Try to keep them in a single layer whichever method you use.

Hazelnuts have thin brown skins. After roasting the nuts, remove most of the skins by rubbing the still-warm nuts against each other in a clean dish towel.

If you are using a food processor to chop toasted nuts, be sure to pulse off and on briefly so you don't turn them into a paste. Otherwise, just chop them with a sharp knife.

Nuts and seeds are high in oil and they turn rancid quickly. Buy the freshest, best-quality nuts and seeds you can find. For freshness, store nuts in the freezer; you can use them directly in the recipes without thawing.

Handmade breadsticks

Sweet Butternut Soup with Thyme Crème Fraîche

{ Makes 6 servings }

One fall day, I got a call at the Dahlia from my father-in-law in Spokane telling me that he had a whole garden full of butternut squash that I could come and get for our newly opened restaurant. When I said that three hundred miles seemed a long way to drive for a couple of baskets of squash, there was a pause. "I got a bit more than a couple of baskets here," he said. "Better bring a truck." I got the point, rented a truck, and drove over the Cascades and down the desert highway, dodging tumbleweeds all the way to Spokane. We then proceeded to load up the truck with more squash than I had ever seen in one place. And it wasn't just butternut. There was acorn, hubbard, spaghetti, delicata, etc., etc., etc.

That was the fall we got creative with squash—for months we cooked and served it every which way—sautéed, baked, pureed, hashed, in fritters and beignets and pies and tarts, and we made lots and lots of squash soup. This soup was the most popular of all the dishes—and we serve it today, especially if my in-laws are in town for a visit.

3½ pounds butternut squash
Olive oil for brushing squash
1 tablespoon unsalted butter
2 tablespoons olive oil
4 cups thinly sliced onions (about 2 onions)
3 cups chicken stock (page 253)
1 cup heavy cream
1½ teaspoons chopped fresh flat-leaf parsley
½ teaspoon chopped fresh sage
½ teaspoon chopped fresh rosemary
½ teaspoon chopped fresh thyme
1 teaspoon sherry vinegar

Kosher salt and freshly ground black pepper
Thyme Crème Fraîche (recipe follows)

1. Preheat the oven to 400°F. Cut the squash in half and scoop out the seeds. Brush the cut edges lightly with oil and place, cut side down, on a baking sheet. Roast the squash until very soft, about 1¼ hours. Remove from the oven. When cool enough to handle, scoop the squash meat from the skin and set aside.

2. While the squash is roasting, caramelize the onions. Heat the butter with the olive oil in a sauté pan over medium-low heat. Add the onions and cook slowly, stirring occasionally until they are soft and uniformly golden brown, 25 to 30 minutes. Set aside.

3. In a food processor, process the squash, onions, and 1 cup of the chicken stock until smooth. Transfer the puree to a large pot. Add the remaining 2 cups chicken stock and heat the soup to a simmer, whisking a few times. Add the heavy cream, chopped herbs, and sherry vinegar. Season to taste with salt and pepper. You can make this soup a few days ahead and store it in the refrigerator. To serve, just reheat.

ON THE PLATE Ladle the hot soup into bowls and serve with a swirl of crème fraîche.

IN THE GLASS A good fruity Viognier from France or California, or a dry Riesling from Washington State or Alsace

Thyme Crème Fraîche

{ Makes ½ cup }

This slightly tart, herb-flavored cream goes perfectly with the sweet flavor of the butternut soup. You can buy commercial crème fraîche, make your own (page 255), or use sour cream, if you prefer.

½ cup crème fraîche
2 teaspoons chopped fresh thyme
Kosher salt and freshly ground black pepper

Place the crème fraîche and thyme in a small bowl and whisk until smooth. Season to taste with salt and pepper.

Using your fingers at the Palace Kitchen

The "Hammering Man" sculpture outside of the Seattle Art Museum

Bento

O N T H E D A I L Y Dahlia menu we have a slot dedicated to bento, a forum that Japanese chefs use to present a whole array of little tastes of their most flavorful foods. The name *bento* literally means "boxed meals," but my favorite part isn't the box. I'm in

love with the concept of small tastes that complement each other and are beautifully presented. Instead of a lacquered box, I use a large rectangular ceramic platter as a palette with plenty of room to show off each item. Our version usually includes a small bowl of miso soup and mix of individual pickles, bits of marinated grilled meat or chicken on skewers, spicy togarashi pepper prawns, and sweet potato tempura. Bento is a way of making a whole meal of appetizers, a bit like Spanish tapas. And with all its little complete tastes, bento is the way I like to eat.

Thanks to the openness and sophistication of diners in Seattle, we can try just about anything and everything in our bento. Peo-

ple here are used to all types of food and are open to trying exotic ingredients like flying fish roe, geoduck, and sea urchin. While you might not want to make a whole meal of herring roe, a bento-size taste is perfect.

It's fun to have beautiful boxes, dishes, and platters for bento. We use small lidded bowls for miso soup and cute little ramekins and tiny porcelain plates for the pickles and condiments. If you get into the bento idea, you can stroll through the aisles of your local Asian supermarket or housewares store where you can spend a little money (or a lot) buying a couple of lacquered boxes here, some lidded bowls there, and ramekins and chopsticks and chopstick holders.

OTHER BENTO DISHES

✳

This chapter offers just a small sample of the items we put on Dahlia's bento.
Some other recipes that would also work in a bento are:

AROMATIC STEAMED RICE (PAGE 159)

LOBSTER AND SHIITAKE POTSTICKERS WITH SAKE SAUCE (PAGE 25)

TINY CLAM AND SEAWEED SOUP (PAGE 36)

GREEN ONION PANCAKES (PAGE 21)

PEACH SAMBAL (PAGE 112)

WOK-FRIED MUSSELS WITH SAKE-GINGER BUTTER (PAGE 75)

ICED SAKE OR COLD BEER WITH BENTO

Many bento dishes are spicy, pickled in rice vinegar, or laced with soy or miso. A lot of flavor is packed into a small amount of food. With bento I suggest drinking chilled sake or beer. If you prefer wine, try a well-chilled fruity Gewürztraminer from Washington State or Alsace, or a light-bodied Pinot Gris from Oregon.

TOGARASHI PRAWNS

{ Makes 4 to 6 servings }

Togarashi is a spicy mixture of peppers, seaweed, sesame seeds, and fragrant orange peel. It is often found in shaker jars on tabletops in Japanese restaurants and used like salt and pepper. We like to make our own, but you can certainly use one of the many commercial versions available.

FOR THE TOGARASHI
1 sheet nori (page 15)
1 tablespoon sesame seeds, toasted (page 39)
1 tablespoon grated orange zest, allowed to dry on a
  paper towel
1 teaspoon red pepper flakes

FOR THE PRAWNS
2 tablespoons peanut oil
1 pound large prawns, shelled and deveined, with
  tails on
Kosher salt and freshly ground black pepper

I. Preheat the oven to 350°F. To make the togarashi, toast the nori on an ungreased baking sheet for 20 minutes in the oven. Allow to cool, then rip the nori into pieces that will fit in your spice mill. Grind the nori, sesame seeds, orange zest, and pepper flakes in batches if necessary, and mix together in a small mixing bowl. Set aside.

2. Heat the oil in a wok over high heat until very hot. Add the prawns and cook 3 to 4 minutes, tossing and turning the prawns as they cook. When they are firm and pink, sprinkle the prawns with the togarashi, salt, and pepper, and toss well to coat.

3. You can also brush the prawns with the oil, sprinkle them with the togarashi, salt, and pepper, and grill or broil them, turning often, until firm and pink, 3 to 4 minutes.

ON THE PLATE   These bright pink prawns are striking displayed on a dark square Japanese plate. Serve them around a heap of Japanese pickled red cabbage (page 56), with grilled Japanese eggplant on the side.

A STEP AHEAD   The togarashi can be made several hours ahead. If stored longer, the orange zest will lose some of its fragrance.

Grilled Chicken Skewers with Tangerine Ginger Glaze

{ Makes 16 skewers; 4 to 6 servings }

In some cities, McDonald's rules, but Seattle is ruled by teriyaki joints. Every place serves its own glaze. I like mine to have a generous ginger tang with tangerine zest.

These flavorful skewers can serve as appetizers, as part of a bento, or as a main course with Aromatic Steamed Rice (page 159) or Spicy Peanut Noodles (page 172). Mirin is a sweet sake often used in Japanese cooking and it's great in marinades. It is available at many supermarkets or from specialty groceries.

Instead of chicken, you could use pieces of salmon or pork, or slices of eggplant.

FOR THE TANGERINE GINGER GLAZE

1 cup fresh tangerine juice
½ cup mirin
¼ cup soy sauce
2 tablespoons firmly packed brown sugar
1 tablespoon granulated sugar
2 teaspoons peeled and grated fresh ginger
½ teaspoon chopped garlic
½ teaspoon grated tangerine zest
1 teaspoon cornstarch plus
    1 teaspoon water

FOR THE CHICKEN SKEWERS

4 boneless skinless chicken breasts
16 bamboo skewers, soaked in water for 30 minutes and drained
Peanut or vegetable oil for brushing
Kosher salt and freshly ground black pepper

1. Combine the tangerine juice, mirin, soy sauce, sugars, ginger, garlic, and zest in a small saucepan over medium heat. Simmer and reduce by half, about 10 minutes. Make a slurry by mixing the cornstarch with the water. Add the slurry to the simmering glaze and allow to simmer another minute. The glaze should be as thick as maple syrup. Reserve one quarter of the glaze in a separate small bowl.

2. Fire up the grill or preheat the broiler. Cut each chicken breast into 4 pieces, about 2 inches by 1 inch each. Thread 1 piece of chicken on each skewer, brush with oil, and season with salt and pepper. Grill or broil the chicken skewers over medium coals, turning often, and brushing 2 or 3 times with the glaze. Watch carefully because the sugars in the glaze can burn; reduce the heat or adjust the grill as necessary. When the chicken is cooked through, after about 7 minutes, remove the skewers from the grill, and spoon the reserved glaze over the chicken just before serving.

A STEP AHEAD The tangerine glaze can be made a few days ahead and stored in the refrigerator. When chilled, the glaze will firm up because of the cornstarch in it. To smooth out the glaze before brushing it on the skewers, warm it up and whisk it.

SAKE-CURED HOT-SMOKED SALMON

{ Makes 8 servings }

Curing salmon gives it a wonderful texture and unforgettable flavor. Cures can be aromatic (with the addition of sake, star anise, sage, fennel, or dill) or simply consist of salt and sugar, leaving no extra flavors behind. The salt and sugar in a cure draw out the natural juices and water in meat and fish and intensify the flavor of the food.

A home-style smoker is a good investment. It can provide you with a whole new world of flavors, especially with fish or seafood. You can hot-smoke this cured salmon in a typical fisherman's smoker, like a Little Chief, which is inexpensive and easy to use. Carefully follow the manufacturer's instructions. Generally, home-smokers need to be used outdoors.

These servings may seem small, but the salmon is very rich. Serve it in combination with other seafood appetizers or as a part of a bento box. Because salmon is best cured overnight (hot-smoking these small pieces of fish took about 1½ hours in our smoker), leave enough time to make this dish.

---

1 cup soy sauce
¾ cup firmly packed brown sugar
½ cup water
¼ cup sake
8 sliced peeled fresh ginger coins (see below),
    ⅛ inch thick
1 tablespoon chopped garlic
2 teaspoons kosher salt

1 pound salmon fillet, cut into 2-ounce pieces, skin
    removed
8 fresh sage leaves

1. In a bowl, whisk the soy sauce, brown sugar, water, sake, ginger, garlic, and salt together until the sugar dissolves. Put the salmon pieces in a nonreactive container and pour the marinade over. Cover with plastic wrap. Allow the salmon to marinate in the refrigerator overnight, turning it occasionally.

2. Remove the salmon from the marinade, saving a little marinade to brush over the salmon just before smoking. Place the pieces on a rack sprayed with nonstick spray set over a baking sheet and let sit, refrigerated, for 2 hours to allow the glaze to set. Place a sage leaf on top of each piece of salmon and brush each one with the reserved marinade.

3. Use a home-smoker to hot-smoke the salmon according to the manufacturer's instructions.

ON THE PLATE   Japanese cucumber pickles (page 56) make a good accompaniment.

A STEP AHEAD   You can make this a few days ahead and store it, covered, in the refrigerator.

HOW TO MAKE GINGER COINS

Ginger coins add a subtle flavor to a dish (peeled and grated ginger will add a more potent flavor). Peel the fresh ginger and cut it crosswise into round slices about ¼ inch thick, or thinner. If you are using the coins in a marinade or in a dish that is going to be strained, you don't need to peel the ginger.

OCTOPUS WITH GREEN PAPAYA SLAW
AND GREEN CURRY VINAIGRETTE

{ Makes 6 servings }

This recipe has some unusual ingredients, but it is not difficult to prepare. Octopus is sold already steamed (and sometimes sliced) and is commonly found in Japanese fish markets, where it is called *taiko*. We get cooked whole octopus tentacles from Harry Yoshimura's Mutual Fish, our fish purveyor. If you can't find it in your area or the thought of eating octopus puts you off, substitute cold poached prawns, or sashimi-grade raw tuna, or just about anything you would find in a sushi bar.

Green papaya is a large, unripe papaya and is used in many kinds of Asian cooking. It is larger than a regular papaya, and the flesh should be light green, not pink or orange. If you can't find green papaya, substitute julienned cucumber or napa cabbage. It's best to use a mandoline to get nice, thin julienned slices (see How to Use a Mandoline, page 158).

FOR THE GREEN CURRY VINAIGRETTE

2 tablespoons finely chopped lemongrass, tender white part only
2 tablespoons finely chopped green onions or scallions, white and green parts
¼ cup chopped fresh basil
2 tablespoons chopped fresh cilantro
2 tablespoons chopped fresh mint
1 teaspoon peeled and grated fresh ginger
¼ teaspoon chopped garlic
1 small Thai chile or serrano chile, seeded and finely chopped (about 2 teaspoons), or to taste
¼ cup rice wine vinegar
1½ teaspoons sugar
1½ teaspoons Asian fish sauce
¼ cup peanut oil

FOR THE SLAW AND OCTOPUS

3 cups peeled, seeded, and julienned (see How to Julienne, page 36) green papaya (about 1 pound)
1 cup julienned carrots
Nuoc Cham Dipping Sauce (page 79)
½ pound cooked octopus (taiko), cut into ⅛-inch-thick slices
Lime wedges for garnish

1. To make the vinaigrette, combine the lemongrass, green onions, herbs, ginger, garlic, and chopped chile in a food processor or blender and puree as finely as possible. Add the vinegar, sugar, and fish sauce and process to combine. Remove to a small bowl and whisk in the peanut oil. Set aside.

2. Place the julienned green papaya and carrots in a bowl and toss with the nuoc cham dipping sauce.

ON THE PLATE   Mound the slaw on 6 plates. Arrange slices of octopus around each mound of slaw and drizzle some of the vinaigrette around each salad. Garnish with lime wedges.

A STEP AHEAD   The vinaigrette can be made a few hours ahead and stored, covered with plastic wrap, in the refrigerator. The dipping sauce can also be prepared a few days ahead and stored, covered, in the refrigerator. You can julienne the green papaya and carrots a few hours before using, cover with plastic wrap, and refrigerate until ready to serve.

MATSUTAKE DASHI

{ Makes 4 servings }

I love to see Peter the Mushroom Man stroll into the Palace Kitchen with that big, bear-greeting grin he gives us when he brings the first treasures of the season. He holds handfuls of the big pine needle–covered mushrooms over his head and shouts out, "Matsuuuutake!" doing his much maligned Toshiro Mifune imitation once again. Matsutake mushrooms are indeed a treasure—you should see the Japanese tourists' jaws drop when they find them in the Pike Place Market at only $30 a pound—in Japan these prized fungi sell for hundreds of dollars.

Matsutakes have a wonderful piney fragrance that you don't want to obscure with a lot of other flavors and smells. At the same time, that pungency is so strong, you only need a little of it. Just pour some delicate hot dashi broth over a paper-thin slice of raw matsutake, in order to cook it, and inhale the perfume. If you can't find matsutakes (they are available seasonally by mail order; see Sources, page 260), use thinly sliced fresh shiitake caps.

Dashi is a fish stock used in Japanese cooking, either alone or as a base for other dishes. The easiest way to prepare it is to use the flavored dried bonito flakes or a dashi base, sold in supermarkets.

---

1 bunch (about 3 ounces) green onions or scallions

8 cups (2 quarts) water

¼ pound shiitake mushrooms, roughly chopped

3 sliced peeled fresh ginger coins (page 47), ¼ inch thick

3 tablespoons packaged dashi (page 13)

1 sheet nori (page 15)

4 paper-thin slices matsutake mushroom or 2 ounces thinly sliced shiitake caps

1. Julienne ¼ cup of the green onions. Set aside. Roughly chop the rest of the green onions.

2. Combine the water, shiitake mushrooms, roughly chopped green onions, and ginger in a saucepan over high heat. Once it comes to a boil, cover and reduce the heat to a simmer for half an hour. Turn off the heat and add the dashi and nori. Allow the broth to steep a few minutes, then strain through a fine-mesh strainer to remove the shiitake mushrooms, green onions, ginger, and nori. Discard the solids.

ON THE PLATE   Set out 4 bowls. Place a slice of matsutake and a few julienned green onions in each bowl. Ladle the hot broth over the mushrooms and green onions and serve immediately.

SHIITAKE THAI STICKS

{ Makes 12 spring rolls; 4 to 6 servings }

These crunchy spring rolls are perfect for party snacks or appetizers. The woodsy, earthy flavors of the shiitakes jump out at you because the mushrooms are sautéed before the Thai sticks are fried.

Deep-frying is a technique that is often neglected by the home cook. It is not difficult (see How to Deep-Fry, page 51) and, if done properly, deep-fried foods are crisp and greaseless.

½ pound fresh shiitake mushrooms, stemmed
3 tablespoons peanut oil
Kosher salt and freshly ground black pepper
1½ teaspoons peeled and grated fresh ginger
½ teaspoon chopped garlic
¼ cup sliced green onions or scallions, white and
    green parts
1 tablespoon rice wine vinegar
1 tablespoon soy sauce
¼ teaspoon sesame oil
1 large egg
1 teaspoon water
12 spring roll wrappers
Peanut oil for frying
Sake Sauce (page 28)

1. Preheat the oven to 400°F. Toss the shiitakes in 2 tablespoons of the oil, coating them evenly, and sprinkle with salt and pepper. Place the mushrooms on a baking sheet and roast until golden, about 20 minutes. Heat the remaining 1 tablespoon oil in a small skillet and cook the ginger and garlic over medium heat, stirring, for a few minutes. In a bowl, combine the roasted shiitakes, ginger, garlic, green onions, vinegar, soy sauce, and sesame oil. Allow the mushroom mixture to marinate for half an hour. Before forming the Thai sticks, place the filling in a fine-mesh strainer and squeeze to remove excess liquid.

2. To make the egg wash, beat the egg with the water. Set aside. Place a spring roll wrapper diagonally on your work surface. Place a thin line of the shiitake filling (about 2 tablespoons) horizontally across the center of the wrapper, leaving a 1-inch border without filling. Brush the top corner with the egg wash. Starting with the bottom point, roll the wrapper up tightly. Once you've rolled just over half the sheet, fold in the ends and continue rolling and seal. Repeat this procedure with the remaining wrappers and filling. Cover the Thai sticks with a clean kitchen towel so they don't dry out.

3. Fill a straight-sided pot with at least 2 inches of oil and heat to 375°F or use a deep-fryer (see page 51). Fry the spring rolls a few at a time until golden, about 3 minutes. It may be necessary to turn them while frying so they brown evenly. Remove them from the oil and drain on paper towels.

ON THE PLATE   Serve hot with a ramekin of sake sauce or other dipping sauce.

A STEP AHEAD   The Thai sticks can be rolled a few hours in advance and held in the refrigerator, wrapped in dry kitchen towels. Fry just before serving.

HOW TO DEEP-FRY

Though there is some time and trouble involved in the process, deep-fried food can be a truly delicious treat. If you fry at the correct temperature with the right kind of oil, the food doesn't absorb a lot of oil and doesn't taste greasy at all.

We prefer peanut, grapeseed, or canola oil for deep-frying because these oils have high smoke points and clean, neutral flavors.

It's important to use a frying thermometer for deep-fat frying. We generally fry foods at 350° to 375°F. When you add a batch of food to be fried, it will lower the temperature of the oil. So before adding another batch, use your thermometer to check that the oil has come back to temperature. Also use your thermometer to check that the oil is not getting too hot, which will burn the food before it is cooked.

The best pot to use for deep-frying is deep, heavy, and straight-sided. It's really convenient to have a fryer basket, but if you don't have one, drop the food in the pot (with tongs or other utensil so the hot fat doesn't splash on your hands) and scoop it out with a small sieve or slotted spoon. You will need at least 2 to 4 inches of oil to deep-fry, but the pot must be big enough to be no more than half full of oil, since the food will cause the oil to bubble up.

Use oil once for frying. Save your empty oil bottle and cap. When you're done and the used oil is cool, funnel it back in the bottle, screw the cap on, and discard.

An electric thermostat–controlled fryer will make your work easier and it generally includes a fryer basket.

Deep-fat frying is potentially dangerous. Work carefully and keep a box of salt or baking soda or a large lid on hand to smother a small fire. Having a working fire extinguisher nearby is always a good idea.

HOW TO DEVEIN AND BUTTERFLY PRAWNS

To devein a prawn, pass the tip of a sharp knife along the back of the prawn and remove the dark vein, which is actually the digestive tract. If your knife is sharp, you can do this with or without the shell on. It's easier to devein prawns with the shells off, but you may prefer leaving them on for certain dishes such as Szechuan Pepper-Salt Prawns (page 67).

To butterfly a prawn, split it lengthwise down the back with or without the shell on, making your incision almost all the way through. Leave the tail attached. Press down on the shrimp to flatten and open it.

SWEET POTATO TEMPURA

{ Makes 4 servings }

The first time I had tempura in a Japanese restaurant, I was surprised to bite into a sweet potato when I thought it was a batter-fried carrot. The sweet potato slice has since become the prize fought over between my daughter and myself whenever a fresh basket of vegetable tempura arrives at our table.

You can also use this batter for prawn tempura. Peel and butterfly the prawns (see page 51) and cook them quickly. Also see How to Deep-Fry, page 51.

Peanut oil for frying
1 sweet potato (about 12 ounces), peeled
Ice cubes
1 cup club soda
¾ cup all-purpose flour
Kosher salt
Sesame seeds, toasted (page 39), for garnish

Fill a straight-sided pot with at least 2 inches of oil and heat to 375°F, checking the temperature with a frying thermometer (see page 51). Cut the sweet potato in half lengthwise and then slice on the bias into ⅛-inch-thick half-moons. Add a few ice cubes to the club soda and allow to chill for a few minutes. Remove the ice cubes. Prepare the tempura batter by combining the iced club soda with the flour in a bowl. Set the bowl of tempura batter in another bowl of ice water. Dip the sweet potato slices in the batter, letting the excess drip off, and fry 2 to 3 minutes, turning as necessary until the coating is crisp. Check that the potato is tender enough to eat by sticking a fork into a slice. Remove from the fryer and drain on paper towels.

ON THE PLATE   Season the fried sweet potato slices with salt, sprinkle with sesame seeds, and serve with a ramekin of sake sauce or other dipping sauce.

Marinated and Seared Tofu

{ Makes 4 servings }

Tofu, fermented soybean curd, comes in a variety of textures, from light and silky to dense and firm. For this recipe, use firm tofu, packed in water. Tofu is so versatile you can prepare it in a variety of delicious ways: in soups, grilled, cold as an appetizer, or stir-fried. Tofu picks up and carries flavors, from mild to really spicy. One of my favorite tofu dishes is served at the counter at Saigon Restaurant in Pike Place Market. The tofu is first deep-fried for flavor and texture, then stir-fried in a tangy blend of tomato, onion, and fish sauce.

Try serving this tofu on a bed of Chilled Miso Spinach (page 55).

¼ cup soy sauce

¼ cup rice wine vinegar

1 tablespoon Asian chile oil

1 teaspoon sesame oil

1 pound firm tofu, cut into ½-inch-thick slices

3 tablespoons peanut oil

¼ cup julienned green onions or scallions, white and green parts

½ teaspoon sesame seeds, toasted (page 39)

1. In a bowl, make the marinade by combining the soy sauce, vinegar, and chile and sesame oils. Add the tofu and marinate for at least half an hour.

2. Heat a nonstick pan over high heat with 1 tablespoon of the peanut oil. Pull the tofu from the marinade and let the excess drip off. Sear the tofu in batches, without overcrowding the pan, until browned, about 3 minutes per side. Add more oil as needed. When all the tofu has been seared, discard any excess oil from the sauté pan and heat a few tablespoons of the marinade in the same pan. Cut each piece of seared tofu diagonally.

ON THE PLATE   Place 3 tofu pieces on each plate, drizzle with the warmed marinade, sprinkle with the green onions and sesame seeds, and serve.

A STEP AHEAD   You can marinate the tofu a few days ahead and store, covered with plastic wrap, in the refrigerator.

IN THE GLASS   For drink suggestions, see page 44.

HOW TO HANDLE CHILES

Always wash your hands after handling chiles—be careful not to touch your eyes with hot pepper juices on your fingers! Or wear thin disposable gloves. The heat varies in individual peppers. Sometimes a relatively mild pepper like an Anaheim can be unusually hot. It's a good idea to taste a tiny bit of a chile before deciding exactly how much you want to add to a dish. The veins and seeds carry the most heat, so (unless you want extra heat) remove them.

ASIAN LONG BEANS WITH
SOY SHALLOT VINAIGRETTE

{ Makes 6 servings }

We like Chinese long beans, which are often 12 inches or longer, for this dish, but of course you can use any type of fresh green bean. Blanching the beans and immediately chilling them in ice water to stop the cooking helps maintain the best color. You can leave the long beans whole and tie them in decorative knots for a dramatic presentation, or you can cut them into more manageable 3-inch lengths.

FOR THE SOY SHALLOT VINAIGRETTE

3 tablespoons sherry vinegar
3 tablespoons finely chopped shallots
4 teaspoons fresh lemon juice
2 teaspoons soy sauce
2 teaspoons Asian fish sauce
1 teaspoon Chinese chile paste with garlic
1 teaspoon sugar
½ teaspoon minced garlic
½ cup peanut oil

FOR THE BEANS

1 pound Chinese long beans or green beans, ends
   trimmed
Kosher salt
2 teaspoons sesame seeds, toasted (page 39)

1. To make the vinaigrette, in a small bowl, combine the vinegar, shallots, lemon juice, soy sauce, fish sauce, chile-garlic paste, sugar, and garlic. Whisk in the peanut oil until well emulsified. Set the vinaigrette aside.

2. Fill a large pot with lightly salted water and bring to a boil. Add the long beans and cook until tender, about 5 minutes. Drain the beans and immediately plunge them in a container of ice water. When the beans are chilled, drain them and pat off the excess water on kitchen towels. In a large bowl, toss the beans with the vinaigrette. Season to taste with kosher salt.

ON THE PLATE   If you've used long beans, you can gather a few together and tie them in a knot. Long beans look nice stacked lengthwise in little bundles. If there's any extra vinaigrette in the bowl, drizzle it over the beans and sprinkle them with the toasted sesame seeds.

A STEP AHEAD   The vinaigrette can be made a few days ahead and stored refrigerated, covered with plastic wrap. You can blanch the beans a few hours before needed and keep them, covered, in the refrigerator.

CHILLED MISO SPINACH

{ Makes 4 servings }

Miso is an intensely flavored paste made from fermented soybeans and other grains (page 14). Japanese cooks use it in soups; as a seasoning for grilled vegetables, meat, and seafood; as a dip; or in salad dressing. There are many types of miso, ranging from light, smooth, and delicate to red-brown, chunky, and pungent. To judge the miso's intensity and flavor, taste a little bit before adding it to any dish.

Black sesame seeds make a nice-looking garnish. We especially like to mix them with equal parts white sesame seeds. Black sesame seeds are similar to white sesame seeds, but have less aroma and an earthier taste.

For a beautiful presentation, roll the spinach into a log and slice it. Or you can simply dress the cooked and chopped spinach with the vinaigrette and sprinkle it with a few sesame seeds for a simpler, but equally tasty dish.

A sushi roller (a small bamboo mat) can help you roll the spinach, or just use a piece of plastic wrap, as described in this recipe.

---

1 pound spinach, washed well and stemmed

FOR THE MISO VINAIGRETTE

2 tablespoons rice wine vinegar

1 tablespoon light miso paste

½ teaspoon soy sauce

¼ cup peanut oil

½ teaspoon sesame oil

2 tablespoons sesame seeds, toasted (page 39)

2 tablespoons black sesame seeds, toasted (page 39)

1. Fill a large pot with water and bring to a boil. Add the spinach and cook until it is wilted, about 1 minute. Drain the spinach and immediately plunge it into a container of ice water. Squeeze as much liquid as possible from the spinach and chop it finely. In a small bowl, combine the vinegar, miso, and soy sauce. Whisk in the oils. Toss half of the vinaigrette on the spinach and let sit for half an hour to marinate.

2. Squeeze the vinaigrette from the spinach. Put a piece of plastic wrap on a work surface and spread with the sesame seeds. Form a log of spinach and place it in the center of the bed of seeds. Roll up the spinach in the wrap, twisting the ends and tying them in knots. You should have a log about 1 inch in diameter. Chill the log in the freezer for half an hour.

ON THE PLATE   Unwrap the log and slice it into eight 1-inch-thick slices. Drizzle each slice with some of the remaining vinaigrette and serve. Another, simpler way to serve this dish is to dress the cooked and chopped spinach with as much vinaigrette as desired and serve it in small mounds, sprinkled with the sesame seeds, either warm or chilled.

JAPANESE PICKLES

{ Makes 4 servings }

Use these mild, slightly sweet pickles in a bento or as a fresh-tasting garnish to many other dishes. This pickling brine is good with other vegetables, such as julienned carrots or thinly sliced radishes.

FOR THE PICKLING BRINE

6 tablespoons rice wine vinegar

2 tablespoons water

4½ teaspoons sugar

1 teaspoon peeled and grated fresh ginger

1. Mix the vinegar, water, sugar, and ginger together in a small saucepan over medium-high heat. Bring to a boil, stirring to dissolve the sugar.

2. *For pickled red cabbage*, thinly slice enough red cabbage to make 1 cup, using a mandoline or a sharp knife. Place the cabbage in a heatproof, nonreactive container (stainless steel or Pyrex) and pour the boiling pickling brine over it. Refrigerate for at least an hour. Drain before using as a garnish.

3. *For cucumber pickles*, prepare a double batch of the pickling brine. Cut 1 English cucumber in half lengthwise and cut slices on the bias ⅛ inch thick. (You don't need to peel or seed a thin-skinned English cucumber, but if you substitute another type of cucumber, peel and seed it.) Place the cucumber slices in a heatproof, nonreactive container and pour the boiling brine over them. Refrigerate for at least an hour. Drain before using.

A STEP AHEAD The pickled cabbage will hold for a week, refrigerated and covered. The cucumber pickles should be used within 1 day.

Since the rough-and-tumble days, when lumberjacks skidded logs down Skid Road and sailors crowded dockside saloons, to the more polite present day with microbrewed ales in every bar and fine-beer lists in restaurants, we've always enjoyed the suds in Seattle. And we've been making good beer and strong ale for quite some time.

Even though we have the Olympia Brewery down near Tumwater, south of Seattle, turning all that pure artesian water into light-bodied lager, the brew of choice in the Northwest has been ale from the start. Ale is old-fashioned beer, made from top fermenting ale yeast and brewed at warmer temperatures to give it a fruity and robust character. It's usually malty and deeply colored, with plenty of bitter hops in the finish. Lager is newfangled beer, introduced into the Midwest by German brewers in the nineteenth century. Cold-fermented and lighter in character, lager became the standard "American"-style beer that has gotten lighter and lighter.

But we in Seattle kept our taste for ale, and for many years Rainier Ale was just about the only American ale you could find anywhere. Rainier Ale was affectionately known by its consumers as "the Green Death," from its bright green bottle and high alcohol level. Rainier was a good product, a copper-colored, hoppy, and bitter ale, a lot better than the most of the thin stuff that passed for beer back then.

In the last fifteen years or so, we've seen a real revolution in beer-making in America, and Seattle and the Northwest have been at the forefront. Some of the finest ales in America are made here, and many of our microbreweries aren't very micro anymore. A few like Redhook Brewery and Pyramid Ales are making significant quantities of flavorful brews that are now available nationwide.

Redhook is one of the oldest and best of the new breweries. The brewery began small, in an old brick trolley barn in the Ballard District, and has been expanding ever since. A brew house and visitors' center has been built in Woodinville, a Seattle suburb that also houses a number of the state's largest wineries, and their facility in Portsmouth, New Hampshire, ensures that ale lovers back East can get their fresh product.

Redhook specializes in full-bodied, hop-flavored ales brewed in a style that goes really well with the foods I like to cook and eat. No wimpy beers here. The ales have a lot of malt character, with good color and a sturdy head, and with plenty of hops to provide a pleasantly bitter finish. My favorite, and one of their most popular ales, is Redhook ESB (Extra Special Bitter), made in an English strong-ale style. This is my beer of choice with the grills and spit-roasted meats we serve at the Palace Kitchen.

Another favorite ale is Redhook IPA (which used to be called Ballard Bitter, after the neighborhood). This full-bodied, brass-colored brew is made in the English India pale ale style, and goes especially well with spicy foods like our hot pepper chicken wings.

Dark ales get their color from crystal malt and other heavily roasted malts that caramelize at higher temperature. Porter is a deep brown ale made in a traditional London style with a toasty, malty flavor and refreshing hop bitterness. Porter is the perfect accompaniment to grilled meats, smoked salmon, and oysters. Stout is a more powerful version of porter that really wakes you up and makes you take notice. Guinness from Dublin is, of course, the most famous brand, but many local ale brewers turn out world-class versions of this strong black ale. The roasted-malt flavors and good dose of bittering hops make stout a good match with spit-roasted prime rib or chile espresso–glazed ham.

The Yakima Valley, just over the Cascades east of Seattle, is famed for its wines of course, but it is even more famous for its hops. Yakima Valley is one of the premium areas in the United States for growing this bitter herb, and its hops are used to make most of America's beers. New varieties like Cascades and Chinook originated here in the valley and one of the reasons Northwest drinkers prefer bitter ales is because of the abundance and quality Yakima Valley hops.

Bert Grant's Yakima Brewing Company is located in the town of Yakima, along with a brew pub. This is a good place to stop off for a taste of the region's ales. Bert's Glorious Golden Ale is dry-hopped with Yakima-grown Chinook hops. Dry hopping is the traditional practice of adding handfuls of fragrant fresh hops to the ale after it has finished brewing. You can smell the pure hop aroma this way and get a delicate taste of the hop flowers. Yakima Brewing also offers seasonal ales, with individual hop varieties identified on the label so you can taste and recognize them.

Pam Hinkley pulling an ale at Redhook Brewery

Always a big selection at the Palace

Shellfish

HERE ON THE edge of Puget Sound, we live in an extraordinary part of the world for shellfish. Washington State is the largest oyster producer in the country. The names of these succulent bivalves could have come directly out of *Star Wars*: Dabobs, Sno-

creeks, Quilcenes, Skookums, Westcotts, Willapas, to name a few. These are place names, some less than half an hour away from Seattle.

The Olympia oyster is a Northwest native; it is the only oyster that is harvested commercially. It is tiny, steely tasting, really sweet, and when full-grown is only about the size of a quarter. The Kumamoto oyster is farmed from Japanese seed on lanterns hanging from floating docks. This oyster is twice the size of an Olympia; it has a deep well in the shell, making for a beautifully plump, lush morsel tasting of the sea. The Pacific oyster originated in Japan, but was brought to Puget Sound in the 1920s; it is cultivated and grows naturally all through the Sound. These are normally harvested right off the beach where

they grow. Pacifics are big, meaty oysters, perfect for barbecuing. As much as I love raw oysters, there's still nothing as tasty as a few dozen Pacifics broiled over a beach fire.

I remember the first time I saw the perfect oyster. I was a sauté cook at a local fish house, checking in the oyster delivery. When I opened up a big Igloo cooler, there were perfectly straight rows of clean, glistening Pacific oysters from Westcott Bay, all lying face up so they wouldn't lose their precious liquor. I had never seen an oyster handled as carefully as a ripe peach before. Local oysters had been always been thrown together in big onion bags, jammed up and sandy, to end up shucked in chowders or panfried. New methods of farming had resulted in these perfect oysters. Now we started selling these beautiful oysters on the half shell, a hundred dozen a week. The selection is unbelievable. The same species, Kumamotos or Pacifics or European varieties, grown in different inlets or bays within a few miles of each other, have distinctive flavors and appearances. At Etta's Seafood on any given day I can offer ten different oysters all farmed in Puget Sound.

However, there's more to seafood here than just oysters. We have Manila clams, razor clams, geoducks, surf clams, and mussels galore. The remarkably delicious singing scallops from Vancouver Island are a prize when you find them during their short season. They get their name because divers claim they make a whistling sound like singing down there in the deeps. Spot prawns, a local shrimp, are also plentiful; I especially like them covered with *togarashi* pepper and roasted in their shells (page 45).

As with all the ingredients in this book, buy only the freshest local shellfish from a trusted purveyor, just as we do. If you don't have access to local fresh seafood or want to try some of our Northwest varieties, give Harry Yoshimura a call at Mutual Fish (see Sources, page 260). He'll tell you what's in the market and if he can air-freight it to you.

GEODUCK

The first time you see a geoduck (pronounced "gooey-duck") you want to hide the women and children. In the Pike Place Market, tourists and newcomers—oohing and aahing, trying to pronounce the name and to keep from laughing at the obvious phallic jokes—gather around pails containing these monstrous local clams with their twelve-inch-long siphons hanging over the edge. These huge clams weigh up to five

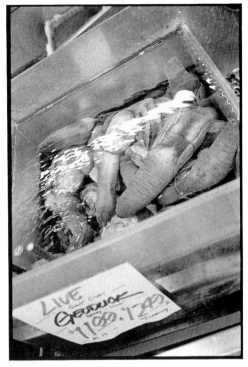

Geoduck

pounds each and are used in everything from sashimi to chowder in local restaurants. From my deck on the edge of the Sound, I can see boats suctioning clams up off the bottom, using what look like huge vacuum cleaners to harvest the tasty geoducks I might be serving the next day at Etta's. We use geoducks sliced thin for sashimi, pounded thin and panfried, or chopped into fritters or chowder.

RAZOR CLAMS

This smaller cousin of the geoduck is a little less alarming to look at and just as tasty. Thousands of people wait each year for extreme low tides so that, during the full moon in midwinter, they can walk out to dig these elusive but delicious clams. You have to be quick with the shovel, though, since the clams can burrow into the sand at the rate of 9 inches a minute.

Razor clams

Razor clams are large, oblong clams, although not as big as geoducks. They are a seasonal treat, and we are really excited when they arrive in midwinter. They suffer from the same overharvesting as many other species of seafood, so we feature them as specials in the restaurants whenever we can get them. Our favorite way to serve them is as fillets dipped in milk, dredged in cornmeal,

Manila clams

then panfried. They are absolutely delicious in sandwiches with tartar sauce and a bottle of Redhook India pale ale.

MANILA CLAMS

These even smaller clams are what you're most likely to find on Seattle menus. Originally from Japan, Manila clams were introduced into local waters early in the twentieth century, and now they are both farmed and growing wild in Puget Sound. Manila clams are steamed, usually with white wine and shallots, or served in chowders. These small, meaty clams are sweet, tender, and versatile, perfect for pasta sauce, soups, and steamers. A similar clam, found all around America's coasts, is the littleneck.

MUSSELS

Two types of mussels thrive in Puget Sound. The indigenous gunmetal-blue mussel was made famous under the name of Penn Cove, an inlet near Whidbey Island, northwest of Seattle, where most are grown. The black Mediterranean mussel is grown in the tide flats of the southern sound near Olympia. The Mediterranean mussels are at their peak in midsummer when the Penn Coves in the north are spawning, thus providing Seattle with fresh local mussels year-round.

SCALLOPS

Weathervane or Pacific scallops are the large and meaty scallops that are featured as "sea scallops" on local menus. They are sold shucked and trimmed and are often grilled or sautéed. Pink or singing scallops are native to Puget Sound and are hand-harvested by divers. Their season is short and sporadic, so whenever we get singing scallops, we put them right on the menus as specials. Singing scallops are always sold in the shell, often with their delicious coral or roe attached. They are very fragile, so we make sure to serve them the day we get them.

SPOT PRAWNS

These large shrimp (three to five inches) have bright white spots on their pinkish-red shells. Most local spot prawns come either from Washington's Hood Canal or southeast Alaska. Because they grow in such cold water, they are mild and sweet and rarely require deveining. We think most shrimp should be cooked in the shell for maximum flavor, but this is especially the case for spot prawns, since their delicate flesh gets torn when they are shelled. Often they are sold with their bright coral-orange roe attached, which gets crispy and salty when grilled.

CRAWFISH

All of the lakes in Washington State give us tons of crawfish, and when the local mud-bugs are in season I love to feast. My idea of a *tail*gate party is to take my boat out early on the day of a University of Washington football game. I anchor in Montlake Cut, just offshore from the football stadium, fill my crawdad traps with chicken necks, and take a nap in the cabin until I hear the band start playing. Then I pull up the traps, fire up my starboard rail barbecue, and steam those little puppies in lots of cayenne pepper, Yakima Valley Semillon, handfuls of garlic, and cubes of butter. At this point I pull out my portable TV and turn on the game. My pals and I kick back and enjoy the game on TV and listen to the roar of the crowd, all from the warmth of our cabin. The Semillon flows, the tails get eaten by the handful, and the Dawgs win.

HOW TO SHUCK OYSTERS

1. Stick the oyster knife in at the hinge while holding the oyster down on the counter with your other hand, then twist the knife.
2. Pull back and clean the knife of dirt or broken shell.
3. Return the knife to the oyster and, with the blade angled toward the top of the shell, slice through the length of the oyster.
4. Remove the top shell.
5. Clean away any dirt or bits of shell on the oyster.
6. Scoop under the oyster and cut the bottom muscle.
7. Last, place the oyster on a bed of crushed ice.

Take your time; don't try to rush things or you may cut into the oyster. In our kitchen, when I'm explaining how to shuck oysters to a young cook, I always say, "Don't wake them up! They should still be sleeping." The important thing is that the shucked oyster is clean and pristine, with no annoying little bits of shell or dirt.

WASHINGTON OYSTERS ON THE HALF SHELL WITH THREE MIGNONETTES

{ Makes 2 servings }

Oysters on the half shell are usually served with a classic mignonette sauce of vinegar and shallots. Here's the recipe, with a couple of variations on the theme.

1 dozen oysters, scrubbed, rinsed, and shucked
  (page 62)
1 lemon, cut into wedges

FOR CLASSIC MIGNONETTE SAUCE
¼ cup Champagne vinegar
1 tablespoon minced shallots
½ teaspoon grated lemon zest
Freshly ground black pepper

FOR TABASCO MIGNONETTE
¼ cup rice wine vinegar
1 tablespoon minced shallots
¾ teaspoon honey
¼ teaspoon Tabasco sauce
1 teaspoon Asian fish sauce
Freshly ground black pepper

FOR SAKE MIGNONETTE
2 tablespoons sake
2 tablespoons rice wine vinegar
1 teaspoon peeled and minced fresh ginger
Freshly ground black pepper

For each mignonette, combine the ingredients in a small bowl.

ON THE PLATE   Serve the oysters on the half shell over a bed of crushed ice with small ramekins of the mignonettes and lemon wedges. The oysters also look beautiful served on a bed of seaweed and ice.

A STEP AHEAD   The mignonettes can be made several hours ahead and stored, covered, in the refrigerator.

IN THE GLASS   Got to go with Champagne.

CORNMEAL-FRIED OYSTER SANDWICH WITH LEMON TARTAR SAUCE

{ Makes 4 servings }

One of my favorite sandwiches is the classic po' boy from New Orleans, a hollowed-out baguette heaped up with fried oysters and slathered with tartar sauce. You don't want bread that's too dense or heavy or one with too hard a crust because it will make the sandwich difficult to eat. If the bread seems too thick, pull some out of the middle to make room for the oysters. You can make this sandwich on un-toasted bread, or you can brush the cut sides with butter and grill them before filling the bread with oysters.

FOR THE LEMON TARTAR SAUCE

1 large egg yolk

2 tablespoons Dijon mustard

1½ teaspoons fresh lemon juice

⅔ cup peanut or vegetable oil

1 tablespoon chopped drained capers

1½ teaspoons finely chopped red onions

1½ teaspoons finely chopped dill pickles

1 tablespoon sweet pickle juice from the jar

1 tablespoon finely chopped fresh flat-leaf parsley

1 teaspoon grated lemon zest

¼ teaspoon Tabasco sauce, or to taste

FOR THE SPICY CORNMEAL FLOUR

2 cups all-purpose flour

½ cup cornmeal

4½ teaspoons cayenne

4½ teaspoons paprika

1 tablespoon kosher salt

1½ teaspoons freshly ground black pepper

1½ teaspoons dried thyme

¼ teaspoon celery seeds

FOR THE SANDWICH

2 dozen Pacific oysters, scrubbed, rinsed, and shucked (page 62)

4 pieces French bread, cut into 6- to 8-inch sandwich lengths

Butter lettuce leaves

Peanut oil for frying

1. To make the tartar sauce, place the egg yolk, mustard, and lemon juice in a food processor or blender. Pulse to combine. With the processor running, slowly add the oil in a steady stream. The mixture will become thick and emulsified. Add the capers, onions, pickles and their juice, parsley, lemon zest, and Tabasco and pulse to combine. Remove to a small bowl and set aside, refrigerated.

2. To make the cornmeal flour, combine the flour, cornmeal, and seasonings in a medium bowl. Set aside.

3. To panfry the oysters, dredge them in the seasoned cornmeal flour. You can leave them in the bowl of flour until you are ready to panfry them. Shake off any excess flour right before frying. Set up your sandwiches so they can be assembled as soon as the oysters are fried. Split the French bread rolls lengthwise. For each sandwich, spread the tartar sauce generously on both sides of the bread. Line the top half of the roll with lettuce leaves.

4. You will need to use two or more nonstick sauté pans or a large sauté pan. Cover the bottom of each sauté pan with a thin layer (1/8 inch) of peanut oil. Over high heat, heat the oil until very hot. Fry the oysters in the hot oil on both sides until golden brown and firmed up, about 4 minutes total. Drain the oysters on paper towels.

ON THE PLATE Place 6 fried oysters on the bottom half of each roll. Put the lettuce-lined half on top to form a sandwich. Serve immediately.

A STEP AHEAD The cornmeal flour can be made a week in advance and stored, covered, at room temperature. The tartar sauce can be made a day ahead and stored, covered, in the refrigerator.

IN THE GLASS Entre-Deux-Mers from Bordeaux, a dry white blend of Sauvignon Blanc and Semillon

---

HOW TO SHAVE CHEESE OR MAKE CHOCOLATE CURLS

Sometimes long shavings of cheese instead of grated cheese make for a more sophisticated look. An ordinary swivel vegetable peeler is all you need to produce these shavings. Just pull the peeler along a chunk of hard cheese, like Parmesan or an aged goat cheese, that you are holding in your hand.

This same technique also works for making chocolate curls. Hold a chunk of chocolate in your hand and scrape it with a vegetable peeler to produce long shavings. This works best if the chocolate is at room temperature.

FIRE-ROASTED OYSTERS WITH
GINGER THREADS AND WASABI BUTTER

{ Makes 4 to 6 servings }

We use *tobiko* (flying fish roe) at all our restaurants because we love the crunchy, sea taste of the tiny eggs and because it looks beautiful on the plate. Plain tobiko is golden orange in color, but there are other variations: black or squid-ink tobiko, green or wasabi tobiko, and chile or red tobiko. I like plain tobiko best for this dish.

After the oysters are cooked, we serve them on a bed of warm rock salt for two reasons: to keep them warm and to keep them upright so their liquor stays in the shell.

Peanut oil for frying
¼ cup fresh ginger threads (see below)
2 dozen oysters, scrubbed and rinsed
3 cups rock salt, warmed in the oven, on the grill,
*   or on the stove*
Wasabi Butter (page 104)
2 teaspoons tobiko or other fish roe
1 lime, cut into 4 to 6 wedges

I. Fire up the grill.

2. Heat ½ inch oil in a medium sauté pan (a cast-iron pan works best) over medium-high heat. When the oil is very hot, fry the ginger a few seconds until golden. Remove with a slotted spoon and drain on paper towels.

3. Grill the oysters over high heat until they "pop" open, 3 to 5 minutes, making sure to put them on the grill flat side up so that the oyster liquor isn't lost. Wearing an oven mitt and using an oyster knife, shuck the oysters (page 62), discarding the top shells and making sure to pick out any pieces of shell or dirt.

ON THE PLATE   Place the oysters on a bed of warm rock salt, then top each oyster with about I teaspoon of the wasabi butter. Garnish each oyster with a small dollop of tobiko and a few fried ginger threads. Serve with lime wedges.

A STEP AHEAD   The ginger threads can be fried a few hours ahead and served at room temperature.

IN THE GLASS   Try a dry Semillon from the Yakima Valley.

HOW TO MAKE GINGER THREADS

For some recipes we like to julienne fresh ginger into superfine, threadlike strips. The ginger threads look nice in the dish, and are also thin enough to eat without being tough and fibrous. We do this by peeling the ginger, then slicing it very thinly, paper thin if possible, on a mandoline or slicer. The slices of ginger are then stacked in little piles and cut into very fine strips with a sharp knife.

SZECHUAN PEPPER-SALT PRAWNS

{ Makes 4 servings }

Our local spot prawns are sweet and tender with great flavor and melt-in-your-mouth texture. As with any prawns, cook them in the shell whenever you can, as the shell provides most of the flavor. Live spot prawns will need to be blanched briefly in boiling water just before you sear them in the wok. If you can't find spot prawns, use any large prawns.

It's important that you get your wok or pan as hot as possible. If you can get it hot enough, you'll be able to cook the shells so crispy that they will actually be edible.

FOR THE SZECHUAN PEPPER-SALT
¼ teaspoon Szechuan peppercorns
¼ teaspoon white peppercorns
½ teaspoon kosher salt

FOR THE PRAWNS
¼ cup peanut oil
1 pound large prawns in the shell, split down the back
    and vein removed
2 tablespoons cornstarch
1 teaspoon chopped garlic
1 teaspoon seeded and minced serrano chile, or more
    to taste

1. To make the pepper-salt, in a small sauté pan over medium heat, toast the Szechuan and white peppercorns for about 3 minutes, shaking the pan. They will smoke and pop like popcorn, but don't let them burn. Let cool, then coarsely grind the pepper in a spice mill and combine with the salt in a little mixing bowl. Set aside.

2. Heat the oil in a wok or large sauté pan over high heat until it is just short of smoking. Toss the prawns in the cornstarch in a bowl and remove the excess cornstarch by shaking the coated prawns in a sieve. Add the prawns to the wok and cook for 2 to 3 minutes, tossing a few times to cook through on both sides. With a large spatula or other implement, hold the prawns in place, tip the wok, and pour off and discard the excess oil. Add the garlic, minced chile, and pepper-salt. Return the wok to the heat and toss the prawns with the spices until the spices release their fragrance and coat the shells, about 1 minute.

ON THE PLATE   These are beautiful served very simply on a pretty plate, garnished with lime wedges. If you can find fresh pea vines in a local farmer's market, arrange them on your platter and set the seared prawns on top.

A STEP AHEAD   The pepper-salt can be made a week or more ahead and kept, covered, at room temperature.

IN THE GLASS   A crisp fruity Northwest Riesling

Singing Scallops with Muscat Sabayon

{ Makes 6 to 8 appetizer servings }

Singing scallops got their name because divers say they whistle through their shells when they are disturbed (and, of course, the name became a good marketing tool). We feature them whenever we can get them because they are a local product with limited availability. Singing scallops are always sold in the shell (like a clam or mussel), which is a beautiful pink. Sometimes they are served simply steamed, but I prefer to steam them first, then trim them down to the scallop muscle and the little half-moon of orange coral, and serve them on the half shell.

If you can't find singing scallops, you could substitute large sea scallops or tiny bay scallops without the shells. Gently poach the scallops until opaque in the wine and aromatics described below until they are just cooked. After you finish the sauce, place the poached scallops on a baking sheet with a dollop of the sabayon on each one and brown them briefly under the broiler. Or put the scallops and sabayon in little decorative ramekins or the scallop shells that are sold for Coquilles Saint-Jacques.

We like to use a good local sweet Muscat, such as Muscat Canelli from Washington State, for the sabayon, but you can substitute another Muscat, such as Beaumes-de-Venise from the Rhône Valley or a California Muscat de Frontignan or other sweet Muscat.

2 cups sweet Muscat wine
3 sprigs fresh tarragon
½ red onion, thinly sliced
1 lemon, sliced into ⅛-inch-thick rounds

2 pounds singing scallops, rinsed, in the shell, or sea or bay scallops (If you are using scallops that don't have shells, you will need only 1 to 1½ pounds)
2 large egg yolks
¼ cup (½ stick) unsalted butter, melted
1 teaspoon chopped fresh tarragon
¼ teaspoon grated orange zest
Kosher salt

1. In a large pot over high heat, combine the Muscat, tarragon sprigs, onion, and lemon slices. Bring to a boil. Add the scallops and cover. Cook the scallops until the shells open, until tender, about 4 minutes. Remove the scallops from the steaming liquid and set aside. Strain the liquid through a fine-mesh strainer to remove and discard the solids. Pour the strained liquid into a small saucepan and boil over high heat until syrupy and reduced in volume by two thirds, about 15 minutes. Set the Muscat syrup aside and allow to cool slightly.

2. Meanwhile, clean the singing scallops, if using. Remove and discard the top shell and cut the scallop away from the bottom shell. Remove everything except the scallop muscle and the coral (the little half-moon piece attached to the scallop muscle). Place the cleaned scallops on their half shells and arrange on a baking sheet. Or put the cooked shelled scallops into ramekins or scallop shells on a baking sheet.

3. Preheat the broiler. Set a pot of water on the stovetop over medium-high heat and bring to a simmer. Using a whisk, combine the egg yolks and the reduced Muscat syrup in a metal bowl. Place the bowl over the simmering water and whisk rapidly until the sauce is light colored, medium thick, has increased in volume, and reached the ribbon stage, where the sauce falls from the whisk in ribbons, 3 to 5 minutes. Remove the bowl from the heat and whisk in the melted butter, chopped tarragon, and orange zest. If the sabayon seems too thick, whisk in a little hot water, a teaspoon at a time. Season to taste with salt.

4. Dollop a little sabayon over each scallop. Place the baking sheet of scallops under the broiler, watching carefully and turning the pan as necessary, until golden-yellow patches appear on the sabayon, about 1 minute.

ON THE PLATE   Divide the scallops among 6 or 8 appetizer plates and serve with cocktail forks. The sauce is a beautiful golden-yellow with golden-brown patches, and the shells are a luminous pink, so this dish needs no other garnish. If you like, you can serve the shells on a bed of warm rock salt.

A STEP AHEAD   The scallops can be steamed and cleaned a few hours ahead. (If you are not using a scallop in the shell, like singing scallops, the only cleaning you will need to do is to remove the small white muscle attached to the side of the scallop.) Loosely cover the cleaned scallops on the half shell with a piece of plastic wrap and keep them refrigerated until you are ready to finish the dish. Warm the scallops for a few minutes in a preheated 350°F oven before putting the sauce on them.

IN THE GLASS   Try Fumé Blanc, a Sauvignon-Semillon blend.

Alki Point Lighthouse, Seattle

UDON WITH SEA SCALLOPS IN MISO BROTH

{ Makes 4 servings }

Udon are thick wheat Japanese noodles that are usually served in a flavorful broth. You could, of course, use other noodles, such as Japanese *soba* (buckwheat noodles), or lovely light green *cha soba* (made with green tea), or popular ramen, or egg noodles.

You can find the dried, and sometimes frozen, leaves of the kaffir lime tree packaged in small plastic bags in Asian and specialty markets. The leaves add a flowery citrus aroma to the broth. If you can't find them, the lemongrass alone will still give the dish a lemony aroma and flavor.

We generally use light miso here because it is mild and not as dominating as dark miso, but follow your own taste. Other garnishes you can add to this soup are enoki mushrooms, shiso leaves, and kiware radish sprouts.

The scallops cook in the hot broth, so the noodles must still be warm and the broth should be boiling. We like our scallops a little on the underdone side. If you don't, cut the scallops into thinner slices so they cook more quickly.

This dish has been on the menu at Etta's since we opened.

---

1 bunch green onions or scallions

1 bunch cilantro

8 cups chicken stock (page 253)

10 peeled fresh ginger coins, ⅛ inch thick

4 stalks lemongrass, tender white part only, chopped (page 14)

3 kaffir lime leaves (optional)

5 tablespoons light miso paste

1 tablespoon soy sauce

½ cup julienned carrots

½ cup soy or mung bean sprouts

¼ cup fresh mint leaves

⅔ pound udon, soba, or other Asian noodles

1⅓ cups baby spinach leaves, washed well and patted dry

1 pound large scallops, sliced in half horizontally

2 tablespoons peeled and julienned (see How to Julienne, page 36) fresh ginger

4 lime wedges

1. Julienne ½ cup of the green onions and set aside. Roughly chop the rest. Pick ¼ cup cilantro leaves off the stems and set aside. Pick off the rest of the leaves and roughly chop them. In a large saucepan, combine the chopped green onions and cilantro, the chicken stock, ginger, lemongrass, and kaffir lime leaves, if using. Bring to a boil, reduce the heat to a simmer, and cover. Let simmer for half an hour. Strain through a fine-mesh strainer to remove the solids and discard (you should have about 7½ cups of flavored stock). Whisk in the miso and soy sauce.

2. Meanwhile, prepare the fresh salad and cook the udon noodles. To make the salad, combine the julienned green onions, carrots, bean sprouts, reserved cilantro leaves, and mint leaves in a bowl and toss together.

3. Cook the noodles in a pot of boiling water according to the package directions until tender but not mushy, about 10 minutes. Drain.

ON THE PLATE   Divide the noodles among 4 soup bowls. Divide the raw spinach and the raw sliced scallops among the bowls, placing on top of the hot noodles. Divide the juli-enned ginger among the bowls. Reheat the stock to the boiling point, then immediately ladle it over the noodles and scallops. Let the hot soup sit for a moment or two to cook the scallops. Mound the fresh salad in the center of each bowl and garnish with lime wedges. If desired, serve with individual ramekins of soy sauce, sesame oil, and spicy *sambal olek*.

A STEP AHEAD   The flavored stock can be made a day ahead and stored in the refriger-ator. Reheat to the boiling point. The fresh salad can be put together a few hours ahead and also stored in the refrigerator, tightly covered.

IN THE GLASS   A Japanese beer like Sapporo or Kirin

One of my favorite walks in the market, Post Alley

CLAM LINGUINE WITH PANCETTA, CHILES, AND GARLIC

{ Makes 4 servings }

I add roasted jalapeños to this classic Italian dish to give it a lift of spice and flavor. It's the perfect dish to order late at night at the bar at Etta's with a glass of Pinot Grigio—it's also a great first course for a big Italian feast. I always put Parmesan on these spicy clams, despite the Italian thing about no cheese with fish. Use grated cheese, if you like, or make Parmesan curls with a potato peeler.

If you don't have a sauté pan big enough to cook 2 pounds of clams, you can split the clams up into 2 pans.

2 jalapeño chiles, cut in half and seeded
¼ cup olive oil, plus more for brushing
Kosher salt and freshly ground black pepper
3 ounces pancetta, diced (½ cup)
1 teaspoon minced garlic
¼ teaspoon red pepper flakes, or to taste
2 pounds clams, scrubbed and rinsed
¼ cup dry white wine
1 pound fresh linguine (page 250) or dried linguine
¼ cup (½ stick) unsalted butter
4 teaspoons chopped fresh flat-leaf parsley
3 teaspoons fresh lemon juice
2 teaspoons grated lemon zest
½ cup fresh flat-leaf parsley
¼ cup shaved (see How to Shave Cheese, page 65) Parmesan cheese
4 lemon wedges

1. Preheat the oven to 400°F and start a pot of salted water boiling to cook the pasta later. Brush the jalapeño halves with oil and sprinkle with salt and pepper. Place them on a baking sheet and roast in the oven for 10 minutes. When cool enough to handle, dice finely.

2. Put a large sauté pan over medium-high heat. Heat the ¼ cup olive oil, add the pancetta, and cook, stirring, until browned, about 2 minutes. Add the jalapeño, garlic, and pepper flakes and cook, stirring, another minute. Turn the heat to high. Add the clams and wine and cover. Cook until the clams open, about 3 minutes. Meanwhile, cook the pasta in the boiling water until *al dente*. Add the butter, chopped parsley, lemon juice, and zest to the clams in the pan and toss until the butter melts into the sauce. Drain the pasta. In a large serving bowl, toss the pasta with the clam sauce and whole parsley leaves. Season to taste with salt and pepper.

ON THE PLATE Divide the pasta among 4 shallow bowls or plates and top with the shaved Parmesan. Make sure the clams mostly end up on top of the pasta, facing up. (Move them around with tongs if you need to.) Discard any unopened clams. Garnish with lemon wedges.

IN THE GLASS Try a Pinot Grigio from the Veneto, in northern Italy.

HOW TO PEEL, SEED, AND DICE TOMATOES

Several of our recipes call for seeding and dicing tomatoes, and you may wonder why we don't peel the tomatoes as well. We do peel tomatoes when we are using them in a cooked sauce or puree, because otherwise the peels come off and give the sauce an unpleasant texture. We may not peel them if we plan to strain the finished product, because that's another way of removing the peels.

If we are using diced tomatoes raw or if there are chunks of diced tomatoes in a briefly cooked dish, we usually don't peel them because the skins won't separate and therefore we don't find them unpleasant. But you can peel the tomatoes if you want.

The easiest way to peel tomatoes is to core them, cut an X in the bottom, then plunge them in boiling water for a few seconds. Remove them from the boiling water with a slotted spoon and immediately plunge them into a bowl of ice water. Remove them from the ice water and you should be able to slide the peels off easily with your fingers or a paring knife.

When dicing tomatoes, always seed them first, because otherwise the watery tomato juices will dilute the dish. One way to seed tomatoes before dicing them is to core the tomato and slice it in half (across the diameter, not through the core), then squeeze out all the seeds, using your fingers or a small spoon to dig out and discard all the seeds and juices. Cut the tomato flesh into dice.

Oven-Roasted Clams with Chanterelles, Bacon, and Tomatoes

{ Makes 4 servings }

Manila clams, geoducks, razor clams, and chowder clams, whatever the size, shape, taste, or texture, they all grow in the Northwest.

If you don't have a sauté pan large enough for 2 pounds of clams, you can divide everything up between 2 pans. There's no salt in this recipe because the clams, bacon, and olives are all pretty salty. Taste the finished dish and add salt if you wish. If you can't get chanterelles, you can substitute crimini mushrooms or fresh shiitakes.

2 ounces (4 slices) bacon, diced (about ½ cup)

2 tablespoons extra virgin oil

⅓ pound chanterelles, cut into bite-size pieces

2 cloves garlic, thinly sliced

2 pounds clams, scrubbed and rinsed

3 ripe Roma tomatoes, seeded and diced, or
    1 half-pint basket cherry tomatoes, cut in half

½ cup good black olives, preferably oil-cured
    (we leave the pits in, but you may want to warn
    your guests)

4 sprigs fresh thyme

6 tablespoons (¾ stick) unsalted butter

3 tablespoons dry white wine

1 lemon, cut into 6 wedges

Preheat the oven to 500°F. Heat a large sauté pan over medium-high heat. Add the bacon and brown, about 3 minutes. Add the olive oil, chanterelles, and garlic and cook, stirring, for 1 minute. Add the clams, tomatoes, olives, thyme, butter, and wine. Squeeze 2 lemon wedges into the pan. Cover the pan and place it in the oven. Roast until the clams open, 10 to 12 minutes.

ON THE PLATE   Divide the clams and cooking juices among 4 shallow bowls. Discard any clams that do not open. Grilled bruschetta or toasted garlic bread is nice with this to sop up the juices. Garnish each bowl with 1 lemon wedge.

IN THE GLASS   A lightly oaked Chardonnay

WOK-FRIED MUSSELS WITH SAKE-GINGER BUTTER

{ Makes 2 to 4 servings }

Mussels, as well as oysters and clams, are aqua-farmed all over the Puget Sound. The local mussels are best eaten during the winter months. My favorites come from Penn Cove Farms on Whidbey Island, just north of Seattle. Recently, a Mediterranean variety has been cultivated in the South Sound, so we now have great mussels year round.

It's fun to use a wok in this recipe, though a large sauté pan will work just as well.

2 pounds mussels
½ cup sake
¼ cup peeled and julienned (see How to Julienne, page 36) fresh ginger
2 dried red chiles (such as chiles de arbol or piquins)
½ cup julienned green onions or scallions, white and green parts
6 tablespoons (¾ stick) unsalted butter
1 teaspoon fresh lime juice
Kosher salt and freshly ground black pepper
2 to 4 lime wedges

1. Scrub and debeard the mussels (see below). Heat a wok or large sauté pan over high heat and preheat the oven to 200°F. When the wok or pan is very hot, add the mussels, sake, ginger, and chiles, cover with a lid, and cook over high heat until the mussels open, 3 to 4 minutes. Toss the green onions with the mussels, then remove the mussels from the wok and place them on a heat proof plater in the oven to keep them warm while you finish the sauce, leaving the liquid in the wok over high heat.

2. Add the butter and lime juice to the liquid and season to taste with salt and pepper; be cautious with the salt, since the mussels may be salty. Continue to cook the sauce, shaking or stirring to melt the butter into the sauce, 1 to 2 minutes.

ON THE PLATE   Divide the mussels among 4 wide, shallow bowls (or 2 large bowls for a dinner portion), pour the sauce over, and garnish with lime wedges.

IN THE GLASS   Try a dry Chenin Blanc from Washington State.

HOW TO DEBEARD MUSSELS

Rinse the mussels and scrub them with a stiff brush. Grasp the beard (the rough, scrubby threads that the mussel uses to attach itself to a surface) of each mussel firmly between your thumb and forefinger and give it a hard yank.

The funky, artsy, eclectic neighborhood of Fremont considers itself "the Center of the Universe."

Crabs, Crabs, Crabs

DUNGENESS, OF COURSE. Most of our crab recipes feature our local delicacy, the Dungeness crab. Dungeness Spit juts out into the Strait of Juan de Fuca, just west of Puget Sound, but the meaty and flavorful crab is found all along the Pacific coast from Mexico to Alaska. The crab season changes up and down the coast, which makes the Dungeness available almost year-round in Seattle.

Dungies, as we affectionately call these large two- to four-pound rock crabs, arrive at our restaurants in many different ways. My favorite way to get the crabs is to climb up on the back of a pickup truck that's been remodeled into a movable aquarium with tanks and pumps and filters. Five-hundred-gallon plastic totes or shipping containers are filled with salt water and live crabs and, sometimes, with local spot prawns. I always go for the largest, liveliest, and heaviest crabs. Dungeness crabs should be heavy for their size and full of meat. I tap on the shells to make sure they don't sound hollow.

The Northwest tradition is to boil the crabs briefly in salted water. The crabs are served hot, or more likely chilled, with melted butter and lemon or mayonnaise. One crab per person is the norm in our house. My daughter Loretta's favorite treat is to have the crabs wok-seared on a very hot burner with ginger, Chinese black beans, and garlic. By the time we're done, we're covered from chin to elbows with crab shells and sticky sauce. You know you've had a successful crab feast when Ruby, our Brittany spaniel, becomes your best friend.

West Coast fishmongers will cook and clean your crab for you, something unheard of in the East with a bushel of small Atlantic blue crabs. Dungeness are often found live in tanks in restaurants and fish markets: You fish them out, boil them up, and fall to. Or you can go to the market and pick up a cleaned cooked Dungeness for dinner or a picnic on the beach.

The king crab is so big and ugly that if Captain Nemo had come across a large specimen he would have gone into another line of work. If you happen to see a live king crab in a Chinatown fish market, you'll know what we mean. These huge spidery creatures are often pimpled with barnacles. They range in weight from nine to a gargantuan twenty-five pounds and can have a leg span of up to six feet.

Most king crab comes from cold northern waters. Fishing for the crab in the Bering Sea is the most dangerous job in the world; the Wall at Fisherman's Terminal in Seattle, where much of the Alaskan crab fleet docks over winter, is filled with names of those lost at sea. The large crab legs, some weighing a pound or more, are usually sold cooked and frozen, the best being cooked and immediately flash-frozen aboard ship. If the frozen legs are slowly and carefully thawed, they are delicious. We don't usually recommend frozen products, but if you buy from a fish purveyor who knows his business, king crab legs are delectable.

Another popular crab from southeastern Alaska is the tanner crab, also called snow crab. It looks like the king crab, but is about one quarter the size. In my opinion, tanner crab doesn't have nearly the flavor of the larger king crab, so I use king or Dungeness.

Most of our recipes feature Northwest crabs, but you can use Atlantic blue crab and other varieties in most cases, since you are always better off using fresh local crab and other shellfish.

Sailing in the Sound

King Crab Legs with Three Dipping Sauces

King crab, which comes from the cold waters of the Gulf of Alaska, is available live in some West Coast markets. Most other parts of the country have to make do with frozen legs, but that's okay. Defrost them slowly in the refrigerator, not at room temperature or under running water. If you buy crab legs, fresh or frozen, as opposed to a whole crab, they will likely already be cooked.

Lemon verbena is an herb that adds a pleasant lemony note to fish and seafood. If you can't find it, substitute lemongrass or grated lemon zest. *Nuoc cham* is a popular Vietnamese dipping sauce.

FOR THE LEMON VERBENA BUTTER
½ cup (1 stick) unsalted butter
1 sprig fresh lemon verbena or 1 stalk lemongrass (tender white part only), roughly chopped, or 1 teaspoon grated lemon zest

FOR THE ROASTED MANGO AND JALAPEÑO SAUCE
1 jalapeño chile, cut in half and seeded
1 ripe mango, peeled, pitted, and cut into wedges
1½ teaspoons fresh lime juice
Kosher salt and freshly ground black pepper

FOR THE NUOC CHAM
¼ cup fresh lime juice
2 tablespoons sugar
2 tablespoons Asian fish sauce
2 tablespoons water

2 teaspoons chopped cilantro
½ teaspoon red pepper flakes
½ teaspoon finely chopped lemongrass, tender white part only

FOR THE CRAB
2 pounds cooked king crab legs, defrosted if frozen
1 lemon, cut into 4 to 6 wedges

1. To make the lemon verbena butter, in a small saucepan over medium heat, slowly melt the butter. Skim to remove the solids on top. (Reheat the butter gently if it cools while skimming.) Add the lemon verbena (or lemongrass or lemon zest) and let steep for half an hour. Strain through a fine-mesh strainer to remove the solids.

2. To make the jalapeño mango sauce, preheat your broiler to high. Place the jalapeño halves, skin side up, and the mango wedges on a baking sheet. Broil until the mango begins to brown and the jalapeño skins are blackened and blistered, about 7 minutes. Remove from the broiler. Puree the mango in a food processor. Peel and mince the jalapeño. In a small bowl, combine the mango, jalapeño, and lime juice. Season to taste with salt and pepper.

3. To make the nuoc cham, whisk together all the ingredients.

4. To prepare the crab, cut each leg in half horizontally. The legs can be served warm or cold. To serve them warm, place them in a

preheated 350°F oven for just a few minutes. Don't overcook or they will become tough and dry.

ON THE PLATE   Serve the crab legs with ramekins of the three dipping sauces and lemon wedges.

A STEP AHEAD   All the sauces can be made a day in advance and stored, tightly covered, in the refrigerator. The mango-jalapeño sauce and the nuoc cham may be served cold, but the lemon verbena butter should be served warm.

IN THE GLASS   A dry-style Riesling from the Northwest or Alsace

Chinatown street theater

Pry the carapace (top shell) from the body. Rinse and set aside.

Rinse and remove the gills.

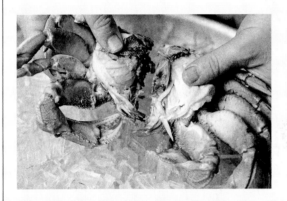

Break or crack the body in half.

Remove the apron (tail) on the bottom shell.

For Wok-Fried Crab, cut the crab into sections and break the claws with a crab-cracker or the back of a knife.

HOT-AND-SOUR SOUP WITH CRAB

{ Makes 4 servings }

This spicy soup makes a terrific first course served in a terrine or a large pot. There's nothing quite like taking the lid off and having the aromatic steam hit your face like a sauna.

For a satisfying main dish on a cold night, you can add enoki mushrooms, cubes of tofu, and beautiful mustard greens.

---

1 ounce dried shiitake mushrooms

6 cups chicken stock (page 253)

3 tablespoons peeled and finely julienned
  (see How to Julienne, page 36) ginger

1 teaspoon chopped garlic

2 teaspoons Chinese chile paste with garlic

¼ cup rice wine vinegar

¼ cup soy sauce

1 cup canned slivered bamboo shoots, drained

1 tablespoon fresh lime juice

2 teaspoons sugar

Kosher salt

1 tablespoon plus 2 teaspoons cornstarch

2 tablespoons cold water

1 large egg, beaten

4 ounces fresh cooked crabmeat (about 1 cup),
  picked over for bits of shell and cartilage

¼ cup green onions or scallions, white and green
  parts, cut on the bias into thin strips or julienned

I. Place the dried shiitake mushrooms in a small heatproof bowl and cover with boiling water. Allow to soak for 30 minutes. Drain, rinse, and cut into thin slices. Set aside.

2. In a large saucepan, heat the chicken stock. Add the ginger, garlic, chile paste, vinegar, soy sauce, reconstituted shiitake mushrooms, and bamboo shoots. Simmer for 10 minutes. Add the lime juice and sugar and season to taste with salt.

3. Make a cornstarch slurry by mixing together the cornstarch and water. Add the slurry to the soup and simmer for a few minutes until the soup thickens. Bring the soup to a boil and slowly pour in the beaten egg, stirring gently a few times with a spoon or with chopsticks. Don't whisk or stir too vigorously—you want nice long shreds of eggs. The egg will cook almost instantly. Remove the soup from the heat.

ON THE PLATE   Ladle the soup into 4 bowls. Top each bowl with an ounce of crabmeat and garnish with the green onions.

A STEP AHEAD   You can make the soup base, without the beaten egg, a few days ahead and store refrigerated. Bring the soup to a boil and add the beaten egg, then ladle into bowls and add the crabmeat and green onions.

IN THE GLASS   A Chinese beer like Tsing tao

CRAB SALAD WITH ASPARAGUS, AVOCADO, AND LIME VINAIGRETTE

{ Makes 4 servings }

There must be six places in the Pike Place Market alone where you can get fresh crab or picked crabmeat. The traditional crab salad from this area is called a crab Louie—mounds of meat piled on lettuce and covered in Thousand Island dressing. Too much gook for me.

This recipe is a very simple entrée salad that we developed for Etta's. It's meant to feature the taste of crab when it's in the prime of the season. If red Bibb lettuce is available, a combination of red- and green-leaved lettuce is attractive. The texture of this salad is very soft, so you may want to serve crisp crackers or toasted bruschetta alongside.

FOR THE LIME VINAIGRETTE

3 tablespoons fresh lime juice
4½ teaspoons rice wine vinegar
2 teaspoons grated lime zest
1½ teaspoons peeled and grated fresh ginger
1½ teaspoons honey
3 tablespoons olive oil

3 tablespoons peanut oil
Kosher salt and freshly ground black pepper

FOR THE SALAD

1 pound asparagus, tough bottoms snapped off
¾ pound fresh cooked crabmeat, picked over for bits of shell and cartilage
2 heads Bibb lettuce (about ½ pound), leaves separated, washed, and dried
2 ripe avocados, halved, pitted, and peeled
1 ruby grapefruit, peeled and cut into segments (see below)

1. To make the vinaigrette, whisk together the lime juice, vinegar, lime zest, ginger, and honey in a small bowl. Whisk in the oils. Season to taste with salt and pepper. Set aside.

2. Bring a pot of water to the boil and cook the asparagus until just tender, about 5 minutes. As soon as the asparagus are tender, scoop them out of the boiling water and immediately plunge into a bowl of ice water.

HOW TO MAKE GRAPEFRUIT SEGMENTS

To make attractive grapefruit segments without any membrane, use a knife to slice off the top and bottom of the grapefruit. Place the grapefruit on the counter with one flat end down, then, with the knife, slice off the peel all around the fruit, removing all the white pith. When the grapefruit is completely peeled, hold it over a bowl to catch the juices and use a small sharp paring knife to cut out and release each segment of grapefruit between the membranes.

When the asparagus are cold, drain and toss them with 3 tablespoons of the vinaigrette. Set aside.

3. Toss the crabmeat with 3 tablespoons of the vinaigrette and set aside. In a large bowl, toss the Bibb lettuce leaves with 3 tablespoons of the vinaigrette.

ON THE PLATE Divide the dressed Bibb lettuce leaves among 4 large chilled plates. Place an avocado half on top of the lettuce on each plate and drizzle the avocado with a little vinaigrette. Arrange a bundle of dressed asparagus next to each avocado half. Divide the dressed crabmeat among the plates, draping it over the avocado and the asparagus. Garnish with the grapefruit segments and serve.

A STEP AHEAD The vinaigrette may be made a day ahead and the asparagus can be cooked (but not dressed) a few hours ahead. Both should be stored, covered, in the refrigerator.

IN THE GLASS Try a Mimosa—orange juice and Champagne.

This winding alley in the Pike Place Market leads to theaters, bars, and little shops.

BLUE CRAB RÉMOULADE WITH
FRIED GREEN TOMATOES

{ Makes 6 servings }

Blue crabs are found in the Chesapeake Bay region where I grew up, and they are delicious steamed, boiled, or stir-fried; in crabcakes and cocktails; and sautéed as soft-shell crabs. This recipe combines the succulent, sweet meat of the blue crab with Creole-style rémoulade, a spicy mayonnaise that goes wonderfully with any cold seafood. We use blue crab here but also Dungeness or any other fresh crabmeat would do as well.

FOR THE RÉMOULADE

2 large egg yolks (see Note, page 24)
2 tablespoons fresh lemon juice
1 tablespoon Creole mustard or whole-grain mustard
1 tablespoon ketchup
1 tablespoon Worcestershire sauce
1½ teaspoons red wine vinegar
1½ teaspoons Tabasco sauce
1½ teaspoons paprika
¾ cup olive oil
¼ cup finely chopped celery
¼ cup finely chopped green onions or scallions, white and green parts
2 tablespoons chopped fresh flat-leaf parsley
2 tablespoons peeled and grated fresh horseradish
1 teaspoon minced garlic
Kosher salt

TO FINISH THE DISH

1 pound fresh cooked blue crabmeat, picked over for bits of shell and cartilage
Fried Green Tomatoes (recipe follows)

6 sprigs parsley (optional)
1 lemon, cut into 6 wedges

1. To make the rémoulade, put the egg yolks in a food processor. Add the lemon juice, mustard, ketchup, Worcestershire, vinegar, Tabasco, and paprika and pulse until combined. Add the oil in a slow steady stream while the processor is running. The mixture will thicken and emulsify. Add the celery, green onions, parsley, horseradish, and garlic and pulse once or twice. Season with salt. Remove the rémoulade from the processor and refrigerate it.

2. Put the crabmeat in a bowl and toss with the chilled rémoulade. The amount of rémoulade in this recipe is just about right for 1 pound of crabmeat.

ON THE PLATE   Arrange three fried green tomatoes on each of 6 plates and top with a portion of rémoulade. Garnish with parsley sprigs, if desired, and lemon wedges.

A STEP AHEAD   The sauce can be made a day ahead and stored, covered, in the refrigerator.

IN THE GLASS   Try a Sauvignon Blanc or a strong beer like Redhook E.S.B.

Fried Green Tomatoes

{ Makes 6 servings }

In Seattle, with our cool and sometimes rainy summers, we never know whether our tomatoes will get ripe or not, so we often end up with lots of green tomatoes. I especially like the flavor of green tomatoes fried in a mixture of half bacon fat and half butter, but you can substitute peanut oil or vegetable oil.

2 cups buttermilk

½ teaspoon cayenne

1¼ pounds green tomatoes, sliced ¼ inch thick (about 18 slices)

1½ cups medium-ground yellow cornmeal

¾ cup all-purpose flour

2 teaspoons kosher salt, plus more for the final seasoning

1 teaspoon freshly ground black pepper

Peanut or vegetable oil for panfrying

1. In a large bowl, combine the buttermilk and ¼ teaspoon of the cayenne. Add the green tomato slices and gently turn them around in the buttermilk so they are completely coated. In a shallow pan, mix together the cornmeal, flour, salt, black pepper, and the remaining ¼ teaspoon cayenne.

2. Using one hand for the dry ingredients and the other hand for the wet ingredients, dip the buttermilk-coated tomatoes in the cornmeal-flour, coating them well and evenly.

3. Heat a few tablespoons of oil in two large sauté pans over medium-high heat. Fry as many slices as will fit comfortably in each sauté pan at a time. Fry the tomatoes on both sides until golden and crisp, about 3 minutes. Drain on paper towels and season with more salt if necessary.

DUNGENESS CRABCAKES
WITH GREEN COCKTAIL SAUCE

{ Makes 8 appetizer or 4 entrée servings }

I brought this East Coast version of crabcakes with me when I moved here from Delaware about twenty-two years ago, but of course in Seattle I make them with the Northwest's sweet and delicious Dungeness crabmeat. Some modern versions of crabcakes are mostly crabmeat lightly bound with egg, but I'm a firm believer that a crabcake should contain bread crumbs. Bread crumbs made from cheap white bread are a key ingredient here: Ordinary store-bought white bread gives the crabcake just the right texture. And, of course, you need perfectly fresh, pristine crabmeat with plenty of big chunks of claw and leg meat.

At both Dahlia Lounge and Etta's Seafood, Dungeness crabcakes is one of our most popular dishes and most requested recipes. Since this is a signature dish, we tend to be a little secretive about the recipe, but, what the hey, here it is.

At Etta's the crabcakes come with French fries, coleslaw, and green cocktail sauce. At Dahlia Lounge we change the presentation often—for example, they can be served with butternut-squash hash and an apple salad with Tabasco vinaigrette.

---

10 slices supermarket white bread (about ½ loaf)
¾ cup chopped fresh flat-leaf parsley
1 large egg yolk (see Note, page 24)
2 teaspoons fresh lemon juice
2 teaspoons Worcestershire sauce
1½ teaspoons Tabasco sauce
7 teaspoons Dijon mustard
½ teaspoon paprika
½ teaspoon dried thyme

½ teaspoon celery seeds
¼ teaspoon freshly ground black pepper
5 tablespoons olive oil
1 pound fresh cooked Dungeness crabmeat, picked over for bits of shell and cartilage with claw meat and large pieces of crab left whole
¼ cup chopped onions
¼ cup seeded and chopped green bell peppers
¼ cup seeded and chopped red bell peppers
Unsalted butter for panfrying, about 6 tablespoons
Green Cocktail Sauce (recipe follows)
4 to 8 lemon wedges

1. Tear up the white bread and pulse the pieces in a food processor to make fine, soft crumbs. (You should have about 6 cups crumbs.) Remove the bread crumbs to a shallow pan and mix in ½ cup of the chopped parsley (reserve the remaining ¼ cup for the crabcake mixture). Set aside.

2. In a food processor, combine the egg yolk, lemon juice, Worcestershire, Tabasco, mustard, paprika, thyme, celery seeds, and black pepper and pulse to combine. With the motor running, slowly add the oil through the feed tube in a steady stream until the mixture emulsifies and forms a mayonnaise. Remove the mayonnaise from the food processor and refrigerate.

3. Place the crabmeat in a cheesecloth-lined sieve set over a bowl. Pull the cheesecloth tightly around the crabmeat and squeeze out as much juice as possible. Place the chopped onions and bell peppers in a sieve set over a bowl and use your hands to squeeze out as much juice as possible. In a large bowl, combine the onions and bell peppers with the remaining ¼ cup parsley. Add the chilled mayonnaise and crabmeat and toss lightly to combine. Add 1 cup of the bread crumb–parsley mixture and combine. Do not overwork the mixture or the crabcakes may get gummy. Gently form 8 patties and roll the patties lightly in the remaining bread crumb–parsley mixture. Leave the crabcakes in the pan of bread crumbs until you sauté them.

4. Preheat the oven to 425°F. Using a nonstick sauté pan and butter as needed, panfry the crabcakes, in batches, until golden brown on both sides and place them on a baking sheet as they are browned. When all the crabcakes are browned, put them in the oven until they are heated all the way through, 5 to 8 minutes.

ON THE PLATE   Serve one crabcake as an appetizer or two as an entrée. Serve with a ramekin of cocktail sauce and a lemon wedge.

A STEP AHEAD   The crabcakes actually hold together better if prepared a day ahead and stored in the refrigerator before cooking. Store them in the pan of bread crumbs, covered with plastic wrap.

IN THE GLASS   A lightly oaked Chardonnay

Etta's Seafood

Green Cocktail Sauce

{ Makes ⅔ cup }

Some people like to serve crabcakes with mayonnaise- or butter-based sauces, but because crabcakes are so rich, we prefer a sauce that's zippy, fresh tasting, and piquant. This spicy, green salsa is just right. This lively sauce also goes well with poached prawns or crab legs—the color combination is stunning.

Tomatillos, a fruit, also called Mexican green tomatoes, are widely used in Mexican recipes. They're not really tomatoes and come in a papery husk that should be removed before cooking. You can find them fresh in many supermarkets and in Latino groceries. Green Tabasco is a fiery sauce made by the McIlhenny Company on Avery Island, Louisiana, from jalapeños.

---

8 ounces tomatillos, husked and cut into quarters

2 tablespoons rice wine vinegar

1 tablespoon sugar

2 teaspoons green Tabasco sauce

1 teaspoon chopped garlic

1 teaspoon mustard seeds, toasted (page 39)

1 teaspoon peeled and grated fresh horseradish

Put the tomatillos in a food processor and process until coarsely pureed. Remove the tomatillo puree to a sieve, drain off the liquid, and discard. Put the drained puree in a small bowl and stir in the vinegar, sugar, Tabasco, garlic, mustard seeds, and horseradish until combined.

A STEP AHEAD This can be made a day ahead and held, covered, in the refrigerator.

Wok-Fried Crab with Ginger and Lemongrass

{ Makes 1 to 2 servings }

Sometimes I can pick up good insights into a technique just by popping my head in somebody else's kitchen. Once while waiting for a table at Sea Garden in Seattle's International District, I saw the cooks "set" the juices of the raw crabs before wok-frying them by quickly dipping them in boiling water (or a deep fryer). This is important because if you wok-fry the crab without doing this beforehand, the crab liquids bleed out and coagulate in your sauce—not necessarily ruining the taste, but changing the texture and the look immensely.

At Etta's the crab is "set," then hacked into convenient pieces and cracked before being wok-fried. We save the top shell in one piece and stir-fry it with the crab so it is warm and has sauce on it—even though it's inedible. Then we quickly "reassemble" the crab on the plate and put the top shell back in place so it looks like a whole crab again. You can try this at home if you want, or just serve the crab in pieces.

A mound of Japanese short-grain rice fragrant with spices (see Aromatic Steamed Rice, page 159) is perfect for soaking up this complex, well-balanced sauce with its bright flavors, sweetness, and gentle spiciness.

FOR THE LEMONGRASS SAUCE

3 tablespoons peanut oil
2 teaspoons finely minced lemongrass, tender white part only
2 teaspoons seeded and minced poblano chiles
2 teaspoons minced shallots
2 teaspoons peeled and grated fresh ginger
1 teaspoon minced garlic
1 cup chicken stock (page 253)
5 teaspoons rice wine vinegar
5 teaspoons soy sauce
2½ teaspoons sugar
2 teaspoons Chinese chile paste with garlic
1 teaspoon coarsely chopped Chinese fermented black beans
2 teaspoons cornstarch dissolved in 1 tablespoon cold water
1 Dungeness crab (about 1½ pounds), cooked, cleaned, and cracked (page 81)
¼ cup sake
2 lime wedges

1. To make the lemongrass sauce, heat 1 tablespoon of the peanut oil in a small saucepan over medium-high heat. Cook the lemongrass, poblano, shallots, ginger, and garlic, stirring, until soft, about 2 minutes. Add the chicken stock, vinegar, soy sauce, sugar, chile paste, and black beans and bring to a simmer for 5 minutes. Add the dissolved cornstarch and simmer, stirring frequently, until the sauce becomes glossy and thickens, about 2 more minutes. Set aside.

2. To wok-fry the crab, heat the remaining 2 tablespoons peanut oil in a wok over high heat until almost smoking. Toss in the crab pieces (including the carapace, or top shell), add the sake, and cover. Allow to steam for 2 to 3 minutes. Add the lemon-

grass sauce and simmer until the crab is heated through and the sauce thickens to the desired consistency, 1 to 2 minutes.

ON THE PLATE On a large plate or platter, arrange the crab with the carapace (top shell) back on top so it looks roughly like a whole crab again and pour all the sauce over and around it. We serve this crab with a big scoop of steamed rice. We also garnish it with pea vines, a sprinkle of julienned green onions, toasted black and white sesame seeds, and a lime wedge. For this very messy and finger-lickin' good dish, you'll need crab-crackers, a side bowl for the shells, a stack of napkins, and bowls of warm lemon water to clean your hands.

A STEP AHEAD The lemongrass sauce can be made up to a few days ahead, refrigerated, and reheated before using. The crab can be steamed, cleaned, and chopped, and chilled earlier on the day you are planning to use it.

IN THE GLASS A dry-style Riesling or Chenin Blanc

The "Bread of Life Mission" in Pioneer Square

The Pike Place Market is a real, functioning farmer's market, not just a tourist attraction.

Finfish

THERE'S A SAYING: "Eating a fish without bones is like kissing a man without a mustache." We are happy to see that people are starting to eat whole fish again, at least in restaurants. There are advantages to buying and eating whole fish. You have a much

better chance of knowing if you're eating a fresh fish—just by looking at it—than if some nameless, boneless, skinless white fillet is placed in front of you.

When you buy fish, get to know your fishmonger and learn to pick out the freshest whole specimens. The eyes should be clear, rounded, and full, not sunken. The gills should be brilliant red and the fish should have no fishy smell. The scales should be clean and bright. Missing scales may mean the fish is old or hasn't been handled properly. Any fishmonger worth his salt will be happy to fillet a whole fish for you.

On our menus it's not enough anymore just to give the names of the fish. We now have "designer" fish, like Campbell River, Yukon River, or Columbia River salmon.

Chefs and fish fanciers wait breathlessly for the arrival of the famous Copper River salmon from Alaska—supermarkets put up signs saying FIRST COPPER RIVER SALMON TOMORROW!!!—and the buying frenzy resembles an internet IPO on opening day.

We not only have to tell our savvy diners which river the fish came from, but even how they were caught: long line, troll caught, gill net, or purse seiner. I think this is a positive trend. The more you know about what you are eating, the better!

Use the KISS method whenever you cook fish: "Keep it simple, stupid." Work hard to find the very best product and then don't screw it up by overcooking or covering it with a gloppy sauce. I especially like to serve fish in an uncomplicated, direct way that highlights the fish itself. Fresh fish grilled over charcoal or broiled in the oven with a simple relish or salsa is as good as it gets.

SALMON

Because of aqua-farming, salmon is available year-round, but its wild season is summer. Salmon are born in fresh water and migrate to salt water for one to four years before they return to their ancestral river to spawn. In Seattle one of the favorite tourist destinations is the Ballard Locks, where you can watch the migrating salmon ascend the fish ladder that gets them around the locks.

Salmon stop eating once they leave salt water, so the best time to catch them is just before they enter fresh water. At this point, their flesh has the highest fat and protein content. The fat content is determined by the length of time they spend in the ocean and the distance they must cover to reproduce. The longer the distance, the more body fat they produce to prepare for the journey. More fat creates better texture and flavor.

PACIFIC SALMON

King: Also known as chinook, this is among the first types available wild, with its season beginning in May. The king salmon has a spotted blue-green back and silver sides. Its distinguishing features are black gums and spotting on its tail. The king salmon has the highest fat content, making it buttery and rich. The fish average fifteen to forty pounds.

Sockeye: The most prized salmon in Japan. It has the most vivid red flesh of all salmon, averages about six pounds each, and has a medium fat content. The fish has a bright blue back with silver sides.

Coho: This has a medium fat content, making its meat more flaky with less flavor. It is distinguished by its metallic blue back, irregular spotting, and a squared-off tail. These fish average six to twelve pounds apiece.

Pink: With its low fat content, it is usually sold canned. Pinks are distinguished by oval spotting. Their season is the early fall. These fish are the smallest, averaging three to five pounds each.

Chum: This has the lowest fat content, which gives it coarse-textured flesh. It is the least expensive type available and is mostly smoked. The fish is distinguished by a V-shaped tail and no spotting on the skin. It's available through October, the latest salmon of the year. These fish average eight to ten pounds each.

Steelhead: These used to be called steelhead trout, but have recently been reclassified as Pacific salmon. The fish has a blue-green back with silver sides and black speckles and has medium fat content. Like the Atlantic salmon, these fish survive after spawning and are often farmed.

Within these types, salmon is also described by how it is caught:

Farm: Salmon raised in net-pens.

Wild: Either troll caught or net caught. We prefer troll caught because the fish are gutted and bled on board, so the meat is firmer.

Salmon are also named for the place they come from. The Copper River in Alaska is among the longest freshwater river runs and the farthest north (making for very cold water). Copper River salmon have a high fat content and firm flesh, which give them a rich flavor and texture. Their season is about three weeks long in the end of May and the beginning of June. Copper River salmon are much sought after in Seattle markets and restaurants during its short season. Yukon River salmon are less well known than Copper River salmon but have similar flavor and texture characteristics.

ATLANTIC SALMON

This is a confusing title because Atlantic salmon are native to the Atlantic, but can be farmed in the Pacific (locally, off Bainbridge Island, for example). Unlike Pacific salmon, Atlantic salmon don't die after they reproduce; they can return to fresh water up to four times. This salmon has a blue back with silver sides. It is distinguished by black spots on its gill cover. These fish are mostly farmed rather than caught wild.

The Space Needle is a survivor of the 1962 World's Fair.

WOK-SEARED ALBACORE TUNA
WITH COCONUT CURRY

{ Makes 2 servings }

This is comfort food: a perfect, soothing one-bowl lunch or supper. The curry sauce also tastes great with grilled or wok-seared prawns or scallops. If you don't have a wok, get one (they're inexpensive), or you can make this in a large sauté pan. The key is a very hot pan—the oil should start to smoke before adding the tuna.

I love the flavor of Southeast Asian sour shrimp paste (*tom yum*). You can visualize nets of tiny shrimp drying on the beaches in Thailand.

1 bunch cilantro, washed

FOR THE COCONUT CURRY
One 13½-ounce can coconut milk (1¾ cups)
½ cup chicken stock (page 253)
¼ cup mirin or sweet sake
1 tablespoon Asian fish sauce
1 tablespoon Thai red curry paste (page 15)
1 teaspoon Asian sour shrimp paste (page 15) or
   1 teaspoon fresh lime juice

FOR THE DISH
3 tablespoons peanut oil
½ pound albacore tuna, cut into 2 × ½-inch strips
1½ cups Japanese eggplant cut ¼ inch thick on the
   bias
1½ cups Napa cabbage cut into 1-inch-wide ribbons
½ cup zucchini cut ¼ inch thick on the bias
½ cup seeded red bell pepper cut into slices ½ inch
   thick
⅓ cup peeled carrots cut into slices ⅛ inch thick on
   the bias
2 lime wedges

Aromatic Steamed Rice (page 159)
¼ cup Thai basil leaves or other fresh basil leaves

1. Pick off ¼ cup of the cilantro leaves and set aside.

2. To make the curry sauce, combine the remaining cilantro leaves and stems, the coconut milk, chicken stock, mirin, fish sauce, curry paste, and sour shrimp paste or lime juice in a medium saucepan. Bring to a simmer, cover, and barely simmer for half an hour. Strain through a fine-mesh strainer. You should have about 1½ cups sauce.

3. Heat a wok with 2 tablespoons of the peanut oil over high heat. When the oil is smoking, add the sliced tuna and sear briefly, tossing, about 1 minute. The tuna should still be rare. Remove the tuna to a plate and set aside. Add the remaining 1 tablespoon peanut oil to the wok, put in the eggplant, cabbage, zucchini, bell pepper, and carrots, and stir-fry for 4 minutes. Add the curry sauce and the tuna, and simmer for 1 to 2 minutes.

ON THE PLATE   Serve in large soup bowls over a big scoop of rice. Garnish with the reserved cilantro, the basil, and lime wedges.

A STEP AHEAD   You can make the curry sauce a day ahead and keep refrigerated, covered tightly.

IN THE GLASS   A crisp Pinot Gris from Oregon

CHARRED AHI TUNA WITH PASTA PUTTANESCA

{ Makes 4 servings }

Some people might find it strange to combine the lush, mild taste of ahi tuna with this pungent and garlicky pasta sauce, but I think the combination really works. We serve the tuna very rare, so use the best-quality and freshest sashimi-grade tuna for this dish.

Most of the time I prefer to use fresh herbs rather than the dried kind. I use dried Greek oregano here because it has an intensity and pungency that tastes right for the sauce. Also, be sure you taste the sauce before adding any extra salt, since ingredients such as olives and anchovies are already salty.

This is a dish where all the cooking is last minute, so you'll want to organize yourself. We suggest that you get all the sauce ingredients together first; the sauce takes only a few minutes to cook. Have a pot of water boiling for the pasta. Then sear the tuna right before you cook the pasta. If you don't want to make fresh pasta, it is perfectly okay to use a good-quality dried linguine. If you use dried pasta, wait until the pasta is only a few minutes from being ready before you sear the tuna.

⅓ cup extra virgin olive oil, plus more for panfrying the tuna

4½ teaspoons minced garlic

½ teaspoon red pepper flakes, or more to taste

½ teaspoon dried Greek oregano

1½ cups seeded and diced fresh Roma tomatoes

½ cup pitted and coarsely chopped Kalamata olives

¼ cup dry white wine

3 tablespoons chopped fresh flat-leaf parsley

2 tablespoons capers, drained

6 anchovies, finely chopped (about 1 tablespoon)

1 teaspoon grated lemon zest

4 lemon wedges, seeded

1 pound fresh sashimi-grade ahi tuna, cut into four 4-ounce portions (thick chunks or steaks are best)

Kosher salt and freshly ground black pepper

1 pound fresh linguine (page 250) or dried linguine

1. Put a pot of salted water on to boil for cooking the pasta.

2. Put a large sauté pan over high heat. Add the olive oil, garlic, pepper flakes, and oregano and cook, stirring, for 1 minute. Stir in the tomatoes, olives, wine, parsley, capers, anchovies, and lemon zest. Squeeze the lemon wedges into the pan and throw them right into the sauce. Let the sauce simmer for 2 to 3 minutes.

3. Season the tuna with salt and pepper and sear it in another sauté pan over high heat using a little olive oil. Sear the tuna rare (raw in the middle), about a minute per side. Set aside.

4. Meanwhile, cook the pasta until it is *al dente*. Drain the pasta and toss it in a bowl with the sauce. Taste the sauce, then season it with salt and pepper.

ON THE PLATE   Divide the pasta and sauce among 4 plates or shallow soup bowls. Slice the tuna portions across the grain and fan the sliced tuna over each serving of pasta.

IN THE GLASS   For a real dare, try a Chianti, or, for tradition, an Italian Vermentino, an herbaceous, lemony wine.

LATE NIGHT SEATTLE

There are a million (okay, a bunch of) places to dine late night in Seattle, which was once, twenty years ago, a wasteland after ten. Here are some favorites:

CHINESE: Tai Tung

NORTHWEST SEAFOOD: Flying Fish

PAN-ASIAN: Wild Ginger

HIP-HOP: Palace Kitchen

ITALIAN: Il Bistro

FUN BAR: Queen City Grill

PIZZA AND POOL: Belltown Billiards

BURGERS DOWN AND DIRTY: Dick's Drive-in

KASU ZUKE BLACK COD

{ Makes 4 servings }

*K*asu paste and Pacific black cod are a match made in heaven. My first taste of kasu zuke black cod came as the ninth course (right after the salmon nose salad—really!) of a fourteen-course traditional Japanese feast I enjoyed for my twenty-second birthday. From that moment, I was hooked. Harry Yoshimura, Japanese-American fish purveyor and newly found friend, explained the long tradition of this classic dish. He also taught me how to make it, and this recipe is inspired by him.

Kasu is the sediment left over from making sake, just like the lees in winemaking, and its fermented flavor makes it an aromatic marinade for fatty fish such as black cod or salmon. With the addition of brown sugar, mirin, and miso, the fish takes on a lovely brown color under the broiler or on the grill. Black cod skin gets especially crispy and delicious with kasu, so be sure to leave the skin on and remove the scales so it can be eaten. Kasu is available at Japanese fish markets and by mail order from Mutual Fish (see Sources, page 260). You can also find premarinated fish at many Japanese fishmongers. Black cod needs to marinate for at least two days before cooking, so plan accordingly. If you can't find black cod, substitute salmon in this recipe—marinate it the same way.

---

1 quart plus 1 cup water

2 tablespoons kosher salt

1½ pounds black cod, cut into four 6-ounce steaks or
   fillets, preferably with skin on

1 pound kasu

½ cup firmly packed brown sugar

2 tablespoons light miso

¼ cup mirin or sweet sake

1. In a large bowl, combine 1 quart of the water and salt and stir until the salt is dissolved. Add the black cod, turning to coat both sides. Cover with plastic wrap and refrigerate for 30 minutes. Remove the black cod from the brine and pat dry with paper towels. Discard the brine. (The brine causes the fish to release water, which makes the fish more firm and the finished flavor more intense.)

2. In another large bowl, combine the kasu, the remaining 1 cup water, the brown sugar, miso, and mirin. Add the black cod, turning the pieces to coat all sides. Cover the bowl and refrigerate for 2 days.

3. Preheat the broiler. Oil a baking sheet or spray with nonstick vegetable spray. Scrape the excess kasu mixture from the black cod, leaving a thin coating of marinade. Arrange the fillets on the baking sheet and broil on both sides, 10 to 12 minutes total per inch of thickness. (The marinade contains sugar, so it will brown well, but be careful not to burn it.)

ON THE PLATE   Serve this with ocean salad (page 15), Japanese cucumber pickles (page 56), or pickled ginger and Aromatic Steamed Rice (page 159).

IN THE GLASS   *Junmai ginjo* sake or a dry Semillon

LING COD IN GRAPE LEAVES
WITH PINE NUT FIG BUTTER

{ Makes 4 servings }

I have grapevines in my garden, so I just go out and pick some leaves in early summer when they're still tender. They just need to be briefly blanched in boiling water and drained. You can, of course, use the Greek grape leaves sold in jars. When fresh figs are in season, just slice them and place them on top of the composed butter (instead of putting the chopped dried figs in the butter) before wrapping the fish in the grape leaves. Ling cod is especially good for this dish, but you could use any firm-fleshed white fish, such as snapper or sea bass.

¼ cup (½ stick) unsalted butter, softened

1 tablespoon chopped toasted (page 39)
    pine nuts

1 tablespoon finely chopped dried figs

1 teaspoon grated lemon zest

¾ teaspoon chopped fresh thyme

Kosher salt and freshly ground black pepper

½ cup dry white wine

½ cup water

1 shallot, roughly chopped

2 sprigs thyme

1½ pounds ling cod fillets, cut into 4 portions

Grape leaves (either from the jar, well rinsed with
    cold water and patted dry, or fresh, blanched, see
    headnote)

4 lemon wedges

4 sprigs thyme (optional)

1. To make the fig butter, mix the butter, pine nuts, figs, lemon zest, and chopped thyme in a small bowl. Season with salt and pepper. Set aside.

2. Preheat the oven to 450°F. In an oven-proof pan large enough to hold all the fish in a single layer, combine the wine, water, shallot, and 2 thyme sprigs. Cover the pan and allow it to slowly simmer over low heat for 20 minutes to make a quick court bouillon.

3. Meanwhile, spread each piece of fish with some of the fig butter. Then lay several grape leaves out on your work surface and place the fish, butter side down, on the grape leaves. Wrap the fish in the leaves and place them, seam side down, in the pan of court bouillon so the buttered side is facing up. Place the pan, uncovered, in the oven until the fish is cooked all the way through, 10 to 15 minutes. Remove the grape leaf–wrapped fish from the court bouillon.

ON THE PLATE   Cut open the grape leaves to reveal the melted butter on the inside, still leaving most of the wrapper intact. Serve with a lemon wedge and a sprig of thyme, if desired.

A STEP AHEAD   The fish can be spread with butter and wrapped in the grape leaves early in the day, and stored, tightly wrapped, in the refrigerator. The fig butter can be made a week in advance and stored, tightly wrapped, in the refrigerator or longer in the freezer.

IN THE GLASS   A light-style Chardonnay from the Alto Adige or Trento, in Northern Italy

Pan-Roasted Halibut with Toasted Bread-Crumb Salad and Green Lentils

{ Makes 4 servings }

Lentils are a major crop in the Pacific Northwest. The flavorful legume is served with all kinds of foods, from braised meats or sausages to grilled or pan-roasted fish. French-style lentils are small and dark green and tend to maintain their shape when cooked. They are much nicer for this dish than regular brown lentils. Alaskan halibut in season is a much-anticipated treat in our restaurants. The rich, subtle flavor of the halibut is complemented by the simple, earthy taste of lentils and the crunch of bread crumbs.

FOR THE GREEN LENTILS
1 cup dried French green lentils, picked over and
  rinsed
2 tablespoons olive oil
1½ teaspoons minced garlic
¼ cup finely diced carrots
¼ cup finely diced celery
¼ cup finely diced onions
1½ cups chicken stock (page 253)
2 teaspoons chopped fresh flat-leaf parsley
1 teaspoon chopped fresh sage
1 teaspoon chopped fresh rosemary
1 teaspoon chopped fresh thyme
1 teaspoon chopped fresh oregano
3 tablespoons cold unsalted butter, cut into chunks
Kosher salt and freshly ground black pepper

FOR THE TOASTED BREAD-CRUMB SALAD
3 tablespoons extra virgin olive oil
1 cup coarse bread crumbs (page 255)
Kosher salt and freshly ground black pepper
⅓ cup chopped fresh flat-leaf parsley

¼ cup loosely packed fresh flat-leaf parsley
1 tablespoon chopped lemon zest
Lemon Vinaigrette (recipe follows)

TO FINISH THE DISH
Olive oil for pan-roasting
1½ pounds halibut fillets, cut into 4 portions
Kosher salt and freshly ground black pepper

1. To prepare the lentils, bring a pot of salted water to a boil. Add the lentils, reduce the heat to a simmer, and cook until tender, about 12 minutes. Drain and set aside. Heat the olive oil in a saucepan over medium-high heat, add the garlic, and cook, stirring, until fragrant, about 1 minute. Add the carrots, celery, and onions and cook, stirring, for another 2 minutes. Add the lentils, chicken stock, and chopped herbs and bring to a boil. Add the butter, stirring until emulsified, and season with salt and pepper. Keep warm.

2. To make the bread-crumb salad, heat the oil over medium-high heat in a sauté pan, then add the bread crumbs and panfry until golden and crunchy, 1 to 2 minutes. Season with salt and pepper. Allow to cool. In a small bowl, combine the bread crumbs, chopped parsley, parsley leaves, and lemon zest. Reserve 1 tablespoon of the vinaigrette for drizzling on the fish later and combine the remaining vinaigrette with the bread crumbs.

3. To pan-roast the halibut, heat a large sauté pan over high heat with a few tablespoons of olive oil until almost smoking. Season the fish with salt and pepper and sear until golden brown, 4 to 5 minutes. Flip and finish cooking, about 2 minutes.

ON THE PLATE   Ladle the lentils into 4 wide, shallow bowls. Place the fish in the center of each bowl, drizzle with a little of the vinaigrette, and top with the bread-crumb salad.

A STEP AHEAD   The lentils can be made a day or two ahead without the 3 tablespoons butter and kept refrigerated. When ready to serve, heat the lentils and whisk in the butter.

IN THE GLASS   Try a New Zealand Sauvignon Blanc. These wines are powerfully crisp, like a good Sancerre.

❉

Lemon Vinaigrette

{ Makes about ¼ cup }

1 tablespoon fresh lemon juice
2 teaspoons minced shallots
2 tablespoons extra virgin olive oil
Kosher salt and freshly ground black pepper

In a small bowl, combine the lemon juice and shallots. Slowly whisk in the oil. Season with salt and pepper.

A STEP AHEAD   This can be made early in the day and held, covered, in the refrigerator.

Sake-Steamed Sockeye Salmon with Sake Butter

{ Makes 6 servings }

I like to use sockeye salmon for this dish—its firm flesh and rich flavors are perfect for steaming. And besides it makes for a great title: Try saying it fast a few times. You could, of course, use other types of salmon, and steaming is a good technique for firm-fleshed fish such as ling cod or halibut. Chinese bamboo steamers work well and are not very expensive, though any steamer setup is fine. I love the aromatic steam you get in this method of cooking: The water's beautiful aroma really permeates the salmon.

---

1 stalk lemongrass, split lengthwise
2 cups water
2 cups sake
10 fresh ginger coins (page 47), sliced ⅛ inch thick
2 star anise pods
Peel of 1 orange
1½ pounds salmon fillet, cut into 4 portions
Sake Butter (recipe follows)
1 lime, cut into 6 wedges

Bruise the lemongrass with the back of a knife to help release the aromatics. Set up your steamer: We use a large saucepan or a wok with a Chinese bamboo steamer set over it. Place the lemongrass, water, sake, ginger, star anise, and orange peel in the bottom of the steamer. Bring to a boil. Lay the salmon fillets in the steamer basket and cover with the steamer lid. Steam until the salmon is just cooked through, 4 to 5 minutes.

ON THE PLATE Place a salmon fillet on each plate. Spoon some sake butter over each portion of fish. Garnish with a lime wedge. Serve with Crispy Sesame Rice Cakes (page 160) or Aromatic Steamed Rice (page 159) and steamed baby bok choy.

IN THE GLASS *Nigori* sake or a classic Oregon Pinot Gris

Sake Butter

{ Makes ⅔ cup }

It is worthwhile to buy a premium sake for this sauce. We use Momokawa Silver, ajunmai, or pure rice sake (see Sake, page 28). This is also delicious on steamed halibut or ling cod.

Beurre blanc is a classic French butter sauce. It is delicate and will "break" or look curdled if you keep it over direct heat for too long. The best ways to keep a beurre blanc warm is to either place the container in a saucepan of hot (not simmering) water for a half hour or so, or pour it directly into a small Thermos and screw the cover on. The Thermos method will keep the beurre blanc warm for an hour or more.

---

2 tablespoons peeled and julienned (see How to Julienne, page 36) ginger
1 tablespoon minced shallots
1 tablespoon unsalted butter
½ cup plus 1 teaspoon quality sake (Momokawa)
1 tablespoon heavy cream
½ cup (1 stick) cold unsalted butter, cut into large dice
½ teaspoon fresh lime juice
Kosher salt

In a small saucepan over medium-high heat, sweat the ginger and shallots in the 1 tablespoon butter for 2 to 3 minutes. Add ½ cup of the sake, bring to a boil, and reduce by two thirds, about 3 minutes. Add the heavy cream, bring to a boil, and reduce by half, about 2 minutes. Add the pieces of cold butter to the sauce, bit by bit, whisking constantly over medium-high heat. The butter will emulsify, creating a thick, creamy sauce. Once all the butter has been incorporated, remove the pan from the heat. Whisk in the remaining 1 teaspoon sake and the lime juice. Season to taste with salt.

TO MAKE *WASABI BUTTER*: Mix together 1 tablespoon wasabi powder and 2 teaspoons cold water until a paste forms. When whisking in the lime juice and sake, add the wasabi mixture to your taste.

Steven's Perfect Panfried Petrale Sole

{ Makes 4 servings }

Steven Steinbock, who has worked with me for over twenty years, makes what I think is the most beautifully crusted panfried sole in the world. His secrets? He uses petrale sole fillets, which aren't too thin and delicate, so the breading has time to cook before the fish is done. Lemon sole or flounder work, too. He puts a nice, even coat of breading on the fish. He uses plenty of peanut oil and butter for frying. He gets the pan nice and hot, almost to the smoking point. He doesn't turn the fish until it is brown and crusty.

We accompany this with the Vietnamese dipping sauce nuoc cham, because it is the perfect, slightly acidic match to the crisp, golden sesame bread crumbs on the panfried fish.

1½ cups fine bread crumbs (page 255)
¼ cup sesame seeds
2 cups all-purpose flour
2 teaspoons kosher salt
1 teaspoon freshly ground black pepper
4 large eggs, beaten
4 petrale sole fillets (about 1½ pounds total)
5 tablespoons peanut oil
2 tablespoons unsalted butter
Kosher salt and freshly ground black pepper
Nuoc Cham dipping sauce (page 79)
4 lemon or lime wedges

1. Mix the crumbs with the sesame seeds in a shallow bowl. Combine the flour with the salt and pepper in another bowl. Place the beaten eggs in a third bowl.

2. Dredge each piece of sole on both sides first in the flour, then in the egg, then in the crumbs, creating a nice even crust. Chef's trick: Use one hand for the dry ingredients (flour and crumbs) and one hand for the wet ingredients (egg) so you don't gum up the works. Lay each piece of breaded sole on a large plate or parchment paper–lined baking sheet until you are finished breading them all.

3. In two large nonstick sauté pans or in one very big frying pan, heat the peanut oil and butter over high heat. The oil and butter should be about ¼ inch deep in the pan. When the oil is hot but not smoking, add the breaded fillets. When the fish is crusty and golden brown on the first side, flip it over to cook the other side. When both sides are crusty and golden, remove the fish from the pan. Total cooking time is about 4 minutes. Drain on paper towels before serving.

ON THE PLATE   Serve the panfried fillets with ramekins of nuoc cham and lemon or lime wedges.

A STEP AHEAD   The sesame crumbs can be made a day ahead and kept at room temperature.

IN THE GLASS   A delicate white Graves from Bordeaux, a blend of Sauvignon Blanc and Semillon

Mr. Joe's Tomato Gravy Catfish with Smoky Bacon and Fried Artichokes

{ Makes 4 servings }

Mr. Joe was our next-door neighbor for eighteen years in Newark, Delaware, where I grew up. (No calling adults by their first names in those days—everyone was Mr. Joe or Mrs. Alice.) Sometimes on weekends he'd have my family over and serve us toast smothered with a gravy he made from bacon grease and canned tomato sauce. I ate huge amounts of Mr. Joe's Tomato Gravy and never forgot it.

No one else in my family ever thought twice about the gravy, though. When I called my parents to get the recipe, I could picture them scratching their heads on the other end of the line. They faxed me a copy of a little scrap of paper, handwritten by Mr. Joe himself. As far as I know, I'm the first—and probably the only—person to get his secret recipe.

We almost never use canned tomato sauce in our recipes, but since Mr. Joe probably never used a fresh tomato for his gravy, we left the canned tomato sauce in when we adapted his recipe as a tribute to the spirit of his cooking. He also used lots and lots of Tabasco, but suit the amount to your taste.

FOR THE TOMATO GRAVY
8 slices bacon (about ¼ pound)
⅔ cup chopped onions
1½ cups canned diced or crushed tomatoes
1 cup canned tomato sauce
1 to 2 teaspoons Tabasco sauce, or more to taste
2 teaspoons sugar
Kosher salt and freshly ground black pepper
1 teaspoon cornstarch dissolved in 1 tablespoon cold water

FOR THE SPICE RUB
2 tablespoons paprika
2 teaspoons kosher salt
1 teaspoon dried thyme
1 teaspoon freshly ground black pepper
½ teaspoon cayenne

TO FINISH THE DISH
1½ pounds catfish fillets, cut into 4 portions
3 tablespoons peanut oil for panfrying, or more if needed
Spicy Fried Artichokes (recipe follows)
4 lemon wedges
1 tablespoon chopped fresh flat-leaf parsley

1. To make the tomato gravy, fry the bacon until crispy. Set aside to garnish the fillets later. Reserve 2 tablespoons of the bacon fat and discard the rest. In the same sauté pan over medium heat, cook the onions in the bacon fat, stirring, about 2 minutes. Add the diced or crushed tomatoes and the tomato sauce and simmer for 10 minutes. Remove the tomato gravy from the pan and coarsely puree in a food processor or blender. Return the gravy to the sauté pan and season with Tabasco, sugar, salt, and pepper. Add the dissolved cornstarch to the gravy and simmer for another 5 minutes, stirring often. Keep warm.

2. To make the spice rub, combine the ingredients together in a small bowl. Liberally sprinkle both sides of each portion of fish with the spice rub (we use about 2 teaspoons per portion; the spice rub is a tad hot, so you may prefer to use more or less).

3. To finish the dish, preheat the oven to 450°F. Heat the oil in a large ovenproof sauté pan over high heat. Panfry the catfish on one side until golden, about 3 minutes. Turn the fillets and put the sauté pan in the oven until the fish is just cooked through, about 3 minutes. While the catfish is cooking, reheat the bacon strips by putting them in another pan in the oven for a few minutes.

ON THE PLATE   Ladle some of the gravy onto each of 4 plates. Put a catfish fillet over the sauce on each plate. Top each fillet with 2 strips of bacon. Garnish each plate with lemon wedges, chopped parsley, and fried artichokes.

A STEP AHEAD   The tomato gravy can be made a few days ahead and stored, covered, in the refrigerator. The spice rub can be made a week in advance and stored, covered, at room temperature.

IN THE GLASS   This is great with a Bloody Mary.

Tom cooking on the line at Palace Kitchen

Spicy Fried Artichokes

{ Makes 4 to 6 servings }

I love how frying removes most of the moisture from the artichokes and intensifies their natural flavor. I could eat a bowl of these just like popcorn.

This recipe works even better with baby artichokes, but sometimes they are difficult to locate. If you are able to get your hands on some, substitute 6 baby artichokes for the 2 large artichokes.

1 cup all-purpose flour
1½ teaspoons paprika
1½ teaspoons kosher salt
1 teaspoon cayenne
¼ teaspoon ground black pepper
1 lemon
2 large artichokes
Peanut oil for frying

1. Combine the flour, paprika, salt, cayenne, and black pepper in a small bowl. Cut the lemon in half and squeeze it into a small bowl of cold water. (The lemon water will help keep the trimmed artichokes from discoloring.) Cut the top inch off the artichokes and then cut them in half. With a paring knife, remove the inner purple leaves, the fuzzy choke, and the outer dark green leaves. Save only the few tender leaves that are *entirely* edible. Also trim the dark green tough part of the stem. Then cut each trimmed artichoke in half, in about 6 thin wedges, and place them in the lemon water.

2. To deep-fry the artichokes, heat 2 inches of peanut oil to 375°F (see How to Deep-Fry, page 51). Remove the artichokes from the water and let drain in a strainer a few minutes before tossing in the flour mixture. Shake off any excess flour and fry until the artichokes are beginning to turn slightly golden, 2 to 3 minutes, but don't let the leaves get too dark. Remove from the oil and drain on paper towels. Serve immediately or, if necessary, hold in a preheated 300°F oven for a few minutes.

A STEP AHEAD The artichokes can be prepped a few hours ahead and held, refrigerated, in the lemon water.

CRUSTED SMELTS WITH SWEET-AND-SOUR ONIONS

{ Makes 4 servings }

My wife, Jackie, loves to tell stories about how many smelt she caught jigging off the side of her great-uncle Frank's sailboat. I don't believe her, but always listen politely. Even so, I love eating them and they certainly are a Northwest tradition. I prefer the tiny silver ocean smelt over the often muddy-tasting river smelt.

I like to serve smelts with the heads and tails on and the bones in. After they are cooked, it's really very easy to remove the bones with your fork. (Some people eat the small fried fish heads, tails, bones, and all.) If you prefer, you can remove the heads and tails of the raw smelts and fillet them by running a small sharp knife under the spine. The sweet-and-sour onions are served at room temperature and the smelts are served hot.

FOR THE SWEET-AND-SOUR ONIONS
1 red onion, halved and thinly sliced (about 2 cups)
1 yellow onion, halved and thinly sliced
  (about 2 cups)
3 tablespoons olive oil
3 tablespoons dry sherry
¼ cup dark or golden raisins
3 tablespoons sugar
6 tablespoons red wine vinegar
1 teaspoon grated orange zest
1 teaspoon grated lemon zest
½ teaspoon red pepper flakes
1 tablespoon chopped fresh flat-leaf parsley
Kosher salt and freshly ground black pepper

FOR THE SMELTS
12 smelts (about ¾ pound)
1 cup all-purpose flour
2 teaspoons kosher salt
1 teaspoon freshly ground black pepper
3 tablespoons olive oil, or more if needed

FOR GARNISH
1 tablespoon chopped fresh flat-leaf parsley
4 lemon wedges

1. To make sweet-and-sour onions, heat the olive oil in a large sauté pan over medium-low heat, then slowly cook the onions until very soft, about 30 minutes, stirring occasionally. While the onions are cooking, heat the sherry in a small saucepan. Remove the sherry from the heat, add the raisins, and allow them to steep in the warm sherry for at least 15 minutes. Add the raisins and sherry, sugar, vinegar, citrus zests, and pepper flakes to the onions and simmer for another 20 minutes. Remove the onions from the heat. Allow to cool, then stir in the parsley. Season to taste with salt and pepper. Set aside to cool to room temperature.

2. To clean the smelts, slit the bellies open and clean out the insides with a small sharp knife. Flush the cavities clean with cold running water.

3. To panfry the smelts, combine the flour, salt, and pepper in a small bowl. Dredge the cleaned smelts in the flour, shaking off any excess. Heat the olive oil over

high heat in a large nonstick sauté pan. When the oil is very hot, panfry the smelts on both sides until golden brown, about 4 minutes total. Cook in batches if necessary to avoid crowding and use more oil, if needed. Place the fried smelts on paper towels on a platter and keep warm in a preheated 300°F oven.

ON THE PLATE Arrange 3 panfried smelts around a mound of onions on each plate. Drizzle a little extra virgin olive oil over the smelts, sprinkle with chopped parsley, and serve with lemon wedges.

A STEP AHEAD The onions can be made a day ahead and refrigerated, covered. Bring them back to room temperature before using.

IN THE GLASS A fresh young rosé from Provence, Washington State, or anywhere, really—just not sweet

RAPID RELISHES

Serving a piece of grilled fish with a simple fruit or vegetable relish is very typical of my cooking style—straightforward, flavorful, and unfussy. It's also a way to feature the flavor of both the fish and the produce, since you don't mask them with a heavy sauce. Of course, you don't have to grill the fish either: You could steam it or pan-sear it or broil it.

Many types of fish go well with these simple relishes. The richness of salmon and tuna is particularly good with fruit. These relishes have the advantage of being relatively quick and easy to prepare as well as being healthy and fairly low in fat.

Once you have the idea, you are likely to think up your own rapid relish. A bowl of roughly chopped blueberries tossed with a few spoonfuls of olive oil, a little bit of balsamic vinegar, and a couple of grinds of the peppermill are all it takes.

Cherry–Walla Walla Onion Relish

Two of our favorite local treats, Washington cherries and Walla Walla onions, are both in season in late spring. This relish gets them together. Delicious on grilled salmon, it would also go well with grilled chicken, pork tenderloin, or even a steak.

1 Walla Walla onion (about 8 ounces)
Olive oil for grilling
Kosher salt and freshly ground black pepper
½ pound sweet cherries, pitted and halved
   (1¼ cups)
1 tablespoon balsamic vinegar

Fire up the grill. Peel and slice the onion into rounds about ⅓ inch thick. Brush the onion slices with olive oil and season with salt and pepper. Grill on both sides, over direct heat, until partially charred and just cooked through, 5 to 10 minutes. Remove the onions from the grill and chop coarsely. In a bowl, combine the onions, cherries, and vinegar and season to taste with salt and pepper. Serve at room temperature.

Nectarine-Basil Relish

{ Makes 4 to 6 servings }

This is a very simple relish and a great way to feature perfectly ripe summer fruit. You could substitute peeled peaches for the nectarines, or red or purple plums. Serve this relish with grilled salmon or halibut and grilled corn on the cob.

3 nectarines, pitted and thinly sliced
⅓ cup thinly sliced fresh basil
1 tablespoon honey
1 tablespoon fresh lemon juice
1 tablespoon extra virgin olive oil
Kosher salt and freshly ground black pepper

In a bowl, combine the nectarines, basil, honey, lemon juice, and oil, tossing well to coat. Season to taste with salt and pepper. Serve at room temperature.

❂

Peach Sambal

{ Makes 4 to 6 servings }

Sambals are traditional Indonesian, Malaysian, or South Indian condiments. *Sambal badjak* is a hot Indonesian condiment made with chile, brown sugar, onion, salt, and other ingredients. You could also make this sambal with nectarines, or peeled papayas or mangoes. Try serving it with grilled halibut and Spicy Peanut Noodles (page 172).

We always peel peaches because of the fuzzy skins, but we don't peel nectarines. This recipe gives a technique for the easiest way to peel peaches. (Use the same technique for tomatoes, if you wish.)

3 tablespoons extra virgin olive oil
¼ cup thinly sliced garlic
¼ cup rice wine vinegar
2 tablespoons sugar
¼ teaspoon ground cinnamon
Pinch of ground allspice
4 ripe peaches
1 tablespoon sambal badjak (page 15)

Tom's Tasty Sashimi
Tuna Salad (page 20)
with Green Onion
Pancakes (page 21) and
Thai Basil and Lime
Kamikaze (page 22)

Tiny Clam and Seaweed Soup
(page 36)

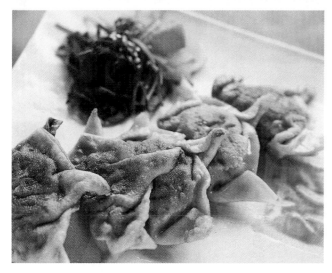

Lobster and Shiitake Potstickers (page 25)
with Sweet-and-Sour Red Cabbage (page 184)

CLOCKWISE FROM TOP RIGHT:
Matsutake Dashi (page 49),
Grilled Chicken Skewers with
Tangerine Ginger Glaze (page 46),
Asian Long Beans with Soy Shallot
Vinaigrette (page 54), Sweet-and-
Sour Red Cabbage (page 184), Sweet
Potato Tempura (page 52), and Sake-
Cured Hot-Smoked Salmon (page 47)

A Cornmeal-Fried Oyster Sandwich with Lemon Tartar
Sauce (page 64) and Poppy Seed Coleslaw (page 183)

A huge platter of
King Crab Legs
(page 79)

A jar of Green Cocktail
Sauce (page 89)

Wok-Fried Crab with Ginger and
Lemongrass (page 90)

Dungeness Crabcakes (page 87)

Rub with Love
Spice Rubs

Mr. Joe's Tomato Gravy Catfish with Smoky
Bacon and Fried Artichokes (page 106)

A Whole Grilled Trout (page 122) and Grilled Apple Rings (page 129)

Basic Barbecued Baby Back Ribs (page 125) with Hoisin Barbecue Sauce (page 128)

Long-Bone
Short Ribs with
Chinook Merlot
Gravy (page 138)
and Rosemary
White Beans
(page 140)

FAR RIGHT:
Dahlia Lounge
neon sign

Riesling Rabbit
with New
Potatoes and
Spring Vegetables
(page 143)

ABOVE : Etta's
Cornbread Pudding
(page 156)

ABOVE LEFT:
A drawing of Tom by
a young friend

Red Beet
Ravioli with
Fresh Corn
Relish
(page 166)

Tuscan Bread Salad with
Fresh Mozzarella and Basil
(page 178)

Plating the White Winter
Salad with Aged Parmigiano-
Reggiano (page 181)

Shaving a chunk of Parmigiano-Reggiano with a vegetable peeler

Grilled Asparagus
with Hazelnut–Star
Anise Mayonnaise
(page 191)

Peach Cornmeal Shortcake with Candied Pecans (page 209)

Triple Coconut Cream Pies (page 216)

Oregon Pinot Noir
Raspberry Sorbet and local
raspberries (page 226)

BELOW LEFT: A stack of
Wild Rice Waffles (page 236)

BELOW: A sheet pan of
Peak-of-Summer Berry Crisps
(page 220)

Grandma Douglas' Schnecken (page 240)

Peruvian papier-mâché
figure of a bread baker

Pepper-Vodka Bloody Mary
(page 244) with Pickled Asparagus
(page 245)

Exotic skewers for grilled meat

A basket of handmade breads
ready for dinner service

Etta's gummy fish and business cards

Slow-Roasted Duck with Huckleberry Sauce (page 145) topped with fried parsnip chips

1. In a small pan over medium heat, heat the oil, then cook the garlic, stirring, until golden brown, about 3 minutes. Set the toasted garlic aside. In another small saucepan, combine the vinegar, sugar, cinnamon, and allspice. Heat over medium-high heat, stirring until the sugar dissolves, about 3 minutes. Set the vinegar mixture aside.

2. Bring a saucepan of water to a boil and fill a bowl with ice water. Cut a small X in the bottom of each peach. Add the peaches to the boiling water until their skins begin to pull away, about 1 minute. Remove the peaches from the boiling water and place in the ice water for a few minutes. Remove the peaches from the ice water. Peel the peaches, cut them in half, remove the pits, and cut into small dice.

3. In a bowl, combine the peaches, toasted garlic, vinegar mixture, and sambal. Serve at room temperature.

❀

TOMATO-OLIVE RELISH

{ Makes 4 to 6 servings }

This fresh tomato *salsa fresca* would work well with pan-roasted ling cod or broiled trout, served on a bed of Sage Tagliarini (page 168).

---

6 ripe Roma tomatoes
Zest from 1 lemon, cut into fine strips
3 tablespoons pitted and roughly chopped Kalamata olives
2 tablespoons extra virgin olive oil
1 tablespoon chopped fresh flat-leaf parsley
5 teaspoons capers, drained
½ teaspoon minced garlic
½ teaspoon fresh lemon juice
½ teaspoon red wine vinegar
Freshly ground black pepper
Kosher salt, if needed

Remove the cores, then cut the tomatoes into quarters lengthwise. With a paring knife, scrape away all the seeds. Cut the tomato flesh into small dice. In a bowl, combine the zest with the tomatoes, olives, oil, parsley, capers, garlic, lemon juice, vinegar, and pepper. Taste the relish before you add any salt, because the olives and capers are already salty. Serve at room temperature.

GRILLED SHIITAKE RELISH

{ Makes 4 to 6 servings }

We especially like to serve this relish with Etta's Pit-Roasted Salmon (page 120), but it would go well with almost any type of fish or meat.

After you fire up the grill, you can grill the mushrooms and make the relish before you cook your fish. Unless the mushroom caps are large, you may want to set a rack over the grill so no mushrooms fall through the grates.

¾ pound fresh shiitake mushroom caps, wiped clean

3 tablespoons olive oil

Kosher salt and freshly ground black pepper

2 tablespoons minced shallots

2 teaspoons minced garlic

½ teaspoon chopped fresh flat-leaf parsley

½ teaspoon chopped fresh sage

½ teaspoon chopped fresh rosemary

½ teaspoon chopped fresh thyme

1 tablespoon balsamic vinegar

2 teaspoons fresh lemon juice

1. Fire up the grill.

2. In a bowl, toss the mushroom caps with 2 tablespoons of the oil and a sprinkle of salt and pepper. Grill the mushrooms on both sides, over direct heat, until cooked through, about 5 minutes total. Remove the mushrooms from the grill and thinly slice. Heat the remaining 1 tablespoon oil in a sauté pan over medium heat. Add the shallots and garlic and sweat them until soft and aromatic, 2 to 3 minutes. Set aside to cool. In a bowl, combine the mushrooms, shallot-garlic mixture, herbs, vinegar, and lemon juice. Season to taste with salt and pepper. Serve at room temperature.

3. If you want to make this relish and you're not planning to grill, you could roast the mushrooms instead. Toss the mushrooms with the oil, salt, and pepper, then spread them on a baking sheet. Roast them in a preheated 450°F oven for 20 minutes.

WASHINGTON STATE WINES

Washington's first commercial grapevines were planted in 1872 on Stretch Island, in southern Puget Sound, and a local grape variety called Island Belle was created by early viticulturists. There was even a village called Grapeview on the mainland nearby.

Grape growing really took off, however, in the early 1900s when the Yakima Valley was transformed from a hot semidesert into a thriving farming region by irrigation water from the Cascade Mountains and the rivers that flowed down the eastern slopes. The Yakima Valley soon became one of the Northwest's most productive areas for fruits and vegetables of all kinds, including grapes.

The Cascades, running north and south, form the great dividing line for the Northwest's climate. West of the mountains, in Seattle and the Puget Sound area, the weather is cool and wet. To the east in the Yakima Valley, and farther east around Walla Walla and Spokane, the land lies in the rain shadow of the mountains and becomes progressively hotter and drier the farther east you go.

Generally, the region to the west of the Cascades is a bit damp and chilly for many wine grapes, although a few enterprising vineyardists are growing grape varieties that can thrive in cool weather. Pinot Noir, which originates in Northern France's Burgundy region, can be grown successfully here, although Oregon's Willamette Valley, south of Portland, has the best microclimates for this grape.

Other grapes that can ripen on islands and along the coast of Puget Sound are Müller-Thurgau, a German white grape created by crossing Riesling with Sylvaner; Madeleine-Angevine, an early-ripening grape that is also grown by sun-challenged English vintners, and Siegerebbe, a cool-weather German variety related to Gewürztraminer. Bainbridge Island Vineyards & Winery, Whidbey Island Vineyards & Winery, and a few others also produce small amounts of Pinot Gris, Chasselas, and various fruit and berry wines. Many of these Puget Sound wineries have tasting rooms and can be visited via ferry boats from the Seattle docks. (Contact the Washington Wine Commission; see Sources, page 260, for more information on visiting these and other Washington State wineries.)

DeLille Winery—the grape crush

Most wineries west of the Cascades purchase the bulk of their grapes from warmer vineyards to the east in the far-ranging Columbia Valley American Viticultural Area, which includes the Yakima and Walla Walla regions. Quilceda Creek Vintners, located in the foothills of the western Cascades, north of Seattle, is gaining note as a maker of full-bodied Cabernet Sauvignon made from grapes grown near Benton City, in the Yakima Valley.

There are a number of wineries located in Woodinville, just east of Seattle—Chateau Ste. Michelle is by far the largest and best known. Chateau Ste. Michelle makes a wide range of quality wines from Columbia Valley grapes: Its single-vineyard Chardonnays and Cabernet Sauvignons are consistently fine. The winery also owns Columbia Crest, located in the Columbia Valley.

Columbia Winery, once known as Associated Vintners, began as an association of home winemakers, a group comprising many professors at the University of Washington. These amateurs turned professional pioneered the making of premium *vinifera* wines in the state. Winemaker David Lake produces remarkable, vineyard-designated wines from the Yakima Valley and other eastern vineyards. His Merlots (especially Milestone Vineyard) and Semillons are among the state's finest. Another Woodinville winery, DeLille Cellars, creates blends from Bordeaux varietals, such as Sauvignon Blanc and Semillon for its whites, and Cabernet Sauvignon, Merlot, and Cabernet Franc for its reds.

The Woodinville wineries are all worth a visit. Their wines, along with other Washington State wines, can be found in restaurants throughout the area and in fine shops in Seattle, such as Pike and Western (see Sources, page 260) near the Pike Place Market.

The area that produces most of the state's best wines and the region I most like to visit is the Yakima Valley, to the east and south of Seattle. The valley is about a three-and-a-half-hour drive from Seattle through the beautiful Snoqualmie Pass. While there are a few good-size wineries in the valley, like Hogue Cellars and Covey Ridge, even these are tiny by comparison to the big California wineries. There are more than twenty wineries in the valley, and most are small and family owned.

The winemaker at Hogue Cellars, Wade Wolfe, also has his own winery, Thurston Wolfe, just down the road. Thurston Wolfe is especially known for its Lemberger, an intensely fruity German grape that some call the Zinfandel of the Northwest. Thurston Wolfe's 1997 Lemberger is a beautiful red wine with cherry, raspberry, and black pepper aromas and just a touch of oak.

When I'm in the Yakima Valley, I always visit Kay Simon and Clay Mackey at Chinook Wines, in the countryside just outside Prosser. They are typical of the creative and dedicated small winemakers and grape growers of the area. Kay, the winemaker, graduated from UC Davis enology school and was the red-wine maker at Chateau Ste. Michelle before she and Clay founded Chinook. Clay has been a grape grower all his life, starting out in the Napa Valley and coming to the Yakima Valley to be a part of its budding wine industry in the late 1970s.

Kay and Clay started Chinook in 1983, married, and released their first wines in 1984. They grow their own Cabernet Franc and purchase grapes from nearby vineyards for their full-bodied, fragrant wines. They are among my favorite winemakers because they love food so much and make their wines to go with our Northwest specialties. The Sauvignon Blanc goes beautifully with oysters, scallops, and seafood from Puget Sound, and their Chardonnay is a perfect match with Dungeness crab.

Near Benton City, at the eastern end of the valley, Kiona Vineyards produces some of the area's best white wines. Their full-bodied oak-influenced Chardonnays and fruity, delicate Rieslings are remarkable for quality and depth of flavor. In 1989, the winery made a memorable ice wine from Chenin Blanc when frost hit the vineyards, a frequent problem this far north.

Farther east, where the Yakima River joins the Columbia near Kennewick, husband-and-wife team Rob Griffin and Deborah Barnard at Barnard Griffin Winery make premium barrel-fermented Chardonnay and Semillon, along with Merlot, Cabernet Sauvignon, and (unusual for the area) a full-bodied Pacific Northwest Zinfandel. Rob, who was winemaker at The Hogue Cellars for some years before setting out on his own, also makes one of the region's best Sauvignon Blancs.

Walla Walla, east of the big bend of the Columbia River, is not only famous for its sweet onions, but for its wine grapes. In the last fifteen years, this new American Viticultural Area has been getting quite a reputation for its big, intensely flavored Cabernets and Merlots, and for some very high prices too.

The weather is quite warm, making for ripe grapes and full-bodied, ample wines. The viticultural region extends up into the cooler foothills of the Blue Mountains, east of the city, giving the area plenty of diverse microclimates. Part of the appellation lies across the border in Oregon, and some Washington wineries (Leonetti, for example) purchase grapes from Seven Hills and other hillside Oregon vineyards.

Rich red wines are the success story in the Walla Walla region: Fully ripe and highly extracted wines are the norm. Leonetti Cellar sets the style with its rich and meaty Cabernets full of varietal fruit like berries and black currants, with plenty of new oak to balance it.

In addition to Cabernet Sauvignon and Merlot, Sangiovese and Syrah are increasingly planted and one grower high up in the Blue Mountains even claims he's found the perfect spot for Pinot Noir. Wineries to look for (and they can be difficult to find) are L'Ecole No. 41, Waterbrook Winery, Woodward Canyon Winery, Canoe Ridge, Glen Fiona, and Walla Walla Vintners.

Mo'Poke, Dadu:
Doing the Charcoal Stroll

MY DAUGHTER, LORETTA, with only a little coaching from me, said, "Mo'poke, Dadu" ("More pork, Daddy") when I offered her another pork rib to gnaw on when she was just a baby. It was the very first sentence she uttered in her young life.

Everybody in my family loves barbecued pork, especially me, and I was happy as a pig in slop to be chosen judge at the Jack Daniel's World Invitational Barbecue Championship in Lynchburg, Tennessee. There were two reasons to be happy: The invitation came with a fifth of the real thing, and I got to pig out on pork shoulder, chicken, ribs, whole hogs, pulled pork, and some of the best sauces God, man, or the Devil ever made.

The night before the judging I went on the Charcoal Stroll, where I got to meet and greet, toss down a few glasses of the local product, and swap lies and recipes with some of the smokiest and most talented grill cooks in the world. Instead of six guns, these good ole boys (and gals) toted spray bottles of spiced cider on their hips, along with basting brushes and tongs and long forks and other tools of the trade.

These grill masters are a revelation. They don't just put a rack of ribs on the grill, they massage it with spice rub and cook it over a smoky fire until it is a real work of art. If Picasso had a Grill Period, this would be it. These grill cooks understand the secret of great barbecuing: Use all your senses to manage the fire and bring the meat to perfection. You listen to the sizzle, feel the fire with your hand, poke the meat with your finger, watch the color of the coals, and, above all, smell that wonderful scent of meat and smoke and sauce until it is just right.

My love of grilling led me to open the Palace Kitchen, where we barbecue whole salmon, baby goats, racks of ribs, whole loins of beef, and entire maple-cured pork loins over a smoky apple-wood fire.

There isn't much of a traditional Southern-style barbecue scene in Seattle, but the Chinese tradition of marinating pork, duck, and chicken in a sweet star anise marinade, then barbecuing them is huge. Window after window of dripping ducks and sides of pork line the streets of the International District. This leads to a weekly competition I put myself through: tasting each version and choosing the Best of Seattle (after all, somebody's got to do it!). Invariably I end up at King's Barbecue House across from the Uwajimaya Market for the buy, and head home nibbling with one hand, holding my greasy steering wheel with the other.

GRILLING

Use all your senses when grilling. Look at the color of the coals, the smoke coming from the vents, the color of the surface of the meat. Listen for the sizzle when the meat hits the grill or for flareups that need attention; lack of sizzle can mean the fire is getting too low. Smell the wood or charcoal smoke, the aromas of the meat or poultry or fish cooking. Feel the heat above the grill on your hand and the texture of the meat when you poke it with your finger. And, of course, there's nothing wrong with sampling meat or fish as it cooks. I like to cut off a piece from the tail of a steak or chop or tear off a bit of fish and taste as I cook.

For me the full experience of grilling includes managing the fire to get the right results. I'm no great fan of the gas grill. Fire is a living thing and the gas flame doesn't give me the results I'm looking for. The flavors that come from wood coals or charcoal are an important part of what I'm trying to create in the food I grill. We use apple wood and other hardwoods in the huge grill at the Palace Kitchen; at home I use a kettle-style barbecue and charcoal.

Fire up the grill any way you prefer. I have a gas igniter in my barbecue which gets the charcoal going, but chimney starters that let you ignite the charcoal with wadded-up paper also work well. I generally avoid kerosene-based liquid starters, but they will do in a pinch. Open up the bottom vents of your barbecue for a good draft and leave the cover off until the coals are uniformly white. Get the fire good and hot before grilling; a hand held just above the grill shouldn't be able to stay past a count of two or three.

For direct cooking, I like to arrange the coals into a hotter spot for searing and quick cooking and a cooler spot for slower cooking. You do this by heaping up coals for more heat and spreading them thinner for less. Leave a portion of the grill without any coals under it for meat or poultry to rest when it is done. Indirect cooking requires the coals to be in two heaps on either side of the center without any coals directly beneath whatever you are cooking. Place a drip pan under the grill between the heaps of charcoal.

I like to highly season meat, poultry, or fish before I grill. You can use one of my spice rubs, Rubs with Love (see page 260), mixed specially for pork, beef, seafood, etc., or create your own. Or you can marinate the food for extra flavor. If you opt for a marinade, make sure you dry the meat or poultry thoroughly before grilling. If you don't use a rub or marinade, sprinkle on plenty of salt and pepper. Forget that old myth about not salting meat before cooking. For vegetables, a little olive oil brushed on them and a generous sprinkle of salt and pepper are usually enough. Take meat or poultry out of the refrigerator about an hour or so before cooking to give it a chance to come to room temperature.

I use direct grilling for chops, steaks, vegetables, and small pieces of poultry, and indirect grilling for roasts, ribs, larger pieces of poultry, and whole birds. I keep the lid on for both methods, although when grilling steaks I'll often use a special basket to hold the meat directly over the coals and leave the lid off for maximum draft and heat.

With indirect grilling the top vent should be centered over the food you are cooking. If vents are off to one side or the other, uneven cooking can result. I prefer to keep track of the cooking temperature with a built-in thermometer. If your kettle grill doesn't have one, you can drill a small hole in the lid and insert your own thermometer. Be sure to get a thermometer with a high enough range, to at least 500°F. Many meat thermometers only go up to 220°F; a candy or a frying thermometer works well.

When cooking by the indirect method, especially when slow cooking for a long time, be sure to shake the grill occasionally to get the ashes off the coals and clear the vents. Otherwise, temperatures can get cooler than you want and the ashes can clog the vents. Add new charcoal when needed to keep temperatures in the desired range. Weather can make a difference; cool or windy days can influence temperatures and cooking time.

ETTA'S PIT-ROASTED SALMON
WITH GRILLED SHIITAKE RELISH

{ Makes 6 servings }

From start to finish, this salmon dish has become a classic in Seattle. Which is exactly what we set out to do.

I developed this spice rub for Etta's signature salmon dish because I wanted to re-create the smoky flavor of the fantastic barbecue I tasted at the Jack Daniel's World Barbecue Invitational Championship event in Tennessee. With this rub and a good smoky fire, you can get great grilling results. You can make the rub in this recipe or purchase some Rub with Love Salmon Rub (see Sources, page 260), which is a bit more complex and includes ingredients like smoked paprika not easily found by the home cook.

Serve this salmon dish with cornbread pudding and shiitake relish. You don't have to work hard to make it look beautiful. The combination of golden-yellow cornbread pudding and reddish pink salmon is stunning. While it grills, the salmon gets a beautiful burnished glow from the sugar and paprika in the rub.

FOR THE SALMON SPICE RUB
3 tablespoons firmly packed brown sugar
2 tablespoons paprika
2 teaspoons kosher salt
1½ teaspoons freshly ground black pepper
1 teaspoon chopped fresh thyme

TO FINISH THE DISH
Six 7-ounce salmon fillets
Olive oil
Etta's Cornbread Pudding (page 156)

Grilled Shiitake Relish (page 114)
1 lemon, cut into 6 wedges
Fresh basil leaves (optional)

1. Fire up the grill.
2. To make the spice rub, combine the brown sugar, paprika, salt, pepper, and thyme in a small bowl. Coat both sides of the salmon fillets with all of the rub. Brush the grill and fish with oil. Grill over direct heat, covered, with the vents open. When the salmon is marked by the grill, flip the fish and finish cooking. I like our salmon medium-rare, which requires a total grilling time of around 10 minutes, depending on the heat of the grill. The sugar in the spice rub can burn easily, so watch it closely.

ON THE PLATE   Spoon the warm cornbread pudding onto 6 plates and rest a salmon fillet up against the pudding. Ladle some shiitake relish over each salmon fillet and garnish with lemon wedges and fresh basil leaves, if desired.

A STEP AHEAD   The spice rub can be made a couple days ahead and stored, tightly covered, at room temperature.

IN THE GLASS   This one's a no-brainer—Oregon Pinot Noir.

PINOT NOIR

It might sound like an odd combination to serve Pinot Noir with salmon, if you believe in the old maxim of red wine with red meat and white with fish. But the smoky-flavored salmon is perfectly matched with a delicate but intense Pinot Noir from Oregon's Willamette Valley, southwest of Portland.

One of my favorite Oregon Pinot Noirs is made by Cristom Vineyards, in Salem. Owner Paul Gerrie is a lover of fine French Burgundy, as I am, and his estate-grown Pinot Noir is spicy and complex like the French wines. Domaine Drouhin is another Oregon Pinot Noir winemaker with a French connection. This 180-acre estate in Yamhill County produces superb Pinot Noirs that are deep, rich, and full bodied, just what I want to accompany salmon, halibut, or lamb.

If you ever get the chance, go to the International Pinot Noir Festival in the town of McMinnville, southwest of Portland. I once cooked the main dinner for a group of Pinot-heads from all over the world, and my greatest pleasure was mixing with winemakers from France, South Africa, New Zealand, Spain, Chile, and even from far-off California. At these events everybody has a great time tasting wine, talking about their main obsession, and eating the good food that wine-loving chefs like myself cook for the crowds of Pinot Noir fanatics.

THANKSGIVING SALMON

On Thanksgiving in our house we have a division of labor: Jackie makes the turkey, I make the salmon, and Loretta makes the crescent rolls. All the other fixin's are brought by a multitude of guests.

We're not the only family in Seattle that thinks that it can't really be a holiday feast unless you have a whole salmon, even on turkey day. My charcoal grill doesn't get put away even in the winter (you don't do much grilling up here unless you are willing to do it in the rain). So I fire up the grill for Thanksgiving and while Jackie puts her twenty-pound turkey in the oven, I put my twenty-pound salmon over the charcoal.

Barbecuing a whole king salmon is not as hard as it might seem. Its belly is stuffed, literally to the gills, with sweet onions, sliced lemons, and the last of the summer sage. The fattened fish goes right on the grill and is slow-roasted with the lid on. Whole roast salmon is a tradition that everybody now looks forward to. It wouldn't be Thanksgiving without it.

WHOLE GRILLED TROUT WITH APPLE CIDER BUTTER

{ Makes 4 servings }

Americans have gotten used to eating only boned fillets of fish, but nothing tastes as good as a whole bone-in fish. It's really easy to slide the cooked trout right off the bone, and the whole fish, with its silver skin marked by the grill, looks beautiful on the plate. If you really can't abide bones, buy whole butterflied boned trout from a careful fishmonger, stuff them, and fold them over to look like whole fish. A nice garnish for this trout would be Grilled Apple Rings (page 129).

The cider butter adds flavor to this trout, or serve the fish more simply, with lemon wedges next to a big pile of Grilled Asparagus (page 191).

Once you master cooking the trout, it's great fun to "move up the fish ladder" and on to salmon or steelhead. For a larger fish, you will need to tie butcher string around the fish to hold in the stuffing. Use a meat thermometer to check for doneness, just like a roast. Cook to about 140°F.

4 whole trout (about 12 ounces each), cleaned
4 sprigs fresh thyme
1 lemon, quartered and thinly sliced
½ onion, quartered and thinly sliced
2 cups all-purpose flour
2 tablespoons kosher salt
1 tablespoon freshly ground black pepper
Olive oil
Apple Cider Butter (recipe follows)
4 lemon wedges

1. Fire up the grill.

2. Stuff the cavity of each trout with a sprig of thyme, and a quarter of the lemon and onion slices. On a plate, combine the flour with the salt and pepper. Dredge both sides of the trout in the seasoned flour, shaking off the excess. Brush the grill and fish with oil. Grill over direct heat, with the grill covered, until cooked throughout, flipping halfway through, about 12 minutes total.

ON THE PLATE   Put a fish on each plate. Ladle the cider butter over the top. Serve with lemon wedges.

IN THE GLASS   A non-oaked Chardonnay from California or Washington State

Apple Cider Butter

{ Makes about 1 cup }

There is something about this sauce that goes great with wood-fired fish. We serve it with whole grilled trout, but it would be equally good with grilled salmon or halibut.

This makes enough sauce for 4 whole trout, or for 6 to 8 (smaller) servings of fish.

---

2 tablespoons minced shallots

1 tablespoon unsalted butter

One 12-ounce bottle hard apple cider (1¾ cups)

2 tablespoons heavy cream

¾ cup (1½ sticks) cold unsalted butter, cut into large dice

Kosher salt and freshly ground black pepper

1. In a small saucepan over medium-high heat, sweat the shallots in the 1 tablespoon butter for 2 to 3 minutes. Add the hard cider, bring to a boil, and reduce by two thirds, 7 to 8 minutes. Add the heavy cream, bring to a boil, and reduce by half, about 4 minutes. Add the pieces of cold butter bit by bit, whisking constantly over medium-high heat. The butter will emulsify, creating a thick, creamy sauce. Once all the butter has been incorporated, remove the pan from the heat. Season to taste with salt and pepper.

2. The best ways to keep this *beurre blanc* warm is to either place the container in a saucepan of hot (not simmering) water for half an hour or so, or pour it directly into a small Thermos and screw the cover on. The Thermos method will keep the beurre blanc warm for an hour or more.

BASIC BARBECUED CHICKEN

This is my favorite barbecued chicken recipe. Make sure you have your sunglasses on, the game playing on the radio, and a bottle of ice-cold Redhook I.P.A. in your hand.

1 chicken, cut into 8 pieces
Kosher salt and freshly ground black pepper or
Rub with Love for Chicken (see Sources,
page 260)
Hoisin Barbecue Sauce (page 128) or Steven's
Traditional American Barbecue Sauce
(page 126)

1. Fire up your grill.

2. Season the chicken pieces generously with salt and pepper or Rub with Love for Chicken. Grill over direct heat, with the grill covered and the vents open, turning the chicken pieces occasionally. When the chicken reaches an internal temperature of 150°F on an instant-read meat thermometer (this usually takes about 25 minutes or so), brush the chicken pieces on both sides with the barbecue sauce of your choice and grill again to caramelize the sauce. Be attentive so the sauce does not burn, turning the pieces frequently until the internal temperature of the chicken reaches 165°F, another 5 to 10 minutes more, then remove from the grill.

ON THE PLATE Pile the chicken on a platter and pass extra sauce. Serve this with Poppy Seed Coleslaw (page 183). Other great accompaniments are "Right on the Grill" Corn on the Cob (page 190), Grilled Asparagus (page 191), Corn and Blueberry Salad (page 149), and Etta's Cornbread Pudding (page 156).

IN THE GLASS California Zinfandel, Washington Syrah, a Rhone-style red, or the ale you started with

Basic Barbecued Baby Back Ribs

{ Makes 2 to 4 servings }

When I make these ribs for my wife, Jackie (she loves them hoisin style), I put several layers of sauce on, grilling the ribs between applications of sauce to create a nice caramelized glaze. If you are making your ribs American style, use a combination of spice rub and sauce—the two work beautifully together.

---

2 racks baby back pork ribs (1½ to 2 pounds each)
Barbecued Pork Spice Rub (page 131); or Rub with
  Love for Pork (see Sources, page 260) and
  Steven's Traditional American Barbecue Sauce
  (page 126); or kosher salt, freshly ground black
  pepper, and Hoisin Barbecue Sauce (page 128)

1. Fire up your grill.

2. Remove the excess fat and membranes from the back of the ribs. If you plan to use the American barbecue sauce, pat the spice rub over both sides of the racks of ribs. If you're planning to use the hoisin barbecue sauce, just sprinkle the ribs generously with salt and pepper.

3. Grill the ribs over direct medium heat, on ash-covered coals with the grill covered and the vents open, for 30 to 40 minutes, depending on the heat of the fire, turning the racks halfway through the cooking time. You should be able to see the meat just begin to separate from the bone. Brush the ribs on both sides with your choice of barbecue sauce and continue grilling, turning frequently, for 4 to 5 more minutes to caramelize and glaze the sauce on the ribs. Watch the ribs carefully so the sauce doesn't burn.

ON THE PLATE   Slice the ribs between the bones, pile them on a platter, and pass extra sauce. If you used hoisin barbecue sauce, you can serve these ribs on Spicy Peanut Noodles (page 172). If you used American barbecue sauce, serve them with Poppy Seed Coleslaw (page 183).

IN THE GLASS   California Zinfandel, Washington Syrah, a Rhone-style red, or a strong Northwest ale

STEVEN'S TRADITIONAL AMERICAN BARBECUE SAUCE

{ Makes 2 cups }

Steven Steinbock and I have worked together for over twenty years. But while I was sure I would trust him to take care of my family if something should happen to me, I wasn't sure I could trust him with my barbecue, until I tasted this tangy sauce.

You can make the sauce as mild or hot as you like. If you are going to combine it with the Barbecued Pork Spice Rub (page 131) as in the baby back rib recipe (page 125), you probably don't want to make it too hot because there is some heat in the spice rub. Another tip from Steven: If you use a smoker or a covered kettle barbecue, put a metal container of this sauce in the smoker or barbecue for a little while to pick up some smoke flavor.

2 tablespoons peanut or vegetable oil
½ cup minced onions
½ teaspoon minced garlic
1⅔ cups canned whole tomatoes with their juice
    (14.5-ounce can)
1 red bell pepper, roasted (page 127), peeled, and
    seeded
¼ cup fresh orange juice
¼ cup balsamic vinegar
¼ cup ketchup
3 tablespoons firmly packed brown sugar
2 tablespoons Dijon mustard
1 teaspoon Worcestershire sauce
1 teaspoon molasses
¾ teaspoon cumin seeds, toasted and ground
    (page 39)

¼ teaspoon ground cinnamon
Pinch of ground cloves
Red pepper flakes
Kosher salt and freshly ground black pepper

In a saucepan, heat the oil over medium-high heat, then cook the onions and garlic, stirring, for 2 minutes. In a food processor or blender, puree the onions and garlic with the tomatoes and roasted bell pepper. Return the puree to the saucepan and add the orange juice, vinegar, ketchup, brown sugar, mustard, Worcestershire, molasses, cumin, cinnamon, and cloves. Slowly simmer until it is as thick as you like it, 20 to 25 minutes. Remove from the heat. Season to taste with red pepper flakes, salt, and black pepper.

A STEP AHEAD This can be made several days ahead and stored, covered, in the refrigerator.

WILD WEST BARBECUE SAUCE

{ Makes 1⅔ cups }

Just over the Cascades, in the Yakima Valley, is one of the hottest places on earth. I'm not talking sun hot, I'm talking hot chiles hot. Who can resist a braid of bright red cayennes, or purple, red, gold, orange, gold orange, and green bells, or chartreuse peperoncini? The crisp green Anaheims make great rellenos, while the waxy yellow banana peppers are good for pickling. When you're looking for heat, sample the Scotch bonnets, jalapeños, habañeros, and serranos. And, like I said, when you've bought too many, make this sauce—a perfect way to use all the leftovers.

The more hot pepper you add to this sauce, the wilder it gets. This is really more of a relish than the kind of barbecue sauce that you mop on the meat. We serve it with our crabcakes, but it's also great with a grilled steak or on a hamburger. Some peppers are hotter than others, so taste and adjust. We serve this sauce at room temperature rather than hot. The flavor improves quite a bit after several hours, or the next day.

1 cup canned whole tomatoes, drained (all the tomatoes from one 14.5-ounce can without the juice)

2 ancho chiles, pureed (page 128)
1 red bell pepper, roasted (see below), peeled, and seeded
⅔ cup minced onions
½ cup seeded and minced Anaheim chiles or poblano chiles
1 teaspoon minced garlic
1 tablespoon chopped cilantro
1 tablespoon fresh lime juice
Red pepper flakes
Kosher salt and freshly ground black pepper

Puree the tomatoes, anchos, and roasted bell pepper in a food processor or blender until smooth. In a saucepan, combine the pureed tomato-pepper mixture with the onions, minced chiles, and garlic. Slowly simmer for 15 to 20 minutes. Remove from the heat and add the cilantro and lime juice. Season to taste with the pepper flakes, salt, and black pepper.

A STEP AHEAD   This can be made 2 to 3 days ahead and stored, covered, in the refrigerator.

HOW TO ROAST AND PEEL CHILES OR BELL PEPPERS

Place the peppers directly over the open flame of a gas burner, turning them until the skin is blackened and charred all over. Or put the peppers under a hot broiler on a baking sheet, turning as needed. Remove them to a bowl, cover tightly with plastic wrap, and allow the peppers to sweat for about 10 minutes to loosen the skins. Take the peppers out of the bowl and scrape away all the skin with a paring knife. Remove the stem and split the peppers in half. Remove and discard the seeds and veins.

HOISIN BARBECUE SAUCE

{ Makes 1 cup }

Hoisin is an incredibly versatile sauce made from soybean paste. The thick, reddish brown, slightly sweet, fragrant sauce is used in China much as ketchup is used here.

Barbara Tropp makes the best stir-fried spicy lamb with hoisin and string beans. Her recipe, published in the *China Moon Cookbook*, has become a staple in our house. Our copy of this much-loved book (named after her café, sadly, now closed) is bedraggled, dog-eared, and food-stained.

I like to use hoisin to make barbecue sauce. It seems perfect with salmon, chicken, spare ribs, or most any meat or fish. Feel free to double or triple the recipe because it keeps beautifully, stored in the refrigerator.

¾ cup hoisin sauce (one 8-ounce jar)
¾ cup rice wine vinegar
1 tablespoon Chinese fermented black beans
1 teaspoon minced garlic
¾ teaspoon red pepper flakes
5 unpeeled fresh ginger coins (page 47),
  sliced ¼ inch thick
2 star anise
Grated zest from ½ orange

In a small saucepan, combine all the ingredients. Slowly simmer for 15 minutes Remove from the heat. Strain through a mesh strainer before using.

A STEP AHEAD This can be made several days ahead or longer and stored, covered, in the refrigerator.

HOW TO PUREE ANCHO CHILES

Split the chiles open and discard the stems and seeds. Place the chiles in a small saucepan and cover with water. Bring to a boil and remove the saucepan from the heat. Allow the chiles to soak for 10 minutes until they are soft. Remove the chiles from the water and puree them in a blender or food processor. Use a little of the soaking water to help you puree them, if necessary. Strain the ancho chile puree through a fine-mesh sieve.

MAPLE-CURED DOUBLE-CUT PORK CHOPS WITH GRILLED APPLE RINGS AND CREAMY CORN GRITS

{ Makes 4 servings }

The maple syrup in this cure does two things; it adds a touch of sweetness as well as an incredible flavor. For me, the smell of the cured chops charcoal-grilling reminds me of my grandma Fogarty's kitchen.

You can also try this cure technique with grilled pork tenderloin (and adjust the grilling time as needed). The pork needs to marinate a day ahead, so plan accordingly.

5 cups cold water
¾ cup firmly packed brown sugar
½ cup kosher salt
½ cup pure maple syrup
2 tablespoons molasses
2 bay leaves
1 teaspoon ground ginger
½ teaspoon ground allspice
½ teaspoon freshly ground black pepper
4 thick-cut (about 1½ inches) pork chops
(about 12 ounces each)
2 apples (Braeburn or Granny Smith)
¼ cup honey
1 tablespoon fresh lemon juice
Creamy Corn Grits (recipe follows)
Sprigs fresh thyme (optional)

I. In a nonreactive pan or bowl, combine the water, brown sugar, salt, maple syrup, molasses, and spices. Add the pork chops, cover, and refrigerate for I day. The pork chops can sit in the brine for I to 3 days, pork tenderloin no more than I day.

2. Fire up the grill. Remove the pork from the refrigerator. Remove the pork chops from the brine and allow them to come to room temperature for 20 minutes before grilling. Grill over direct heat, covered, with the vents open. Smoke should be flowing from the vents, which means the fire is hot, and you should be able to hear the pork sizzling. Brown both sides of the pork chops. If the surface is burning, move the pork chops to an area of indirect heat on the grill. Pull the pork from the grill when it reaches an internal temperature of 140° to 145°F on an instant-read meat thermometer. It should take approximately 25 minutes total. Let the pork chops rest about 5 minutes.

3. Meanwhile, core the apples, leaving the peel on, and slice into rings about ¼ inch thick. In a small bowl, combine the honey and lemon juice. Brush this mixture on the apple rings and grill them over direct heat, with the lid off, until caramelized, about 4 minutes. You don't want to cook them so much that they fall apart; the goal is simply to caramelize them.

ON THE PLATE   Spoon the corn grits in the middle of 4 plates. Lean a pork chop against the mound of grits. Garnish with the grilled apple rings and a sprig of fresh thyme, if desired.

IN THE GLASS   Try a Côtes-du-Rhône, maybe from the small town of Vacqueyras. They are quite fruity in nature.

Creamy Corn Grits

{ Makes 4 servings }

This is a luscious, creamy dish similar to soft polenta. Grits are made of coarsely ground hominy—dried corn kernels from which the hull and germ have been removed. I like to make this with real grits—the slow-cooking kind, like Hoppin' John's from South Carolina (see Sources, page 260). These grits are perfect with maple-cured pork chops, but also would be delicious with roast chicken or grilled sausages.

4 cups milk
2 cups water
1 cup grits (not instant)
1 cup grated Cheddar cheese (about 4 ounces)
2 tablespoons (¼ stick) unsalted butter
Kosher salt and freshly ground black pepper

In a saucepan over high heat, bring the milk and water to a boil. Gradually whisk in the grits and reduce the heat to a slow simmer. Cook until the grits are soft and creamy, whisking occasionally, about 1 hour. Whisk in the cheese and butter. Season to taste with salt and pepper. If the grits are too thick, add more water to adjust to the desired consistency.

BARBECUE PORK BUTT TACOS

{ Makes 6 servings }

One year, for a Christmas party at our house, Jackie and I put together a great taco bar, which included a huge platter of this delicious, tender shredded pork. We ordered excellent hand-made corn tortillas from a nearby local restaurant and Eddie, our Mexican prepster, made the best pico de gallo I've ever tasted.

FOR THE BARBECUED PORK SPICE RUB

1 tablespoon firmly packed brown sugar

2 teaspoons paprika

2 teaspoons cumin seeds, toasted and ground (page 21)

2 teaspoons coriander seeds, toasted and ground (page 21)

2 teaspoons kosher salt

1 teaspoon ancho chile powder or chili powder

½ teaspoon freshly ground black pepper

¼ teaspoon cayenne, or more to taste

FOR THE BARBECUE

One 3-pound pork butt (either bone in or bone out)

2 cups water

1 cup apple cider

1 orange, sliced

1 onion, sliced

TO SERVE

½ cup vegetable oil

12 corn tortillas

Pico de Gallo (recipe follows)

1. Fire up your grill.

2. Combine all the spice rub ingredients in a bowl. Rub the pork butt all over with the spice mixture. Grill the pork butt over indirect heat, with the grill covered and the vents fully open. To help keep the meat moist, fill a small metal pan with the water, cider, and orange and onion slices and place it under the meat to catch the drippings and provide steam. If your grill has a thermometer, keep the temperature of the grill at about 350°F. Barbecue the pork slowly, turning it occasionally and adding coals as necessary, for 2½ to 3 hours, until the meat is very tender and shreds easily with a fork.

3. Remove the pork from the grill and wrap it in aluminum foil. Allow the meat to rest for at least 10 minutes, then slice it across the grain, pulling off and discarding any large chunks of fat. Using a large knife or Chinese cleaver, chop the sliced meat into ½-inch chunks.

4. While the meat is resting, you can fry the tortillas. Heat the oil in a sauté pan over medium-high heat. Fry the tortillas until crispy, about a minute per side. Drain on paper towels.

ON THE PLATE Set out the crispy tortillas, a platter of chopped pork, and a bowl of pico de gallo, allowing everyone to make their own tacos. If you like, you can also set out bowls of sour cream, diced avocados, chopped lettuce, cooked pinto or black beans, and grated pepper Jack cheese.

You can make the spice rub ahead and keep it in a jar at room temperature.

NOTE: This pork is great cooked over indirect heat in a covered grill, but if you prefer, you can also roast it in the oven. Place the spice-rubbed pork butt on a rack in a baking dish and roast it at 350°F for 2½ to 3 hours.

IN THE GLASS A good, stiff, limey Margarita

❁

Pico de Gallo

{ Makes 3 cups }

This simple sauce is wonderful on tacos, sandwiches, and salads, wherever you want a fresh, spicy taste.

6 Roma tomatoes, seeded and diced small
½ cup finely diced onions
¼ cup chopped cilantro
1 jalapeño chile, or more to taste, seeded and minced
2 tablespoons fresh lime juice
Kosher salt

In a small bowl, toss together the tomatoes, onions, cilantro, jalapeño, and lime juice. Season to taste with salt. This is best if used the same day.

CHILE-CRUSTED GRILLED TURKEY

{ Makes 10 servings }

It's fun to roast a whole turkey on the grill. It's not difficult and doesn't take nearly as long as you might expect. You get those wonderful smoky flavors and juicy, tender white and dark meat. Use leftovers from this turkey to make tacos, as described in the Barbecue Pork Butt Tacos (page 131).

When you cook a large bird like this over indirect heat, be sure you turn the turkey around from time to time so it cooks evenly, because your coals may be unevenly hot. Serve this with grilled corn and baked yams. You could cook everything on the grill, but it's best not to overcrowd it; leave room for heat to circulate.

FOR THE CHILE RUB

3 tablespoons firmly packed brown sugar
4½ teaspoons kosher salt
4½ teaspoons ancho chile powder or regular chili powder
4½ teaspoons paprika
4½ teaspoons cumin seeds, toasted and ground (page 21)
2¼ teaspoons freshly ground black pepper

FOR THE TURKEY

One 10- to 12-pound turkey
½ onion
½ orange
3 star anise
Kosher salt and freshly ground black pepper

1. Fire up the grill. Combine all the chile rub ingredients in a small bowl.

2. Rinse and pat the turkey dry with paper towels. Cut away any excess fat and discard the innards (or save them to make stock). Place the onion, orange, and star anise in the cavity of the turkey and season the cavity with salt and pepper. Generously pat the chile rub all over the outside of the turkey.

3. Grill over indirect heat, covered, with the vents open. If your grill has a thermometer, hold the grill temperature around 350°F. Grill until the turkey reaches an internal temperature of 165°F on an instant-read meat thermometer, about 2 hours. Add more coals and move the turkey around as necessary to allow all sides to cook evenly. Let rest for 10 minutes before carving.

ON THE PLATE   Slice the turkey and place on plates. We like to serve this with grilled corn and roasted yams.

A STEP AHEAD   The chile rub can be made several days ahead and stored, covered, at room temperature.

IN THE GLASS   Lemberger, a favorite Northwest red wine much like Zinfandel

Rib Eye Steak with Garlic Bruschetta and Aged Balsamic Vinegar

{ Makes 4 servings }

I love the rich (in more ways than one) balsamic vinegar from Modena that has been aged in barrels, but less expensive balsamic vinegar will also work well here. The sweetness of the balsamic vinegar reminds me of old-fashioned Southern-style barbecue sauce on grilled steak. Serve this steak on a piece of grilled garlic bruschetta so the bread can soak up all the delicious juices.

Four 14-ounce rib steaks, about 1 inch thick
10 cloves garlic, peeled and smashed
3 sprigs fresh rosemary, leaves roughly chopped
  (about 2 tablespoons)
½ cup extra virgin olive oil, plus more for grilling
Black pepper
Kosher salt
Four ½-inch-thick slices rustic bread
Balsamic vinegar

1. Fire up the grill.
2. Place the steaks in a single layer in a shallow dish. Sprinkle 6 cloves of the garlic and the rosemary on and around the steaks, reserving the rest of the garlic for the bruschetta. Pour the ½ cup oil over the steaks and coarsely grind pepper over the top. Let marinate in the refrigerator a few hours, covered with plastic wrap.
3. Scrape off any excess oil before placing the steaks on the grill to prevent flare-ups. Heavily season the steaks with salt and pepper. Grill over direct heat with the lid off to the desired level of doneness, turning often with tongs. A 1-inch-thick steak will take about 8 minutes total for rare.
4. Rub each slice of bread with a smashed clove of garlic. Generously brush the slices with olive oil and season with salt and pepper. Grill the bread over direct heat with the lid off until golden and crusty, about 1 minute per side.

ON THE PLATE   Place a garlic bruschetta on each plate. Place a steak on each bruschetta, partially covering it. Drizzle each steak with balsamic vinegar and some more extra virgin olive oil.

IN THE GLASS   A full-bodied Barbaresco from Northern Italy; a super-Tuscan red composed of any or all Cabernet Sauvigion, Sangiovese, or Merlot; or a Washington Nebbiolo

Bengal Spice-Rubbed Lamb
with Cool Cucumber Yogurt

{ Makes 12 servings }

Every couple of weeks, Julie, from Wild Currant Farms, on Lopez Island in the San Juan Islands, sells us half a dozen of the most delicious lambs you've ever tasted. Our recipe features the leg, but most any part of the lamb can be substituted, though cooking times may change.

Because different groups of muscles in the leg vary in thickness, it's difficult to cook a whole butterflied leg of lamb to the same degree of doneness at one time. What I do is divide the leg into 3 pieces and remove them all from the grill when the thinnest one is cooked to medium. Thus the other, thicker pieces are medium-rare and rare, so you have different degrees of doneness for everyone's tastes.

This flavorful lamb would be delicious with Seed Bread (page 35) or warm pita bread. It would also be good served with our Smoky Eggplant (page 34). The lamb needs to marinate at least 4 hours or overnight in the refrigerator, so plan accordingly.

FOR THE LAMB

8 green onions or scallions, white and green parts, roughly chopped

Leaves from 1½ bunches cilantro (about 3 cups picked leaves)

1 jalapeño chile, seeded and roughly chopped

3 tablespoons peeled and grated fresh ginger

2 tablespoons minced garlic

1 tablespoon cumin seeds, toasted and ground (page 21)

1 tablespoon coriander seeds, toasted and ground (page 21)

1 tablespoon kosher salt

2 teaspoons mustard seeds

2 teaspoons freshly ground black pepper

½ teaspoon ground cinnamon

½ teaspoon ground cardamom

¼ teaspoon ground cloves

¼ teaspoon cayenne, or more to taste

½ cup olive oil

One 6½-pound leg of lamb, boned and butterflied, most visible fat removed, and separated into 3 pieces

FOR THE COOL CUCUMBER YOGURT

1 cucumber (about 14 ounces)

Kosher salt

3 cups plain yogurt

¼ cup chopped cilantro

¼ cup chopped mint

2 tablespoons fresh lime juice

Freshly ground black pepper

1. Combine the green onions, cilantro, jalapeño, ginger, and garlic in a food processor or blender and process until finely chopped. Add the seeds, salt, and all the spices and process to combine. With the motor running, add the olive oil in a slow, steady stream and puree everything to a paste. Remove the paste to a small bowl.

2. Place the 3 pieces of lamb in a large nonreactive pan and spread the paste over all sides with a rubber spatula. Allow to marinate, refrigerated, for at least 4 hours or overnight, covered with plastic wrap.

3. Fire up the grill. Remove the lamb from the refrigerator about half an hour before grilling to allow it to come to room temperature.

4. While the grill is heating, make the cucumber yogurt. Peel and seed the cucumber. Grate the cucumber and place it in a strainer set over a bowl. Generously salt the cucumber and let drain for half an hour. Squeeze the liquid out. In a small bowl, combine the cucumber, yogurt, cilantro, mint, and lime juice. Season to taste with salt and pepper.

5. Grill the lamb over direct heat with the lid on and the vents fully open to the desired level of doneness, about 30 minutes, moving the pieces around as necessary to cook evenly.

If your grill has a thermometer, keep the temperature of the grill between 375° and 400°F. Remove the lamb as described in the headnote above. Let the meat rest for 5 minutes.

ON THE PLATE Slice the lamb across the grain and place on a platter. Spoon the cucumber yogurt alongside.

A STEP AHEAD The cucumber yogurt can be made a day ahead and stored, covered, in the refrigerator until serving.

IN THE GLASS A big fruity Merlot or Cabernet Franc from the Yakima Valley or Walla Walla

Al fresco dining near Boeing Field

Slow Dancing:
Braising and Roasting

ONE OF MY favorite pastimes while I'm chopping the garlic and browning the short ribs for the feast to come is to put on the CD from that food movie *Big Night*. I sing along with Louis Prima and Rosemary Clooney, and take a turn or two, slow dancing with my wife around the kitchen island. There's something sensuous about slow cooking, just like slow dancing. You enjoy it and savor it and you don't want to hurry it along. Jackie and I take another turn or two, we sing another song (this time with Claudio Villa), peek into the oven from time to time, sipping martinis, waiting for the tenderness that only time can bring.

Luscious, slow-cooked braises are the perfect antidote to our long, gray soggy winters up here in the Northwest. Slow-roasted and braised foods have a warmth and comfort factor that can create high noon any dreary day. Browning the meat first provides a caramelized surface that gives a dish that rich, meaty flavor, and long, slow cooking in a flavorful liquid like wine or beer creates a silky and delicious sauce. And when braising, try to use the same wine in the dish that you have on the table (and hopefully in the cook). This makes for a delicious match when you sit down to eat.

Slow roasting is another satisfying way to cook game or fowl. I love duck, but I'm no fan of the current trend of rare breast meat. I like to roast duck the Eastern European way, long and slow. The meat should be almost falling off the bone, but still have a crisp skin.

LONG-BONE SHORT RIBS WITH CHINOOK MERLOT GRAVY AND ROSEMARY WHITE BEANS

{ Makes 6 servings }

I love the awesome look of big short rib bones lying across the plate—some of our cooks refer to these as Flinstone bones. But you could use the short-cut or English-cut short ribs instead. This is a great rib-sticking (excuse the pun) dish for our long, gray, drizzly winters.

My friends Kay and Clay, who own Chinook Wines (see pages 114–116) in Prosser, Washington, make great Merlot, and it's a tradition in our house to drink and cook with it when we make this dish. Of course, another Merlot will do if you can't get Chinook.

This recipe takes a long time to cook, but can easily be made the day before and reheated before serving. In fact, like most braises, it will taste even better.

1½ cups all-purpose flour
1 tablespoon kosher salt
1 teaspoon freshly ground black pepper
6 long-bone short ribs (about 1½ pounds each) or other short ribs
¼ cup olive oil
2 onions, roughly chopped (about 3½ cups)
2 carrots, roughly chopped (about 1 cup)
1 tablespoon chopped garlic
2 teaspoons chopped fresh thyme
2 bay leaves
1 teaspoon black peppercorns
2 cups Chinook Merlot or other dry red wine
3 cups chicken stock (page 253)
Kosher salt and freshly ground black pepper
Rosemary White Beans (recipe follows)
Horseradish Gremolata (page 23)

1. Preheat the oven to 325°F. On a baking sheet, combine the flour, salt, and pepper. Coat the short ribs evenly with the seasoned flour, shaking off any excess. In a large roasting pan over high heat on the stovetop, heat the oil, then brown the ribs on all sides (in batches if necessary), about 15 minutes. Remove the ribs from the roasting pan and set aside.

2. To the same pan, add the onions and carrots and cook, stirring until softened, about 10 minutes, adding the garlic, thyme, bay leaves, and peppercorns for the last few minutes. Return the short ribs to the roasting pan, bone side up. Pour the Merlot and chicken stock over the ribs. Bring the liquids to a simmer on top of the stove, then cover the pan with aluminum foil (or a lid) and braise in the oven until the meat begins to pull away from the bone, about 2½ hours. Carefully remove the roasting pan from the oven. Reduce the oven temperature to 200°F. Lift out the ribs and place them in a clean pan. Cover this pan and keep the ribs warm in the oven while you finish the sauce.

3. Pour the braising liquids from the roasting pan through a sieve into a deep, tall container (like a large pitcher), pressing on the vegetables to get as much liquid as possible. Discard the vegetables. Allow the liquids to rest about 5 minutes, then skim off all the fat with a ladle and discard. (A tall container makes it easy to remove the fat in one deep layer.) Short ribs are fatty, so there will be quite a bit of fat to remove at this point.

4. Pour the strained and skimmed braising liquid into a large sauté pan and reduce over high heat until thickened, about 15 minutes. You should end up with about 2 cups sauce. You want this to be a sauce, not glue, so don't overreduce it. It should be the consistency of heavy cream, just thick enough to cling to the meat when you ladle it over. Season with salt and plenty of freshly ground black pepper.

ON THE PLATE   Spoon the white beans and some of their broth into 6 large, shallow bowls. Remove the short ribs from the oven and place a short rib in the center of each bowl. Ladle the sauce over each rib. Garnish with the gremolata. You can also remove the meat from the bone so that it is easier to eat.

A STEP AHEAD   You can braise the ribs a day ahead and store them, covered, in the refrigerator. Store the sauce separately, covered, in the refrigerator. When you are ready to reheat the short ribs, preheat the oven to 400°F. Place the ribs in a pan with 1 cup hot chicken stock. Cover the pan and place it in the oven for about 25 minutes until the meat is warmed through. Heat the sauce to a simmer in a small saucepan on the stovetop.

IN THE GLASS   For me, it has to be Chinook Merlot.

REDUCING SAUCES

A tip: using a large, wide pan helps reduce sauces more quickly. Also, if your pan is large enough to fit over two burners, turn both burners on high.

Rosemary White Beans

{ Makes 6 servings }

Serve these beans in wide, shallow soup bowls with our Long-Bone Short Ribs (page 138). Or pair them with other roasted meats, birds, or sausages.

For the best flavor, cook the beans in chicken stock. The beans need to start soaking the day before, so plan accordingly.

---

2 cups dried white beans, picked over and rinsed
¾ cup diced bacon (2 thick strips, about 3 ounces)
1 cup chopped onions
1 teaspoon chopped garlic
4 cups chicken stock (page 253)
4 cups water
2 tablespoons chopped fresh rosemary
2 tablespoons (¼ stick) unsalted butter
Kosher salt and freshly ground black pepper

1. Generously cover the beans with cold water and allow to soak overnight, refrigerated. The beans will double in volume (at least), so put them in a container that can hold them and at least twice their volume of water.

2. The next day, heat the bacon in a large pot over medium-high heat until the fat is rendered and bacon crisp, 8 to 10 minutes. Add the onions and cook until soft, stirring, 8 to 10 minutes. Add the garlic and cook, stirring, 1 minute longer. Add the chicken stock and water and heat to a simmer. Drain the beans of their soaking liquid and add them to the pot. Cook the beans over medium heat until soft, about 1½ hours.

3. By the time the beans are soft, there should be just enough liquid left in the pot to make the beans slightly brothy. If the beans seem to have too much liquid, turn the heat to high and reduce the cooking liquid a bit. Stir in the rosemary and butter and season to taste with salt and pepper.

A STEP AHEAD The beans can be cooked a day ahead and stored, covered, refrigerated. Add the butter and rosemary when you are reheating them.

MUSTARD-GLAZED RIB ROAST

{ Makes 6 to 8 servings }

This is my version of my father's favorite dish: prime rib—thick cut, rare, and on the bone. At the Palace we thread it on the rotisserie and turn it slowly over smoldering apple wood. What a treat! Sometimes rib roasts are sold with a net over them. I always remove it before cooking to keep the crust intact.

½ cup Dijon mustard
⅓ cup minced shallots
2 tablespoons minced garlic
4 teaspoons chopped fresh rosemary
1 teaspoon kosher salt
1 teaspoon freshly ground black pepper
One 3-bone rib roast (6 to 7 pounds)

Preheat the oven to 400°F. To make the rub, combine the mustard, shallots, garlic, rosemary, salt, and pepper in a small bowl. Place the roast on a rack in a roasting pan. With a rubber spatula or your hands, spread the rub all over the roast. Place in the oven for 20 minutes, then reduce the oven temperature to 350°F. Roast for another 40 minutes, and check with an instant-read meat thermometer. When the internal temperature reaches 115°F, the rib roast will be rare. Continue cooking if you like it more well done. Remove from the oven and let the roast sit for 5 to 10 minutes to rest, loosely tented with aluminum foil, before removing the rib bone and slicing the meat into servings.

ON THE PLATE Sprinkle each slice of beef with salt and pepper. We also like to grate peeled fresh horseradish over each slice, which is optional. We serve this with Red Bliss Mashers (page 162) or Masa Onion Rings (page 161).

IN THE GLASS Try one of the good Washington State Cabernets like Woodward Canyon.

COOKING ROAST BEEF TO PERFECTION

Here are two tricks for perfect roast beef (or any meat for that matter): Use an instant-read digital meat thermometer, and let the meat sit for at least 5 and up to 15 minutes (depending on its thickness) before serving. The internal temperature of the meat will rise 5 to 10 degrees while it sits, and the juices and temperatures inside the meat will redistribute and stabilize.

Suggested Internal Temperatures for Removing Roast Beef from Oven
Rare: 115°F   Medium Rare: 125°F   Medium: 135°F

Black Pepper—Crusted Venison with Potato-Turnip Gratin and Cranberry Jam

{ Makes 6 servings }

The creamy potato and turnip gratin, the crust of black pepper on the venison, the bright red cranberry jam all look beautiful on the plate and taste great together. We get our venison from game farms, and I like to cook this flavorful meat medium rare, but you can cook it longer. And, if you prefer, beef tenderloin would also be delicious for this recipe.

The cranberry jam yields more than you need to garnish the venison, but it is also excellent on turkey sandwiches, or with roast chicken, duck, goose, or grilled pork tenderloin.

FOR THE CRANBERRY JAM
1 tablespoon unsalted butter
1 tablespoon peeled and grated fresh ginger
1 tablespoon fresh orange juice
1 tablespoon fresh lemon juice
1 teaspoon grated orange zest
1 teaspoon grated lemon zest
One 12-ounce bag fresh cranberries (about 3¾ cups), picked over for stems and rinsed
½ cup sugar
½ cup water
¼ cup port wine
¼ teaspoon ground cinnamon
2 tablespoons olive oil
One 2-pound boneless venison loin, cut into 6 portions
Kosher salt
¼ cup black peppercorns, coarsely ground
Potato-Turnip Gratin (page 158)

1. To make the cranberry jam, in a small saucepan over medium heat, heat the butter, then cook the ginger, stirring, for a few minutes. Add the citrus juices and zests, cranberries, sugar, water, port, and cinnamon. Simmer just until the cranberries begin to pop, about 5 minutes. Remove from the heat. You should have about 2½ cups jam.

2. To prepare the venison, heat a large sauté pan with the oil over high heat. Season each piece of venison with a sprinkling of salt. Crust each piece of venison with the pepper. Brown well all the sides of the venison. We like to cook it rare, which takes 8 to 10 minutes.

ON THE PLATE Slice the venison across the grain about ¼ inch thick. Place a square of the hot potato-turnip gratin in the center of each plate. Fan the venison over the gratin and top with a generous spoonful of the cranberry jam.

A STEP AHEAD The cranberry jam can be made several days ahead and stored in the refrigerator, covered. Bring it back to room temperature before using.

IN THE GLASS A sturdy red like Châteauneuf-du-Pape

Riesling Rabbit with
New Potatoes and Spring Vegetables

{ Makes 2 to 4 servings }

Even though this is a braised dish, it has a light, springlike feel to it. The sauce is light-bodied, more like a substantial broth than a heavy sauce. I make this dish with Yukon Gold potatoes, blue potatoes, or fingerlings. If you can find tiny new potatoes, definitely use them here.

Also, use whatever spring vegetables you can find in the market or harvest from your garden, such as tiny fennel bulbs or baby zucchini. Just blanch them in boiling water until tender before adding them. Fava beans would be perfect. They take time to peel (since you have to remove both the outer pod and the thin skin around each bean), but the quantity called for is not large. You could also substitute freshly shucked English peas for the favas; blanch them only a minute or two.

---

3 tablespoons olive oil

1 rabbit (about 2 pounds), cut into 8 pieces

Kosher salt and freshly ground black pepper

2 ribs celery, roughly chopped

1 onion, roughly chopped

1 carrot, roughly chopped

2 bay leaves

1 teaspoon black peppercorns

2 cups dry Riesling

3 cups chicken stock (page 253)

¾ pound new potatoes, peeled and halved, or
    quartered if large

1 pound fresh fava beans (½ cup shucked beans) or
    English peas

1 cup pearl onions

2 bunches baby carrots, peeled

3 baby turnips, cut in halves or quarters

Sprigs fresh chervil, thyme, or chive blossoms, or
    lavender blossoms, for garnish

1. Preheat the oven to 325°F. Heat the oil in a large, ovenproof straight-sided sauté pan over high heat. Season the rabbit pieces with salt and pepper. Brown the rabbit well on both sides, 5 to 10 minutes. Remove the seared pieces from the pan and set aside. In the same pan, add the celery, onion, and carrot and cook, stirring, until they begin to caramelize and brown, about 3 minutes. Add the bay leaves, peppercorns, and wine. Return the seared rabbit to the pan. Let the wine simmer for a few minutes. Add the stock, cover, and place in the oven until the meat begins to fall off the bone, about 1 hour.

2. Remove the pan from the oven. Reduce the oven temperature to 200°F. Take the rabbit out of the braising liquid and place it in a clean pan. Cover and keep warm in the oven. Strain the braising liquid through a sieve to remove the solids. Skim to remove the fat. Return the braising liquid to a large sauté pan over high heat and reduce by half, about 15 minutes. Even though you are reducing the braising liquid, you will not end up with a thick, glossy sauce; the liquid will be more like a substantial broth. You should have about 2 cups Riesling broth.

3. While the rabbit is cooking, prepare all the vegetables. Place the potatoes in a small pot of cold salted water, bring to a simmer, and continue to simmer until the potatoes are cooked through, about 15 minutes. Drain and set aside. For the favas, pearl onions, carrots, and turnips, set up a small pot of boiling salted water. Set a strainer filled with the pearl onions in the pot of boiling water for about 4 minutes. Remove the onions from the water. When they are just cool enough to handle, trim the onions of their roots and peel them. Set aside. Shuck the favas or English peas from their outer pods and boil the beans or peas in the strainer. Favas will need to blanch for 3 minutes. Peas will need to blanch only a minute or two. Remove from the water. When the favas are cool enough to handle, pop them out of their skins (this won't be necessary for the peas). Set aside. Then boil the carrots and turnips together in the same strainer until just done, about 3 minutes. Drain and set aside.

ON THE PLATE   Divide the vegetables among wide, shallow bowls and cover with the Riesling broth. Top with the rabbit pieces and garnish with herb sprigs.

A STEP AHEAD   The rabbit can be braised a day ahead and stored, refrigerated. The Riesling broth can also be reduced a day ahead and stored, refrigerated. The vegetables can be blanched ahead and stored, refrigerated. Warm the rabbit and vegetables in the Riesling broth on top of the stove over medium-high heat.

IN THE GLASS   This calls for a big Alsatian Riesling like Zind-Humbrecht.

ROAST DUCK WITH HUCKLEBERRY SAUCE AND PARSNIP-APPLE HASH

{ Makes 4 servings }

Slow-roasted duck is a signature dish at the Dahlia Lounge. I am not a fan of a rare duck breast. I like ducks well roasted, to render off most of the fat, leaving a rich, tender meat and a crisp skin.

I feel lucky that huckleberries grow wild in the Cascade Mountains. When the huckleberry season arrives, at the height of summer, I buy as many as I can get my hands on. Warren Webster, the character who sells them to us, comes in year after year with the same story: "Man, the bears sure were thick out there today." Or maybe, "A lot of bears out there today." He says it with such a straight face that I'm sure he's not kidding!

You are going to need some reduced stock for the huckleberry sauce. At the restaurant, we have duck and chicken stock on hand. At home, you can enrich chicken stock with duck trimmings to make the sauce, as explained on page 254. See the photographs on page 146 on trimming and carving the ducks.

The fruitiness of both the huckleberry sauce and the parsnip-apple hash works really well with the rich duck meat.

---

2 ducks (about 4½ pounds each)
4 sprigs fresh thyme
4 shallots, quartered
½ orange, cut into chunks
Kosher salt and freshly ground black pepper

FOR THE HUCKLEBERRY SAUCE
   AND TO SERVE
1 pint fresh or defrosted frozen huckleberries (or red currants, blackberries, or raspberries)
4 cups Duck-Enriched Chicken Stock (page 254)
1 tablespoon unsalted butter
2 tablespoons minced shallots
2 teaspoons crème de cassis
Kosher salt and freshly ground black pepper
Parsnip-Apple Hash (page 163)
4 small sprigs fresh rosemary (optional)

1. To trim the ducks, remove the necks, hearts, and gizzards from the duck cavity and set aside for stock. The livers can be saved for another use (see Duck Liver Pâté, page 148). Trim and discard any extra skin and fat from the neck and tail end. Stuff each cavity with half of the thyme sprigs, shallots, and orange. Season the outside of the ducks with salt and pepper. Do not truss the birds. Let the ducks sit, uncovered, in the refrigerator for 30 minutes so the salt can dehydrate the skin for a crisper finished bird.

2. To roast the ducks, preheat the oven to 500°F. Set the ducks on a rack in a large roasting pan to catch the fat during cooking, and be sure they are separated from each other so the heat circulates evenly around the ducks, allowing all the skin to render its fat. Roast the ducks for 30 minutes, then turn the oven temperature down to 350°F and cook for another 45 minutes. To test for doneness, carefully tilt each duck to allow the

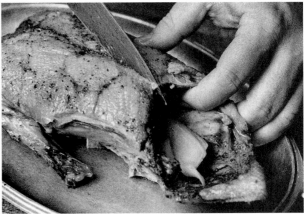

Place the duck back side down, with the legs pointing toward you, and use your knife to cut into the natural division between the leg and the body. Bend the leg away from the body and cut through the joint. Repeat to remove both leg-thigh portions from the duck.

To remove the breasts, turn the duck around so the wishbone (neck end) is facing you. Run your knife down the central breast ridge and follow the angle of the wishbone.

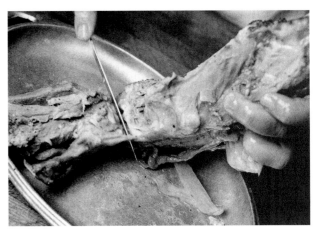

With your thumb, gently pull the breast meat away from one side of the rib cage, freeing the meat with your knife as necessary.

Cut the breast free from the body at the wing joint, leaving the wing bone attached to the breast. Repeat on the other side.

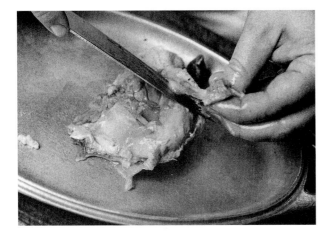

Trim any fat or gristle from the 4 pieces (2 leg-thigh portions, and 2 breast portions).

juices to run from the cavity. They should be pink-gray instead of red. An instant-read meat thermometer inserted into the thigh should read between 150° and 160°F. We cook our ducks until they are slightly pink at the joint because we cook them again after carving. Remove the ducks from the oven and allow them to cool for about half an hour.

3. While the ducks are roasting, make the duck-enriched chicken stock (page 254).

4. To make the sauce, reduce the stock to 2 cups. Reserve ¼ cup of the whole huckleberries or other berries. Puree the rest of the berries in a food processor, then force them through a fine-mesh strainer. In a small saucepan, heat the butter, then cook the shallots over medium-high heat, stirring, for 2 minutes. Add the reduced stock and the berry puree and slowly simmer until the sauce thickens, about 30 minutes, skimming as necessary. Add the crème de cassis and reserved huckleberries. Season to taste with salt and pepper. You should have about I cup sauce.

5. Carve the ducks as described on page 146. Use immediately or refrigerate the duck pieces for later use.

6. To finish the dish, preheat the oven to 450°F. On the stovetop, heat an ovenproof sauté pan over medium-high heat. Put the duck pieces into the pan, skin side down, and cook until the skin is golden and crispy and more of the fat has been rendered, about 5 minutes. Flip the pieces and put the pan into the oven for another 10 minutes until the duck is heated through. If you don't have a pan large enough to accommodate all the duck pieces, you can brown them in batches on the stove. Then transfer the duck pieces to a baking sheet and put the baking sheet into the oven.

ON THE PLATE   We stack a breast-wing piece on a leg-thigh piece on top of a mound of the parsnip hash. Ladle some huckleberry sauce on each plate and garnish with a sprig of rosemary, if desired.

A STEP AHEAD   The sauce can be made, and the ducks roasted and carved, a day ahead. Store both in the refrigerator, covered with plastic wrap.

IN THE GLASS   Try a Petite Sirah from California or a Syrah from Washington State.

DUCK LIVER PÂTÉ

{ Makes 1 cup }

Duck livers are delicious and it's a shame to throw them away or feed them to your cat when you are roasting a duck. You can make this quick pâté from two duck livers and serve it as an appetizer with crackers or crostini. Or dress some arugula with Lemon Vinaigrette (page 102) and make appetizer salads, topping each one with a couple of duck-liver toasts, or use duck liver toasts to garnish a plate of roast duck.

1 tablespoon olive oil
2 duck livers, trimmed of fat and gristle
1 tablespoon minced shallots
2 tablespoons dry sherry
9 tablespoons unsalted butter, cut into bits, at room
  temperature
¼ teaspoon chopped fresh thyme
Kosher salt and freshly ground black pepper

I. Heat a small nonstick sauté pan with the olive oil until it is very hot. Add the livers, being careful, because they will sputter when they hit the fat. Sear the livers on both sides and cook them to medium rare (cut one open to check), I to 2 minutes. Remove the livers from the pan and set aside. Add the shallots to the same pan and cook, stirring, until fragrant, about I minute. Add the sherry, scraping the bottom of the pan with a wooden spoon to dissolve any caramelized bits. Allow the sherry to boil until it is reduced by half, about I minute. Set aside to cool. It is important that the livers, shallots, and sherry are cool or they will break the butter in the following step.

2. Puree the cooled livers, shallots, and sherry in a blender or food processor. While the machine is running, gradually add bits of the butter until it is all incorporated. Add the thyme. Season to taste with salt and pepper.

ON THE PLATE   Spread the pâté on toasted crostini (see below) or crackers, or serve with slices of bread, such as walnut bread. . . . delicious!

A STEP AHEAD   Store in the refrigerator, covered, for 2 or 3 days. Allow the pâté to come to room temperature before spreading it.

IN THE GLASS   A dry fino sherry

CROSTINI

These toasts make a great base for just about any kind of appetizer: pâté, cheese, caponata, roast garlic, thinly sliced prosciutto or coppa, or what you will. Brush thin (¼-inch) slices of French bread (baguettes preferably) with olive oil and bake on a cookie sheet at 350°F for 15 minutes. Let cool slightly before using.

BUTTERMILK-FRIED QUAIL
WITH CORN AND BLUEBERRY SALAD

{ Makes 4 servings }

My wife, Jackie, loves these tasty little birds, and she likes to make a delicious summer salad from tender new greens from our garden, and local blueberries. The buttermilk helps keep the quail moist and provides a pleasant tang, and quick frying creates a crisp and delicious crust.

---

1 cup corn kernels, cut from the cobs
4 quail (semiboneless are usually available where
  quail are sold)
1 cup buttermilk
2 cups all-purpose flour
2 tablespoons kosher salt
2 teaspoons freshly ground black pepper
Vegetable oil for frying
6 cups arugula, trimmed, washed, and dried
1 cup fresh blueberries, picked over for stems
¼ cup basil leaves, cut into thin strips
Lemon Vinaigrette (page 102)

1. Bring a small saucepan of salted water to a boil and set up a bowl of ice water. Add the corn to the saucepan and cook for 2 minutes. Strain the corn and immediately plunge it into the bowl of ice water. Drain the corn and set aside.

2. Clean the quail by clipping any excess fat around the neck or tail end and clipping off the first two joints of the wings. Put the birds in a bowl with the buttermilk. In another bowl, combine the flour, salt, and pepper. Remove the quail from the buttermilk and dredge them in the seasoned flour, turning to coat them evenly and tapping them to remove any excess.

3. Preheat the oven to 400°F. On the stovetop, heat ¼ inch oil in a heavy pan. Brown the quail on all sides in the hot oil, 5 to 6 minutes total. Transfer the quail to a roasting pan and place in the oven. Roast the quail until it is cooked through, about 15 minutes. You can check with an instant-read meat thermometer for an internal temperature of 160°F or cut into a thigh to make sure it is no longer red.

4. In a bowl, toss together the corn, arugula, blueberries, basil, and vinaigrette.

ON THE PLATE   Place a mound of the salad in the center of each plate and lean a quail up against it.

IN THE GLASS   A good fruity Beaujolais Nouveau or a vineyard-designated Beaujolais like Moulin-à-Vent

HOW TO CHIFFONADE BASIL LEAVES

Chiffonade is another way of saying "cut into very thin strips." An easy way to cut basil leaves is to stack several leaves in a pile, then roll the pile of leaves up. Use a sharp knife to cut the roll of leaves, crosswise, into very thin strips.

Roasted Lemon Thyme Chicken with Sweet-and-Sour Red Cabbage and Brown Butter Spätzle

{ Makes 4 servings }

Is there anything more delicious than a simple roasted chicken? I like to serve it with brown butter spätzle and sweet-and-sour red cabbage but you can serve roast chicken with anything that sounds good to you.

When I was in Munich, I saw some cooks salting chicken and letting it sit overnight, a sort of dry-brining technique. After roasting, the chicken was moist and delicious with an especially crispy skin. I thought I would give it a try, and everybody seems pleased with the results.

1 chicken (about 3 pounds)
1 tablespoon kosher salt
1½ teaspoons freshly ground black pepper
2 tablespoons chopped fresh thyme or lemon thyme
(save the stems for putting in the cavity)
1 lemon, quartered
4 cloves garlic, peeled
3 tablespoons unsalted butter, melted
Brown Butter Spätzle (recipe follows)
Sweet-and-Sour Red Cabbage (page 184)
4 small sprigs thyme (optional)

1. Trim the excess fat from the chicken and clean out the cavity. Rinse under cold running water and pat dry with paper towels. Mix together the salt, pepper, and chopped thyme and pat this mixture all over the skin of the chicken. Set the chicken on a rack over a baking pan and place it, uncovered, in the refrigerator overnight.

2. The next day, preheat the oven to 400°F. Put the quartered lemon, garlic, and thyme stems in the cavity of the chicken and place it on a rack in a roasting pan. Brush the chicken with some of the melted butter and put the bird in the oven to roast. Baste every 15 to 20 minutes, using the melted butter, until enough fat has collected in the bottom of the roasting pan to use that. The chicken is done when an instant-read meat thermometer inserted in the thickest part of the thigh reads 175°F and the juices run clear from the cavity and from the thigh when sliced into. Remove the chicken from the oven and let rest for 5 to 10 minutes. Carve the chicken into breast and leg portions.

ON THE PLATE On each dinner plate, spoon some of the spätzle and some of the red cabbage and put a quarter portion of the chicken on top. Garnish with thyme sprigs, if desired.

IN THE GLASS This is one of the few times I would suggest a rich, buttery Chardonnay, or a Valpolicella from the Veneto, in Northern Italy—Quintarelli is a fine producer.

Brown Butter Spätzle

{ Makes 4 servings }

Spätzle is a tiny homemade noodle (the name means "little sparrow" in German). Spätzle is easier to prepare than you might think, and sort of fun to make, and always popular with guests. Cook in butter until they become golden and crusty. Spätzle go well with roast chicken or any roast meat.

You can buy a special piece of equipment to push the spätzle dough into the boiling water, but a metal colander with medium-size holes (not a fine-mesh sieve) works fine. When you're not scraping the dough through the colander, don't leave it sitting over the pot of boiling water. If the colander gets too hot, it will cook the dough and the holes will get plugged.

---

2 cups all-purpose flour

2 tablespoons chopped fresh thyme

1 tablespoon grated lemon zest

1 teaspoon kosher salt

½ teaspoon freshly ground black pepper

3 large eggs

1 to 1¼ cups milk, or as needed

¼ cup (½ stick) unsalted butter

I. In a large bowl, combine the flour, thyme, zest, salt, and pepper. In a small bowl, combine the eggs and milk (start with the smaller quantity of milk and add more as needed to the final batter). Blend the egg-milk mixture with the flour mixture, combining well to form a batter that looks like a thick pancake batter. Add more milk if needed.

2. Bring a large pot of salted water to a boil and set a bowl of ice water near the stove. Place a metal colander with medium holes over the pot. Working in two batches, use a plastic spatula to force half of the dough through the holes and into the boiling water. Allow the spätzle to cook in the boiling water until the little dumplings float to the surface and the water comes back to a boil, about 2 minutes. Remove the spätzle with a slotted spoon and place them in the bowl of ice water. Repeat with the other half of the dough. When all the spätzle are done, strain them from the ice water.

3. Heat the butter in a large nonstick sauté pan over medium-high heat until it bubbles and is beginning to brown. Add the spätzle and cook until hot, golden, and a little crispy, stirring only occasionally to let them brown, about 8 minutes. Season to taste with salt and pepper.

A STEP AHEAD Spätzle can be made and boiled early in the day and stored, covered, in the refrigerator. Brown them in the butter just before serving.

STAR ANISE GAME HENS

{ Makes 2 to 4 servings }

There is a tiny café in the Pike Place Market called Saigon Restaurant, where Ving, like her sister Lucy before her, makes incredible ginger chicken from the humblest of ingredients. Even though I've eaten there probably more than any place in Seattle, I have never managed to get the recipe from them. That hasn't stopped me trying to figure it out, and this is a really good version.

Caramelized sugar gives these hens a beautiful golden color. The marinade is delicious, so we set some aside to serve with the birds and put on our aromatic rice. You can also use the marinade on chicken or on pork tenderloins. These game hens are best when marinated overnight, so plan accordingly.

---

2 Cornish game hens (about 1½ pounds each)

FOR THE STAR ANISE MARINADE
¾ cup sugar
¼ cup water
1 cup sake
Zest from 1 orange, cut with a peeler into
  ½-inch-wide strips
3 star anise, crushed with a rolling pin
2 tablespoons peeled and grated fresh ginger
⅓ cup soy sauce
¼ cup Asian fish sauce
⅓ cup honey
⅓ cup peanut or vegetable oil

TO SERVE
Aromatic Steamed Rice (page 159)

1. Trim any excess fat from the Cornish game hens. Cut out the backbones and split the hens in half through the breastbones. Place in a nonreactive baking pan and refrigerate.

2. To make the marinade, in a heavy-bottomed saucepan over medium-low heat, combine the sugar and water, stirring until the sugar is completely dissolved. Raise the heat to high and cook, undisturbed, until the sugar caramelizes to a golden-brown color, 5 to 8 minutes. As soon as the sugar is caramelized, remove the saucepan from the heat and add the sake. *Be careful because the mixture will sputter.* When the mixture settles, return the saucepan to medium-low heat and stir until any hardened strands of caramel melt (see How to Caramelize Sugar Safely, page 195).

3. Remove the saucepan from the heat and pour the caramel syrup into a bowl. Stir in the zest, star anise, ginger, and soy and fish sauces. Whisk in the honey and oil. Allow the marinade to cool. Reserve 1 cup of the marinade, then pour the rest over the game hens, turning them in the marinade to coat completely. Cover with plastic wrap and refrigerate overnight.

4. Preheat the oven to 375°F. Set aside ½ cup of the reserved marinade for basting and pour the rest into ramekins for serving with the hens. Remove the game hens from the marinade and place them on a baking sheet. (For easier cleanup, line the baking sheet with aluminum foil because the excess marinade will drip off and burn.) Roast the hens

in the oven for 25 to 30 minutes, basting with the reserved marinade occasionally, until the hens are cooked through. An instant-read meat thermometer inserted into the thickest part of a thigh should read 165°F and the juices should run clear from the cavity and the thigh when sliced into. Remove the hens from the oven and preheat the broiler. Place the hens under the broiler for a minute or two to caramelize the glaze, turning the baking pan as needed. Watch carefully because the glaze burns easily.

ON THE PLATE Place one or two game hen halves on each plate next to a mound of the rice. Serve with ramekins of the reserved marinade.

A STEP AHEAD The marinade can be made a few days ahead and stored, covered, in the refrigerator.

IN THE GLASS A Gewürztraminer from the Yakima Valley or Alsace

Seattle's brand-new open-air ballpark—Safeco Field

Starch Stacking

I REALLY LOVE starches—potatoes, pasta, rice—because of their earthy flavors and their ability to soak up sauces and gravies. This has led to a process my family and friends know as starch stacking, or making a whole meal of the tastiest carbos we can whip up. The first

time I ever starch-stacked was in a restaurant in Italy when I couldn't make up my mind what to eat. On the menu were rigatoni with Bolognese sauce, velvety Gorgonzola-coated gnocchi, creamy polenta with spicy sausages, plump pumpkin-filled ravioli, and garlic-and-rosemary-roasted potatoes. So I compromised. I ate them all.

From then on I was hooked on the idea of starch stacking. If you come to dinner at my house, you might start out with a first course of seafood risotto and finish with an entrée of wild mushroom ravioli, and, in between, some tiny new potatoes and fresh green beans from the garden, tossed with butter and fresh dill. We've even had special starch-stacking dinners at our restaurants over the years: all-risotto dinners or meals consisting entirely of different forms of pasta.

The very first menus we wrote for Dahlia Lounge listed all the starches first (for example, Crusty Potatoes with Red Chile Mussels or Creamy Polenta with Fennel Sausages) because the starch was our favorite part of the meal. When I'm in a restaurant, I often order my entrée based on the starch that comes with it. I get the veal chop because I lust after the risotto Milanese that will be on the plate with it. Creamy mashed potatoes or perfectly cooked rice fragrant with spices are essential parts of our cooking and presentation.

Did I ever meet a potato, noodle, or dumpling I didn't like? Not yet, but I'll keep trying.

ETTA'S CORNBREAD PUDDING

{ Makes 6 servings }

Bread pudding was invented as a tasty way to use up old bread and it's usually served as a dessert. We've come to love these puddings so much that we bake different "breads" (like gingerbread or chocolate cake) just so we can put together a bread pudding. In another twist, we've created savory puddings to accompany our poultry and seafood dishes. We found ourselves baking special breads just to make them into pudding, in this case cornbread.

The cornbread pudding here is made with dry Jack cheese, which is nuttier and tangier than regular Jack cheese. Our favorite is Vella Dry Jack from Sonoma, California (see Sources, page 260). Or use sharp Cheddar instead; while the flavor of the cornbread pudding would change, it would be equally delicious. We serve this luscious pudding with Etta's Pit-Roasted Salmon (page 120), but it would also be great partnered with roast chicken.

This recipe makes more cornbread than you need to make the pudding. You can freeze the extra cornbread for future batches or, if you're like us, you can snack on it while it's warm, spread with butter and honey.

FOR THE CORNBREAD
1 cup all-purpose flour
¾ cup medium-ground yellow cornmeal
½ cup grated pepper Jack cheese (1½ ounces)
1 teaspoon baking powder
1 teaspoon salt
2 large eggs
1 cup milk
3 tablespoons honey

¼ cup (½ stick) unsalted butter, melted, plus a little more for buttering the pan

FOR THE PUDDING
1 tablespoon unsalted butter, plus a little more for buttering the pan
1 cup thinly sliced onions (about ½ large onion)
¾ cup grated dry Jack cheese
2 teaspoons chopped fresh flat-leaf parsley
½ teaspoon chopped fresh rosemary
½ teaspoon chopped fresh thyme
2¼ cups heavy cream
4 large eggs
1 teaspoon kosher salt
½ teaspoon freshly ground black pepper

1. To make the cornbread, preheat the oven to 425°F. Butter an 8-inch square baking dish. Combine the flour, cornmeal, cheese, baking powder, and salt in a large bowl. In a mixing bowl, whisk together the eggs, milk, and honey. Add the wet ingredients to the dry ingredients, stirring until just combined. Add the melted butter and stir into the mixture. Pour into the prepared pan and bake until a toothpick comes out clean, 15 to 20 minutes. When cool enough to handle, cut into 1-inch cubes. You should have about 8 cups cornbread cubes, but you only need one third of the cornbread cubes (or 2⅔ cups) for this recipe.

2. To make the pudding, reduce the oven temperature to 350°F. Put the 2⅔ cups of cornbread cubes in a buttered 8-inch square baking dish. Set aside. Heat the 1 tablespoon butter in a sauté pan over low heat and cook the onions very slowly until soft and golden brown, at least 20 minutes, stirring occasionally. Remove from the heat. Scatter the onions, cheese, and herbs over the cornbread cubes. Whisk together the heavy cream and eggs with salt and pepper in a mixing bowl and pour over the cornbread cubes. Let sit for 10 minutes so the cornbread absorbs some of the custard. Bake until set and golden, about 40 minutes. Serve hot.

A STEP AHEAD   You can make the cornbread and store it in the freezer, covered tightly in plastic wrap, for a few weeks until you are ready to make the cornbread pudding. The onions can be caramelized a day ahead and stored, covered, in the refrigerator. The cornbread pudding can be baked a day in advance and stored in the refrigerator, covered. Before serving, reheat the cornbread pudding, covered with aluminum foil, in a preheated 375°F oven until warmed through, 35 to 40 minutes.

POTATO-TURNIP GRATIN

{ Makes 6 servings }

The best part of a gratin is the crusty top, so, in order to get mostly crust, we make very thin gratins on big restaurant-size baking sheets. You could use a jelly-roll pan or any baking sheet with a 1-inch rim. Put the gratin under the broiler after the vegetables are cooked through to get a beautiful golden crust.

Try this with all sorts of root vegetables, including celery root, rutabaga, even fennel bulbs. The slicing of the vegetables is done best on a mandoline.

3 tablespoons unsalted butter

¼ cup chopped fresh flat-leaf parsley

2 teaspoons chopped fresh rosemary

2 teaspoons chopped fresh sage

2 teaspoons chopped fresh thyme

6 cups peeled and thinly sliced russet potatoes, about ⅛ inch thick (about 4 large potatoes)

Kosher salt and freshly ground black pepper

1 cup freshly grated Parmesan cheese

1 cup heavy cream

2 cups peeled and thinly sliced turnips, about ⅛ inch thick (about 2 turnips)

1. Preheat the oven to 400°F. Butter a jelly-roll pan or 10 × 15-inch baking pan with a 1-inch rim, using about 1 tablespoon of the butter. In a small mixing bowl, combine the herbs and set aside. Spread half the potatoes in a single layer over the bottom of the pan. Season the potatoes with salt and pepper. Sprinkle 2 tablespoons of the chopped herbs and ¼ cup of the Parmesan over the potatoes. Drizzle ¼ cup of the heavy cream evenly over the layer of potatoes. Spread out all the turnip slices in a single layer over the potatoes. Season with salt and pepper, sprinkle 2 tablespoons of the herbs and ¼ cup of the Parmesan over the turnips, then drizzle with ¼ cup of the cream. Spread the rest of the potatoes over the turnips. Season with salt and pepper and sprinkle with the rest of the herbs and the remaining ½ cup Parmesan. Drizzle with the remaining ½ cup cream and dot the remaining 2 tablespoons butter over the top.

2. Cover the pan with aluminum foil and bake for 35 minutes. Take the pan out of the oven and remove the foil. Turn on the broiler and broil for 5 minutes, turning the pan as needed to get an even golden-brown crust. Cut the gratin into 6 pieces and serve hot.

HOW TO USE A MANDOLINE

Several recipes call for ingredients to be very thinly sliced. Of course, you can just use a sharp knife, but a mandoline will make the job easier and give you a very uniform result. A French stainless-steel mandoline costs about $150, but there are much less expensive plastic slicers available in kitchenware shops, in Japanese specialty stores, and by mail order. It's best to purchase a slicer that comes with a safety guard, because it's all too easy to cut your fingers using these devices.

Aromatic Steamed Rice

{ Makes 4 to 6 servings }

Lemongrass, ginger, star anise, and orange zest infuse this rice with a lovely aroma. I like to use aromatic herbs, spices, and vegetables to add subtle depth to certain dishes. Sometimes a little steamed-in orange perfume from the zest is all you need to bring a simple dish to perfection.

If you have an electric rice cooker, definitely use it here. Rice cookers cook rice exactly right and keep it warm for a long time. If you decide to buy one, go for the Teflon kind, because you'll never have to clean a dirty pan of stuck-on rice again.

There are many types of rice available today: long grain and short grain, brown rice, red rice, and even black rice. We use California-grown Japanese short-grain rice for this dish, a slightly glutinous rice often used in Japanese cooking.

---

2 cups Japanese short-grain rice

2½ cups cold water

1 stalk lemongrass

3 slices unpeeled fresh ginger coins (page 47),
   ⅛ inch thick

3 star anise

Zest from 1 orange (large strips cut with a vegetable
   peeler are best)

Place the raw rice in a fine-mesh strainer and rinse under cold running water until the water runs clear. In a small pot, combine the rice and water. Smash the stalk of lemongrass with the back of a knife to release the aromatics, and then slice it thinly. Wrap the lemongrass, ginger, star anise, and zest in a small piece of cheesecloth and tie up the bundle with a piece of kitchen twine. Add the cheesecloth bundle to the pot of rice and bring to a boil. Reduce the heat to a simmer, cover the pot, and cook gently until all the water is absorbed, about 20 minutes. Turn off the heat and leave the lid on for 5 minutes to fluff the rice. Remove the cheesecloth bundle and serve hot.

CRISPY SESAME RICE CAKES

{ Makes 6 servings }

Because of the slightly glutinous quality of Japanese short-grain rice, these rice cakes hold together well. You can cut them into squares or triangles or rounds. Be sure you panfry them toasty-brown for the unique taste of toasted rice. We like to use a combination of black and white sesame seeds here because the seeds show up better against the white rice. *Sambal olek*, a hot Indonesian chile paste, is available at well-stocked supermarkets or by mail order (see Sources, page 260).

2 cups Japanese short-grain rice

2½ cups cold water

⅔ cup sliced green onions or scallions (about 3),
*   white and green parts*

4 teaspoons peeled and grated fresh ginger

4 teaspoons rice wine vinegar

1 tablespoon sesame seeds, toasted (page 39),
*   preferably a combination of black and white*
*   sesame seeds*

1 tablespoon Asian fish sauce

1 teaspoon sesame oil

1 teaspoon fresh lime juice

1 teaspoon sambal olek (page 15) or other Asian
*   chile paste, or more to taste*

Peanut oil for panfrying, about ¼ cup

1. Place the raw rice in a fine-mesh strainer and rinse under cold running water until the water runs clear. In a small pot, combine the rice and water. Bring to a boil, then reduce the heat to a simmer, cover, and cook for 20 minutes. Remove from the heat and let sit, covered, for 5 minutes.

2. In a bowl, combine the cooked rice with the green onions, ginger, vinegar, sesame seeds, fish sauce, sesame oil, lime juice, and sambal olek. Spray a jelly-roll pan (a 14 × 10-inch baking pan with a 1-inch rim) with non-stick vegetable spray or grease it with a little peanut oil. Press the rice into the pan with a rubber spatula. This amount of rice will not fill the whole pan. Just be sure to press the rice into an even ¾-inch-thick layer. Chill the rice, covered with plastic wrap, for at least 1 hour. When chilled, cut into 6 squares.

3. Heat the peanut oil in a large nonstick sauté pan over medium-high heat. Panfry the rice cakes on both sides until golden brown, about 3 minutes per side.

ON THE PLATE   Place a rice cake on each plate and serve as part of a bento (page 43), or serve as a side dish to Kasu Zuke Black Cod (page 99) or Basic Barbecued Baby Back Ribs with Hoisin Barbecue Sauce (page 125).

A STEP AHEAD   Cover the filled baking pan with plastic wrap and refrigerate for a day or two before cutting the rice cakes into squares and panfrying them.

MASA ONION RINGS

{ Makes 4 to 6 servings }

Babe Shepherd was, for many years, one of our great waitresses. When she opened her own place, Red Mill Burgers, in Seattle's Phinney Ridge district, she was set on serving the perfect onion ring. So she and I developed these onion rings together. This recipe is similar to the one she uses, but not exactly the same.

We serve onion rings as a garnish to many dishes at our restaurants—for example, the Palace Burger Royale. In the summer the rings taste even better because we use sweet Walla Walla onions.

Masa harina is a flour made from *nixtamal*, corn that has been leached in lye, then dried and ground to make tortillas. It has a wonderful, penetrating fragrance, and even the small quantity in this recipe makes a noticeable difference in the taste of these onion rings. Masa harina is available in Mexican specialty markets and in well-stocked supermarket in cities with large Latino populations.

---

2 onions (about 1½ pounds)
4 cups all-purpose flour
2 cups buttermilk
1 cup medium-ground yellow cornmeal
¼ cup masa harina
1 tablespoon paprika
1 tablespoon kosher salt
2 teaspoons cayenne
1 teaspoon dried thyme
½ teaspoon freshly ground black pepper
Peanut oil for deep-frying

I. Peel the onions and cut them into ½-inch-thick slices. Separate the onions into rings. Discard the inner center pieces, which are too small, or reserve them for another purpose. You will need three bowls for breading the onion rings. In the first bowl, place 2 cups of the flour. Pour the buttermilk in the second bowl. In the third bowl, combine the remaining 2 cups flour with the cornmeal, masa harina, paprika, salt, cayenne, thyme, and black pepper. Line two baking sheets with parchment or wax paper. As you bread the onion rings, use one hand for the dry ingredients and one hand for the wet ingredients to avoid a gloppy mess on your hands. In batches, dip the onions in flour, then buttermilk, and then seasoned flour mix. When necessary, to keep the flour clean and easy to work with, sift the seasoned flour mix and discard any clumps of batter. Place the breaded rings on the baking sheets and place the sheets in the refrigerator for 1 hour to set.

2. Heat a straight-sided pan with at least 2 inches of oil, no more than halfway up the sides, to 350°F, checking with a deep-fry thermometer (see How to Deep-Fry, page 51). Fry the onion rings without crowding them until golden yellow, then drain on paper towels. The onion rings should be light in color; be careful because the cornmeal can burn if you fry them too long. Season to taste with salt and serve immediately. (If you are frying the onion rings in batches, you can hold them on a baking sheet in a preheated 300°F oven while you finish frying all of them. But don't leave them in the oven too long, or they will get soggy.)

RED BLISS MASHERS

{ Makes 4 servings }

Red Bliss potatoes are a type of small, red potato. I like to leave their skins on. This dish is a lush, rich version of mashed potatoes with butter, cream, sour cream, and Parmesan cheese. To mash the potatoes, use a potato masher, a ricer, or a food mill, but don't use a food processor or the potatoes will turn to glue. If you can't find Red Bliss potatoes, use any other kind of red potato you like.

2½ pounds red or other new potatoes, washed
6 tablespoons (¾ stick) unsalted butter
1 tablespoon minced garlic
½ cup heavy cream
6 tablespoons freshly grated Parmesan cheese
¼ cup sour cream
Kosher salt and freshly ground black pepper

1. Leaving the skins on, cut the potatoes in halves or quarters and put them in a large pot of cold salted water. Bring the water to a boil and cook the potatoes until they are soft, about 25 minutes total, depending on their size. Drain the potatoes well and put them in a bowl.

2. Meanwhile, heat the butter in a small saucepan over medium heat, then add the garlic. As soon as the garlic is aromatic but not browned, pour the heavy cream into the pan and allow it to gently heat through. Add the warm garlic-cream mixture, Parmesan, and sour cream to the potatoes, then mash them. Season to taste with salt and pepper. Serve immediately.

A STEP AHEAD You can make this up to an hour ahead and keep it warm, covered, in a double boiler over simmering water.

PARSNIP-APPLE HASH

{ Makes 4 servings }

Washington State is the number one apple producer in the United States. Our produce purveyors carry over a dozen local varieties at the peak of the apple season: Braeburns, Criterions, Jonagolds, Granny Smiths, crab apples, lady apples, to name just a few.

Pairing apples with parsnips brings out the earthy sugars of these underappreciated root vegetables. This dish is best made just before serving to highlight the contrast of the soft, sweet parsnips with the crunchy, tart apples. You can serve this hash with slow-roasted duck (page 145) as we do or with a big, juicy grilled pork chop and hot sweet mustard.

½ cup diced bacon (about 2 ounces)

3 tablespoons unsalted butter

1 onion, cut into ¼-inch dice (about 1 cup)

2 parsnips, peeled and cut into ½-inch dice (about 2⅔ cups)

1 apple, peeled, cored, and cut into ½-inch dice (about 1¼ cups)

1 red bell pepper, seeded and cut into ¼-inch dice (about 1 cup)

2 teaspoons chopped fresh thyme

Kosher salt and freshly ground black pepper

In a large sauté pan over medium-high heat, brown the bacon until crisp, about 3 minutes. Remove the bacon and set aside, leaving the bacon fat in the pan. Add the butter and onion and cook, stirring, until translucent, about 2 minutes. Add the parsnips and cook, stirring, until soft and golden brown, about 10 minutes. Add the apple, bell pepper, and thyme and continue to cook, stirring, until they caramelize a bit, about 5 minutes. Stir in the reserved bacon, season to taste with salt and pepper, and serve hot.

POTATO GNOCCHI WITH ROASTED TOMATOES AND GORGONZOLA CREAM

{ Makes 4 servings }

Every restaurant is made up of a cast of characters and every day they are expected to "bring something to the table." Shelley Lance (our pastry chef) has always brought a sense of food history; she's a real food scholar, constantly coming up with new recipes and food lore. That's why she helped write this book and also why, when I decided I wanted to serve the best gnocchi in Seattle, I went to her to develop the recipe and then translate the technique to the rest of the staff.

The gnocchi dough is easier to make and turns out best if you work with the potatoes while they are still hot. Use a dish towel or oven mitt to hold the hot baked potatoes while you scoop the pulp from the skin. As soon as you put the potatoes through a food mill or potato ricer, start making the dough. Use only as much flour as needed to form a soft dough that you can work with; you will be using more flour on the work board, which adds a little more to the dough. Try to handle the dough as little as possible (this is good advice for most doughs except bread doughs). It's easiest to shape the dough if you keep your board, hands, and board scraper (an indispensable little item) lightly filmed with flour.

FOR THE GNOCCHI
1 pound russet potatoes (2 medium russets)
2 tablespoons unsalted butter, softened
½ teaspoon kosher salt
Pinch of freshly ground black pepper
1 large egg
¾ to 1 cup all-purpose flour, as needed

FOR THE ROASTED TOMATOES
1 pint cherry tomatoes (about 1 pound, or 40 cherry tomatoes), stemmed and cut in half
4 teaspoons extra virgin olive oil
½ teaspoon kosher salt
¼ teaspoon freshly ground black pepper

FOR THE GORGONZOLA CREAM
½ cup heavy cream
1½ ounces Gorgonzola cheese (or substitute a good-quality blue cheese), crumbled
Freshly ground black pepper

TO FINISH THE DISH
¼ cup extra virgin olive oil
1 teaspoon minced garlic
2 tablespoons pine nuts, toasted (page 39)
½ cup thinly sliced fresh basil

1. To make the gnocchi, preheat the oven to 400°F. Bake the potatoes until very soft, about 1 hour. Remove from the oven. While the potatoes are still hot, split them in half and use a large spoon to scoop the potato from the skins. Pass the potato pulp through a food mill (fitted with the coarse plate) or a potato ricer. While the potato is still warm, make the dough. Add the butter, salt, and pepper and mix together with a rubber spatula until the butter melts. Mix in the egg with the spatula. Gradually add the flour, starting with the smaller amount and adding only as much flour as necessary to make a soft dough.

2. Turn the dough out onto a floured work board. If the dough seems too sticky, work in a little more flour, kneading gently with your hands. Shape the dough into a rough rectangle about 2 inches thick and cut the rectangle lengthwise into 4 ropes, using a floured metal board scraper or a floured knife. Gently roll each rope on the floured board until it is about 12 inches long, ¾ inch wide, and ¾ inch thick. Cut each rope into ¾-inch segments, or gnocchi. Place the gnocchi on baking sheets lined with floured parchment or wax paper.

3. To make the roasted tomatoes, preheat the oven to 400°F. Put the tomatoes in a bowl and toss them with the the olive oil and the salt and pepper. Arrange the tomatoes, cut sides up, on a rack over a baking pan. Place the pan in the oven and roast until the tomatoes look plumped and slightly browned on the cut edges, about 40 minutes. Remove them from the oven and set aside.

4. To make the Gorgonzola cream, bring the heavy cream to a low boil in a small saucepan and reduce it by one third. Remove the pan from the heat and stir in the Gorgonzola. Season to taste with pepper. Set aside.

5. Set a large pot of salted water over high heat and bring to a boil. Add the gnocchi to the boiling water and boil them until they are cooked through. After the gnocchi float to the top of the water, they will need to cook another 2 or 3 minutes, for a total cooking time of 5 to 6 minutes. Meanwhile, set a large sauté pan over low heat and gently warm the olive oil and garlic together for a few minutes. Add the roasted tomatoes and turn off the heat. When the gnocchi are cooked, skim them out of the water with a slotted spoon and add them to the pan of tomatoes. Add the pine nuts and basil and toss everything gently together with a rubber spatula.

ON THE PLATE   Divide the gnocchi among 4 plates. Drizzle each serving with some of the Gorgonzola cream.

A STEP AHEAD   You can make the dough and shape and cut the gnocchi early in the day. Store them, refrigerated, on floured parchment paper–lined pans, loosely covered with another piece of parchment paper. Use the gnocchi the same day they are made; the texture changes over time and they won't be good the next day. The tomatoes can be roasted a day ahead and held in the refrigerator. The Gorgonzola cream can be made a few days ahead and held in the refrigerator, tightly covered. Warm gently before serving.

IN THE GLASS   A young, fresh Dolcetto from Piedmont in northern Italy

Red Beet Ravioli with Fresh Corn Relish

{ Makes 4 servings }

I was inspired by Marcella Hazan's recipe for beet ravioli to come up with this dish. I love her hearty and honest approach to cooking, and I own (and use) all of her books all the time. My own touch is to serve the ravioli with a fresh corn relish. This is a really beautiful dish, with the bright yellow corn, green herb leaves, and the scarlet beet filling showing through the thin sheets of pasta. Shavings of an aged dry goat cheese goes well with this—but you could substitute thin shavings of Parmesan if you like.

FOR THE RAVIOLI
½ pound red beets
1 tablespoon unsalted butter
1 tablespoon minced shallots
2 tablespoons fine bread crumbs (page 255)
Kosher salt and freshly ground black pepper
Fresh Pasta Dough (page 250)

FOR THE FRESH CORN RELISH
2 ears corn, kernels cut from the cobs
  (about 1½ cups)
¼ cup fresh chervil
¼ cup fresh chives cut into ¾-inch lengths
¼ cup chopped fresh flat-leaf parsley
2 teaspoons Champagne or other white wine vinegar
1 teaspoon fresh lemon juice
3 tablespoons extra virgin olive oil

TO FINISH THE DISH
¼ cup (½ stick) unsalted butter
1 teaspoon grated lemon zest
Kosher salt and freshly ground black pepper
¼ cup shaved aged goat cheese or Parmesan cheese

1. To make the beet ravioli, preheat the oven to 400°F. Place the beets in a baking dish covered with aluminum foil and roast in the oven until soft, 1½ to 2 hours.

2. Meanwhile, in a sauté pan over medium-high heat, heat the butter, then cook the shallots, stirring, about 2 minutes. Add the bread crumbs and cook, stirring, until golden and crunchy, about 4 minutes. Set aside.

3. Peel the beets when they are cool enough to handle. Grate them using the large holes of a cheese grater or the grater attachment of a food processor. Wrap the grated beets in cheesecloth and squeeze to remove excess moisture. In a bowl, set aside two thirds of the grated beets. Place the remaining third in a food processor with the shallots and toasted bread crumbs and process to mince the beets and combine everything well. Add this mixture to the bowl of reserved grated beets and season to taste with salt and pepper.

4. Prepare the pasta dough, roll it out, and fill it as instructed for ravioli (page 251).

5. Bring a large pot of salted water to a boil and set up a small bowl of ice water. Cook the corn kernels in the boiling water until just cooked through, 2 to 3 minutes. Remove the corn from the boiling water with a sieve, saving the pot of boiling water to cook the ravioli in later. Plunge the corn kernels in the bowl of ice water, drain, and place the corn in a small bowl. Add the herbs, vinegar, lemon juice, and olive oil, toss, and season to taste with salt and pepper. Set aside.

6. Cook the ravioli in the boiling water until they are cooked through and the edges are tender to the bite, about 3 minutes, then drain. Meanwhile, melt the butter in a large sauté pan over medium heat. Add the lemon zest and ravioli and season to taste with salt and pepper. Toss to coat the ravioli in the butter.

ON THE PLATE Divide the ravioli among 4 plates. Spoon a mound of the relish in the center of each plate. Sprinkle the shaved aged goat cheese over the top.

A STEP AHEAD The beet filling can be made a few days ahead and held, covered with plastic wrap, in the refrigerator.

IN THE GLASS Orvieto, a light dry white wine from Umbria in Italy, is the perfect match.

SAGE TAGLIARINI

{ Makes 4 to 6 servings }

A big dish of noodles with butter and Parmesan is one of my daughter Loretta's favorite things in the world (which is why we have My Kid's Favorite Oodles of Noodles on the menu every day at Dahlia). Here we have added the classic Italian touch of crispy, fried sage leaves.

For this we use the finest Parmigiano-Reggiano, and we often take a little chunk of it and shave it with a vegetable peeler directly over the pasta for nice-looking curls.

---

1 pound tagliarini, fresh (page 250) or dried, or
    linguine or spaghetti
½ cup (1 stick) unsalted butter
3 sprigs fresh sage (about 3 tablespoons leaves)
Kosher salt and freshly ground black pepper
¼ cup freshly shaved Parmigiano-Reggiano or other
    dry cheese (about 1 ounce)

Bring a large pot of salted water to a boil. Cook the pasta until *al dente*. Meanwhile, melt the butter in a sauté pan over medium-high heat. When the butter is melted, add the sage leaves and fry them for a few minutes until they start to get crisp. Drain the pasta and toss it with the sage, butter, and salt and pepper to taste in a large bowl.

ON THE PLATE   Divide the pasta among the plates. Shave the cheese over each serving.

IN THE GLASS   A Barbera d'Alba from Piedmont, in northern Italy

WILD MUSHROOM RAVIOLI WITH ARUGULA SALAD

{ Makes 4 servings }

Sitting between the Olympic and Cascade mountains and surrounded by forests, Seattle is classic mushroom country. Mycologists and weekend warriors jealously guard their secret hunting grounds. While many successful hunters show up at our restaurant's back door more than willing to sell their bounty for top dollar, my favorite sources for wild mushrooms are friends who come to dinner willing to share their trophies which they found with blood (nettles), sweat (hiking for miles), and tears (sheer joy of the game.)

Some of the mushrooms we use in our dishes are chanterelles, shiitakes, yellow foot, lobster, oyster, or porcini. Select whatever kind you can find in local markets.

If you are lucky enough to get hold of an Oregon (or Italian or French) truffle, shave a little of it over the finished pasta. Arugula tastes best when it is still fairly young and small—older leaves can become hot and bitter.

1½ pounds any combination wild and cultivated
  mushrooms
¼ cup olive oil
Kosher salt and freshly ground black pepper
6 tablespoons (¾ stick) unsalted butter
¼ cup minced shallots
1½ teaspoons minced garlic
2 teaspoons finely chopped fresh flat-leaf parsley
1 teaspoon finely chopped fresh rosemary
1 teaspoon finely chopped fresh thyme
1 teaspoon finely chopped fresh sage
Fresh Pasta Dough (page 250)
5 cups loosely packed arugula, washed, dried, and
  stems trimmed

Lemon Vinaigrette (page 102)
¼ cup shaved Parmesan cheese

1. Clean the mushrooms by wiping off any dirt with a damp cloth. Trim off tough bottoms. Cut ½ pound of the mushrooms into attractive-looking bite-size pieces for roasting for the salad. Thinly slice the rest of the mushrooms for the filling.

2. To roast mushrooms for the arugula salad, preheat the oven to 400°F. In a bowl, toss the ½ pound mushroom pieces with enough of the olive oil to lightly coat them (about 2 tablespoons). Season the mushrooms with salt and pepper. Arrange them on a rack over a baking sheet and roast in the oven until brown and crisp around the edges, about 20 minutes. Remove from the oven and set aside.

3. To make the ravioli filling, place a large sauté pan over medium-high heat with about 2 tablespoons of the butter and the remaining 2 tablespoons olive oil. Add the remaining 1 pound sliced mushrooms and the shallots and cook, stirring, until soft, about 10 minutes, adding the garlic for the last few minutes of cooking. Be sure all the mushroom juices have evaporated before you remove the mushrooms from the heat. Place the sautéed mushrooms in a food processor and process until very well minced. Remove the minced mushrooms to a bowl, mix in the chopped herbs, and season to taste with salt and pepper. Set aside.

4. Prepare the pasta dough, roll it out, and fill it with the mushroom mixture as instructed for ravioli (page 251).

5. Place a large pot of salted water over high heat and bring it to a boil. Cook the ravioli in the boiling water until they are cooked through and the edges are tender to the bite, about 3 minutes. Place a large sauté pan over low heat, melt the remaining 4 tablespoons butter, and remove from the heat. When the ravioli are cooked, scoop them out of the boiling water with a slotted spoon or small sieve and place them in the sauté pan with the melted butter. Gently toss the ravioli to coat them with the butter and season to taste with salt and pepper. Meanwhile, in a bowl, toss the arugula with the roasted mushrooms (the mushrooms don't need to be warm, room temperature is fine) and enough lemon vinaigrette to coat everything.

ON THE PLATE　Divide the ravioli among 4 plates or wide, shallow pasta bowls. Spoon a mound of the arugula salad in the center of each serving and sprinkle shaved Parmesan over the top. Serve immediately.

A STEP AHEAD　The ravioli filling can be made a few days ahead and stored, covered with plastic wrap, refrigerated. The mushrooms for the salad can be roasted a few hours ahead and held at room temperature.

IN THE GLASS　I love this with Peter Dow's Cavatappi Nebbiolo from Washington State.

WILD MUSHROOMS

The weather and landscape in the Northwest are ideal for wild mushrooms. Our damp climate and thick, mossy forest floors provide a perfect environment for the growth of all kinds of fungi. More than two thousand varieties of mushrooms grow here, many of them edible, although only ten or twelve of these appear regularly in our markets.

Wild mushrooms are truly "wild." Some, such as shiitakes and oyster mushrooms lend themselves to cultivation and are easily found in local markets. Others are gathered by foragers who roam the mountains and meadows with their baskets and walking sticks, searching for the gleam of a golden chanterelle or the pale ivory of a boletus among the leaves and pine needles. When they find their treasures, they never reveal the spot where wrinkled slender morels or unbelievably fragrant and valuable matsutakes come up year after year.

The weather is the real key. A few days of sun after the rain, days not too hot and nights not too cold, make for abundant mushrooms in good condition. When you buy mushrooms in your produce market, look for dry and firm mushrooms, unbroken and without any slime or decay. They might be dirty and even have some pine needles sticking to them, but don't worry. Just use a soft brush or cloth to clean them, but don't get them wet, as they can deteriorate when damp.

We're lucky in Seattle because where else could you walk into a farmer's market and fill a paper bag with lovely chanterelles, at the height of their season, for $3.95 a pound? Tourists who are mushroom lovers often walk out of the Pike Place Market with shopping bags filled with wild mushrooms to bring home for feasts or to dry for later use.

Here are some of our favorites mushrooms:

- Chanterelles are the most plentiful mushrooms in the Northwest. Late summer and fall are the times we get case after case of these golden beauties. Their mild flavor makes them versatile to use in a simple ragout, to dress up a pasta, or to serve heaped over a steak or a chicken breast.
- Morels have a more intense, more pungent flavor than chanterelles. Try leaving them whole, especially if they are small and shapely. I roast them over a wood fire, which seems to concentrate their flavor and add a delicious smokiness.
- The "King of Mushrooms," the Northwest's boletus, is related to Italy's prized porcini. I love the meaty-tasting flesh of this mushroom, but I am always careful to check for worms.
- We probably use shiitakes more than any other variety of mushroom. Because they can be cultivated, they are always available. They're perfect in Asian-influenced dishes, showing up in our hot-and-sour soups and in our potstickers.
- Lobster mushrooms have a mild, earthy flavor and a beautiful bright orange-red color. I like to sauté them in butter with a splash of Madeira.
- Matsutake mushrooms are prized by the Japanese, so they tend to be expensive and in high demand. Because they have a superstrong, potent flavor and a piney aroma, they should be used sparingly, putting only a thin sliver or two in a cup of light chicken broth.
- Not many people know that truffles grow in the Northwest. You don't see them very often, but when I come across an Oregon truffle, I grab it so I can shave it over a bowl of fresh pasta.

SPICY PEANUT NOODLES

For ten years at Café Sport, and now five at Etta's, this dish has followed us like a lost puppy. Once again, like many of our dishes, this one is based on a classic of another culture. We still make buckets of the peanut dressing every day.

Brightly colored pickled red cabbage makes a good, tart foil to the rich-tasting wheat noodles.

FOR THE PEANUT DRESSING

¼ cup smooth peanut butter

3 tablespoons water

3 tablespoons soy sauce

¼ cup tahini

2 tablespoons peanut oil

2 tablespoons sesame oil

⅓ cup rice wine vinegar

2 tablespoons dry sherry

3 tablespoons honey

2 teaspoons chopped garlic

2 teaspoons peeled and grated fresh ginger

½ teaspoon red pepper flakes

Kosher salt

FOR THE NOODLES AND TO SERVE

¾ pound Chinese wheat noodles (see page 13)

1 tablespoon peanut oil

Pickled red cabbage (page 56)

¼ cup green onions or scallions, white and green
    parts, cut on the bias into thin strips or julienne

¼ cup chopped roasted peanuts

I. To make the peanut dressing, put the peanut butter in a bowl and, using a whisk, add the rest of the dressing ingredients in the order given. Start with the water, then add the soy sauce, tahini, oils, vinegar, sherry, and honey, whisking well after each addition. Whisk in the garlic, ginger, and red pepper flakes and season to taste with salt. Set aside.

2. Bring a large pot of salted water to a boil. Cook the noodles, stirring occasionally, until soft, 4 to 5 minutes. Drain in a colander and rinse under cold running water. Drain well. Toss the noodles with the peanut oil to prevent them from sticking together and chill.

3. When you are ready to serve the cooked and chilled noodles, place them in a large bowl and toss with the peanut dressing.

ON THE PLATE   Divide the sauced noodles among 4 plates. Garnish each serving with pickled cabbage, sliced green onions, and roasted peanuts. Try serving this with grilled Japanese eggplant or grilled chicken breasts that have been marinated in Honey Soy Glaze (page 188).

A STEP AHEAD   The peanut dressing will keep about a week in the refrigerator, tightly covered. The noodles can be cooked, chilled, and stored, covered with plastic wrap, in the refrigerator a day ahead. But dress the noodles right before serving them.

Toasted Penne with Herbs, Goat Cheese, and Golden Bread Crumbs

{ Makes 6 servings }

I got the idea for toasting dry pasta in a hot oven, before boiling, on a trip to Italy years ago. This technique is quite easy and gives the pasta a slightly different color and texture than untoasted pasta.

---

1 tablespoon extra virgin olive oil

⅔ cup fine bread crumbs (page 255)

Kosher salt and freshly ground black pepper

⅓ cup finely chopped fresh flat-leaf parsley

1 tablespoon grated lemon zest

1 pound penne

2 tablespoons (¼ stick) unsalted butter

¼ cup minced shallots

1 teaspoon minced garlic

¼ teaspoon red pepper flakes

2 cups heavy cream

1 teaspoon chopped fresh rosemary

1 teaspoon chopped fresh thyme

1 teaspoon chopped fresh sage

3 tablespoons freshly grated Parmesan cheese

5 ounces soft, fresh goat cheese

1. To make the toasted bread crumbs, heat a medium-size sauté pan over medium-high heat with the olive oil. Add the bread crumbs and stir until the crumbs begin to brown and get crunchy. Season with salt and pepper. Allow to cool. Once the bread crumbs are cool, combine with the parsley and lemon zest. Set aside.

2. Bring a large pot of salted water to a boil and preheat the oven to 400°F. Place the penne on a baking sheet and bake until the pasta just begins to brown, 5 to 6 minutes. Watch carefully, because it goes from yellow to brown very fast. Allow the pasta to cool off for a few minutes, then dump it into the pot of boiling water and cook until it is just *al dente*, 10 to 12 minutes. Drain.

3. Meanwhile, make the sauce. Heat the butter in a large wide-bottomed saucepan or a deep straight-sided sauté pan over medium heat and cook the shallots, stirring, about 3 minutes. Add the garlic and the pepper flakes and cook, stirring, for another minute. Add the heavy cream and simmer until it reduces by a third, about 5 minutes. Add the herbs, penne, and Parmesan and remove the pan from the heat. Crumble the goat cheese into the pasta and toss, seasoning to taste with salt and pepper.

ON THE PLATE   Divide the penne and sauce among 6 shallow bowls and sprinkle with the toasted bread crumbs.

IN THE GLASS   Try a Sangiovese from Umbria, a richer style than Tuscany, or a Sangiovese from Washington State.

One of Seattle's famous P-Patch gardens

Not Just Peas and Carrots

No one has to tell me to eat my greens, which is a good thing because they grow well here and don't mind the rain at all. I love kale, escarole, spinach, turnip greens, beet greens—greens of all kinds—blanched and tossed in olive oil and garlic or drenched in delicious browned butter. Ruby chard is my all-time favorite, and we always offer it on the menu at Etta's.

I also enjoy the simplicity of grilling vegetables. Most are full of natural sugars that caramelize to a golden brown on the fire. Just brush vegetables with olive oil, add a dash of salt and pepper, and toss them on the grill. For a real treat, grill fat asparagus or fresh corn out of the husk.

I may be one of the few chefs with a compost bin named after him—at my neighborhood P-Patch (Seattle's community gardens). Tasting the sweetness and flavor of vegetables grown in compost with no other fertilizer and no pesticides made a lasting impression on me. For our restaurants over the years, we have sought out produce grown by small farmers. We have an ever-growing interest in supporting organic farming and sustainable agriculture in the Seattle area.

Vegetables are never just an afterthought on our menus. We put as much love and care into preparing green beans as we do in grilling steaks. Local farmer's markets in the area keep getting bigger and better, with the Pike Place Market still the city's heart and soul.

SPINACH, PEAR, AND FRISÉE SALAD WITH SMOKED BACON AND CURRIED CASHEWS

{ Makes 6 servings }

This has been on Etta's menu since we opened; it's probably the restaurant's most popular salad. There are many wonderful varieties of pears in the Northwest, and we vary them throughout the year. This salad is also a way to feature the beautiful grapes we get in the fall: the muscats or the big purple-black Ribiers, plump Black Beauties, or sweet Red Globes. The colorful presentation combines sweet, salty, and savory flavors. Try to find small, organic baby spinach leaves and the smallest, most tender frisée (or curly endive). We use a very smoky slab bacon from Bavarian Meats in the Pike Place Market. Find the best slab bacon you can and slice it thickly.

FOR THE HONEY SESAME VINAIGRETTE

3 tablespoons white wine vinegar

3 tablespoons Dijon mustard

2 tablespoons honey

3 tablespoons sesame seeds, toasted (page 39)

1 teaspoon minced garlic

Kosher salt and freshly ground black pepper

½ cup vegetable or peanut oil

FOR THE CURRIED CASHEWS

¾ cup cashews (about 3 ounces)

1 tablespoon unsalted butter, melted

1 teaspoon chopped fresh rosemary

1 teaspoon curry powder

1 teaspoon dark brown sugar

½ teaspoon kosher salt

⅛ teaspoon cayenne, or more to taste

FOR THE SALAD

½ pound bacon, sliced (about twelve ¼-inch-thick slices)

12 cups loosely packed spinach leaves, washed well, dried, stems trimmed, and torn into pieces if leaves are large

6 cups loosely packed frisée, stems trimmed, washed, dried, and torn into bite-size pieces

⅔ cup thinly sliced red onions

3 small pears, halved, cored, and thinly sliced

6 small bunches grapes

1. To make the vinaigrette, whisk together the vinegar, mustard, honey, sesame seeds, garlic, and salt and pepper to taste in a bowl. Gradually whisk in the oil. Set aside.

2. To make the curried cashews, preheat the oven to 400°F. On a baking sheet, toast the cashews until golden, 8 to 10 minutes. Meanwhile, combine the melted butter, rosemary, curry powder, brown sugar, salt, and cayenne in a bowl. Add the toasted cashews while they are still hot and toss with a rubber spatula so they are thoroughly coated with the spices and butter. Leave the oven on to cook the bacon.

3. Put the bacon on a baking sheet, place it in the oven, and cook until crisp, 8 to 10 minutes. Remove the bacon from the pan and cut the slices into 1-inch pieces. Keep the bacon warm.

4. In a large bowl, combine the spinach, frisée, red onions, and sliced pears. Toss with enough vinaigrette to coat everything well.

ON THE PLATE Divide the salad among 6 plates. Garnish each salad with pieces of warm bacon and spiced cashews. Set a grape cluster on the side of each salad.

A STEP AHEAD The bacon can be cooked ahead, stored in the refrigerator, and reheated. The cashews can be cooked early in the day and stored at room temperature. The vinaigrette can be stored refrigerated, tightly covered, for several days.

TUSCAN BREAD SALAD
WITH FRESH MOZZARELLA AND BASIL

{ Makes 4 servings }

This salad has been on the menu at Dahlia Lounge since day one. We figured the best part of a salad is the vinaigrette-soaked croutons, so a salad that was made up mostly of vinaigrette-soaked, grilled bread croutons would be even better. A good densely textured rustic or European-style bread is essential for this recipe.

This is a perfect salad to make when you have the grill going for some barbecue. You can put a piece of rotisserie chicken or a grilled rib-eye steak right on top of the salad and let the croutons absorb some of the meat juices.

We like to use a small amount of flavorful greens. Don't use soft lettuces—something with a hardier leaf and a little more assertive flavor, such as arugula, is called for here. Or use small spinach leaves, mâche, watercress, baby mustard greens and kales, radicchio and other endives—either one type of green or a mix. But the bread should dominate.

We love the way the grilled bread tastes in this salad, but you can also brush the bread with olive oil and toast it on both sides under the broiler until golden brown, then add it to the salad.

FOR THE MUSTARD VINAIGRETTE

2 tablespoons red wine vinegar
1 teaspoon Dijon mustard
1 teaspoon minced shallots
½ teaspoon chopped fresh thyme
½ teaspoon minced garlic
⅓ cup extra virgin olive oil
Kosher salt and freshly ground black pepper

FOR THE SALAD

4 slices rustic bread, 1 inch thick
Extra virgin olive oil
24 good black olives, preferably oil-cured
½ pint cherry tomatoes, cut in half, or 5 ripe Roma tomatoes, cut into eighths
6 ounces fresh mozzarella, sliced
4 cups loosely packed flavorful salad greens (see headnote), washed, dried, stems trimmed, and torn into pieces if large
1 tablespoon Pesto (recipe follows) or ½ cup thinly sliced fresh basil
⅓ cup freshly grated Parmesan cheese
¼ cup pine nuts, toasted (page 39)
4 lemon wedges
Freshly ground black pepper

1. To make the vinaigrette, combine the vinegar, mustard, shallots, thyme, and garlic in a bowl. Slowly whisk in the oil in a steady stream until the dressing emulsifies. Season to taste with salt and pepper. Set aside.

2. Fire up the grill. Liberally brush both sides of the bread with oil. Grill the bread on both sides until golden and nicely marked by the grill. Remove the bread from the heat and use a serrated knife to cut the bread into bite-size cubes. Put the bread in a serving bowl with the olives, tomatoes, mozzarella, and greens. Whisk the pesto or basil leaves into the vinaigrette. Pour the vinaigrette over the salad and toss well. There should be enough vinaigrette to soak into the bread, but the salad greens should not be

drenched—use a little more or less vinaigrette as needed.

ON THE PLATE Divide the salad among 4 plates. Scatter the Parmesan cheese and pine nuts over the top of each salad and garnish each salad with a lemon wedge. Pass a pepper grinder at the table.

A STEP AHEAD The vinaigrette can be prepared and stored, tightly covered, in the refrigerator up to a week ahead. Whisk well before using.

Pesto

{ Makes about ½ cup }

There's no Parmesan in this pesto because there's freshly grated cheese in the Tuscan bread salad. You can add a few tablespoons of freshly grated Parmesan to the pesto if using it in another dish. Since the bread salad calls for only a tablespoon of pesto, make a batch anytime, divide it up into small portions, and freeze them, thawing only what you need. A handy way to do this is to spoon the pesto into a plastic ice cube tray, freeze, and then store the cubes in a plastic bag in the freezer until ready to use.

3 cups loosely packed fresh basil, washed and dried
2 tablespoons pine nuts, toasted (page 39)
½ teaspoon minced garlic
½ teaspoon fresh lemon juice
⅓ cup extra virgin olive oil
Kosher salt

Process the basil, pine nuts, garlic, and lemon juice together in a food processor until smooth. Slowly add the olive oil though the feed tube and process until well combined. Season with salt to taste. Use the pesto the same day or freeze for the best color.

WHITE WINTER SALAD
WITH AGED PARMIGIANO-REGGIANO

{ Makes 4 servings }

This salad is a winter staple at Palace Kitchen. Use the finest aged Parmigiano-Reggiano cheese here. This is the highest grade of imported Parmesan and it is well worth the high price and extra effort to find it. Use a vegetable peeler to get nice curls of the rich, dry cheese. Slice the fennel bulb very, very thinly on a mandoline. The smallest and most tender heads of frisée are best. If you have truffle oil, drizzle some on the salad just before serving.

---

3 tablespoons extra virgin olive oil

2 cloves garlic, peeled

3 Belgian endives

3 cups loosely packed frisée, trimmed, washed, and dried

2 cups peeled and seeded cucumber, sliced ⅛ inch thick

2 cups thinly sliced fennel bulb

5 teaspoons fresh lemon juice

Kosher salt and freshly ground black pepper

½ cup shaved Parmigiano-Reggiano

1. To make garlic oil, combine the olive oil and garlic in a small saucepan over medium heat. When the garlic starts to sizzle, remove from the heat and let sit for half an hour. Discard the garlic cloves and set the oil aside.

2. Cut the endives in half lengthwise, remove the cores, and slice into strips ½ inch wide. In a medium bowl, toss the endives, frisée, cucumber, and fennel with the garlic oil, lemon juice, and salt and pepper to taste.

ON THE PLATE Divide the salad among 4 plates and top with shaved Parmigiano-Reggiano.

A STEP AHEAD The garlic oil can be made early in the day and stored, tightly covered, in the refrigerator.

TOM'S MOM'S HARVARD BEETS WITH BEET GREENS

{ Makes 6 servings }

These sweet-and-sour beets were the only way my mom could get me to eat beets. The only difference between her recipe and mine is the sautéed beet greens. I often put these on the menu for Valentine's Day because my wife, Jackie, loves them.

If your beets don't come with a good-size head of greens, you may need to steal some from off another bunch. Or you could add a bunch of red chard.

---

2 bunches beets with plenty of nice greens (about 2 pounds beets with about 15 cups loosely packed greens)
¾ cup fresh orange juice
¾ cup water
3 tablespoons firmly packed brown sugar
2 tablespoons cider vinegar
1 teaspoon grated orange zest
1 teaspoon cornstarch dissolved in 1 tablespoon water
Kosher salt and freshly ground black pepper
2 tablespoons olive oil
½ teaspoon minced garlic
2 tablespoons toasted (page 39), skinned, and finely chopped hazelnuts

1. Separate the greens from the beets. Discard the stems and wash thoroughly and dry the beet greens. Peel the beets, cut them in half, and thinly slice them into half-moon shapes ⅛ inch thick.

2. In a medium saucepan over medium heat, combine the orange juice, water, brown sugar, vinegar, and zest. Once the sugar has melted, add the beets to this mixture and cook, covered, until tender but still retaining a little crunch, about 20 minutes. Stir in the dissolved cornstarch and simmer a few minutes. Season with salt and pepper.

3. Meanwhile, heat the olive oil in a large sauté pan over medium-high heat, then cook the greens until wilted, about 3 minutes, stirring in the garlic halfway through. Season with salt and pepper.

ON THE PLATE   Arrange the wilted beet greens on 6 salad plates. Arrange the beet slices over the greens. Garnish each salad with the toasted hazelnuts.

A STEP AHEAD   You can cook the beets early in the day, omitting the cornstarch, and store them, covered with plastic wrap, refrigerated. Add the cornstarch slurry when you are reheating the beets. But don't cook the beet greens until the last minute.

POPPY SEED COLESLAW

{ Makes 4 servings }

The lightly sweet and mildly tart flavor of this slaw makes it just the right pairing for my favorite food—barbecue. The speckles of poppy seeds add color interest and extra flavors to the finely shredded cabbage. Use all red cabbage or half green and half red.

---

1 large egg yolk (see Note, page 24)
2 tablespoons chopped onions
2 tablespoons Champagne vinegar or cider vinegar
1 tablespoon sugar
1 cup vegetable oil
1½ teaspoons poppy seeds
Kosher salt and freshly ground black pepper to taste
1 pound red cabbage, cored and thinly sliced
   (5 cups or ½ head)

In a food processor or blender, combine the egg yolk, onions, vinegar, and sugar. Slowly add the vegetable oil in a steady stream until the dressing is emulsified. Pour the dressing into a large serving bowl and stir in the poppy seeds. Season to taste with salt and pepper. Add the cabbage to the bowl and toss to combine.

A STEP AHEAD   The poppy seed dressing can be made early in the day and stored, tightly covered, in the refrigerator.

SWEET-AND-SOUR RED CABBAGE

{ Makes 4 servings }

The caraway seeds are the key to this dish. They add a distinct flavor that is often found in Czechoslovakian cooking. I like to serve this spiced cabbage with Roasted Lemon Thyme Chicken (page 150). It would also be delicious with roast duck or grilled pork chops. Use a mandoline (page 158), if possible, to slice the cabbage.

¼ cup (½ stick) unsalted butter
6 cups cored and thinly sliced red cabbage
   (⅛ inch thick)
¾ cup cider vinegar
½ cup sugar
1½ teaspoons caraway seeds
Kosher salt and freshly ground black pepper

Melt the butter in a large sauté pan over medium-low heat. Add the cabbage, vinegar, sugar, and caraway seeds. Cover and allow to cook until the cabbage softens, about 45 minutes, stirring occasionally. Season to taste with salt and pepper.

A STEP AHEAD You can cook the cabbage early in the day and store it, covered, refrigerated. Gently reheat it before serving.

Ruby Chard with Garlic, Chile, and Lemon

{ Makes 4 servings }

At Etta's we change vegetable side dishes seasonally (corn in the summer, acorn squash in the winter), but this chard dish is always available, since greens can be grown year-round in our mild climate. Ruby chard is a variety with red stems and red-veined leaves, but other types of chard work just as well. It's important to clean the greens well under cold running water and to separate the tough stems from the tender leaves. We like to squeeze lemon wedges over the wilting chard and then throw the squeezed lemons right into the pan. It's important to add the lemon at the last minute or the chard will discolor.

For this amount of chard, you will either have to cook it in more than one pan or in a really large pan, or cook it in batches. A tip for preparing larger quantities: There is a lot of volume in chard leaves (and greens in general). If you want to make chard for more than four people, blanch it first in a big pot of boiling water, shock it in ice water, then squeeze all the water out. Then, when you are ready, reheat the chard by sautéing it in the olive oil and garlic, and you won't need quite as much pan space.

Stem and wash the chard well. Shake off any excess water. Heat a large sauté pan with the oil and red pepper flakes over medium-high heat. Add the chard and garlic. Wilt the leaves over medium-high heat, stirring occasionally, 3 to 5 minutes. When the leaves are wilted, season to taste with salt and pepper and squeeze the lemon wedges into the pan. Throw the squeezed wedges into the pan. Divide the chard among 4 plates and serve immediately.

3 bunches ruby or other chard (about 2 pounds, or 12 cups loosely packed, cleaned leaves)
¼ cup olive oil
¼ teaspoon red pepper flakes
2 teaspoons minced garlic
Kosher salt and freshly ground black pepper
4 lemon wedges

GRILLED AND ROASTED WALLA WALLA SWEET ONIONS WITH PINE NUT BUTTER AND CHARD

{ Makes 4 servings }

Walla Walla is a town about four hours east of Seattle that produces some of the world's sweetest onions, hence the name Walla Walla Sweets. These onions are so mild that you can eat them raw. Sliced them, and then pile them up on a piece of pumpernickel bread spread with sweet butter. You'll see.

We chauvinistically believe our Walla Wallas are superior to all other onions, but if you can't get your hands on the real thing, try this recipe with Vidalias, Mauis, or Bermudas.

At the Dahlia Lounge, after grilling and roasting Walla Walla Sweets, we rub them with a knob of pine nut butter, then rest them on a bed of sautéed ruby chard and present them as an appetizer. The onions could also be served on soft polenta or grilled bread to soak up the butter.

At the restaurant, it's easy both to grill and roast the onions because there's always a fire going right next to the oven. We love the flavor our apple-wood fire adds to these onions, but if you don't feel like firing up the grill, you can get color on the onions by searing them in a heavy pan before roasting.

FOR THE PINE NUT BUTTER

½ cup pine nuts (about 2½ ounces), toasted
   (page 39)
6 tablespoons (¾ stick) unsalted butter, softened
1 teaspoon grated lemon zest
½ teaspoon chopped fresh rosemary
¼ teaspoon freshly ground black pepper
¼ teaspoon kosher salt

TO FINISH THE DISH

4 Walla Walla onions
Olive oil
Ruby Chard with Garlic, Chile, and Lemon
   (page 185)
2 tablespoons shaved Parmesan cheese
   (we use a vegetable peeler)
4 lemon wedges

1. To make the nut butter, chop half of the pine nuts.

2. With a wooden spoon mix together the whole and chopped pine nuts, the butter, lemon zest, rosemary, pepper, and salt in a small bowl. Set aside.

3. Fire up the grill and preheat the oven to 400°F. Peel and cut the onions in half. Be careful to leave the root ends intact so the onions hold together. Brush the onion halves with olive oil and grill, cut side down, until lightly marked, about 3 minutes. Place the onion halves, cut side up, on a baking sheet, place in the oven, and roast until soft and cooked through, 30 to 40 minutes. To sear the onions instead of grilling them, heat an ovenproof frying pan over medium-high heat with 2 tablespoons olive oil. Sear the cut sides until brown, about 3 minutes. Flip the onions and place in the oven to roast as directed. Meanwhile, prepare the chard with garlic, chile, and lemon.

4. Remove the onions from the oven. Spread the cut halves liberally with the nut

butter. Return to the oven to melt and "bake in" the butter, about 5 minutes.

ON THE PLATE Divide the chard among 4 plates. Put 2 onion halves on top of each plate of chard. Sprinkle the shaved Parmesan over the onions and garnish with lemon wedges.

A STEP AHEAD The nut butter can be made a few days ahead and held, tightly wrapped, in the refrigerator or for a few weeks in the freezer. The onions can be grilled and roasted a few hours ahead and kept at room temperature. Return them to the oven to warm them through before spreading with the nut butter.

Grilled Japanese Eggplant with Honey Soy Glaze

{ Makes 4 servings }

With so many varieties of eggplant available these days, we don't have to rely only on the big globe eggplant anymore. My favorite is the light purple, long, and spindly Japanese variety, but any variety will do.

FOR THE HONEY SOY GLAZE
¼ cup honey
¼ cup vegetable or peanut oil
¼ cup fresh lemon juice
¼ cup soy sauce
½ teaspoon minced garlic
¼ teaspoon red pepper flakes

FOR THE EGGPLANT
4 Japanese eggplant (about 5 ounces each) or 1 globe eggplant
2 teaspoons sesame seeds, toasted (page 39)

1. Whisk together the glaze ingredients. Set aside.

2. Fire up the grill. Cut each eggplant in half lengthwise, leaving the stem on. Then partially cut each half several times lengthwise, like a fan. If using a globe eggplant, slice it into ½-inch-thick rounds.

Pour half the glaze over the eggplants in a medium bowl and let them marinate for 10 minutes. Remove the eggplants from the marinade. Allow any excess marinade to drip off, to prevent a flare-up when you place them on the grill. Grill the eggplants, turning as necessary, until tender, 4 to 6 minutes.

ON THE PLATE   Place 2 eggplant halves or 2 slices of eggplant on each plate and drizzle with a bit of the remaining glaze. Garnish with the sesame seeds; we also like to serve this with pickled red cabbage (page 56).

A STEP AHEAD   The glaze will keep about a week, tightly covered, in the refrigerator.

GRILLED CHICKEN BREASTS WITH HONEY SOY GLAZE

The glaze is a very versatile marinade for grilling. Both the grilled eggplant and grilled chicken breasts would be delicious with Spicy Peanut Noodles (page 172).

4 chicken breasts
Honey Soy Glaze (page 188)

In a baking dish, marinate the chicken breasts in the glaze for 30 minutes. Drain off the excess marinade. Grill or broil the breasts on both sides until cooked through, about 10 minutes total on the grill, about 16 minutes total in a preheated broiler. Be careful not to burn the chicken because the honey in the marinade can char easily. Move the chicken to a cooler part of the grill, if necessary. Cut into a breast to make sure no pink remains.

"Right on the Grill" Corn on the Cob with Molasses Chile Butter

{ Makes 6 servings }

Wonderful fresh corn from all over Washington is delivered to our kitchens just about every day in season. Most people don't realize they can put fresh corn on the cob right on the grill. You don't have to leave the husks on or wrap the cobs in foil. The corn comes out tender and sweet with an appealing smoky taste and just a little crunch from the grill marks. After the cobs are grilled, rub them with a flavored butter like this one. They are beautiful—golden orange from the butter with patches of deep brown and bright yellow.

This corn makes a perfect side dish for any barbecue. Serve it with everything from spit-roasted prime rib to grilled chicken or down-home ribs.

FOR THE MOLASSES CHILE BUTTER
½ cup fresh orange juice
½ cup (1 stick) unsalted butter, softened
1 ancho chile, pureed (page 128)
1 tablespoon molasses
1 teaspoon grated orange zest
1 teaspoon kosher salt
Freshly ground black pepper

FOR THE CORN
6 fresh ears corn, shucked

1. In a small saucepan over high heat, reduce the orange juice until it is a thick syrup and yields 1 tablespoon, about 5 minutes. Let cool. In a food processor or by hand, combine the reduced orange juice, butter, ancho puree, molasses, orange zest, salt, and pepper. Remove the flavored butter to a small bowl and set aside.

2. Fire up the grill. Grill the corn until done, about 8 minutes over medium heat, turning as necessary to brown evenly. Remove the corn from the grill and slather with the chile butter.

A STEP AHEAD   The butter can be made a week ahead and held, tightly wrapped, in the refrigerator or for longer in the freezer. It is also great spread on grilled halibut, grilled summer squash, or cornbread.

Grilled Asparagus
with Hazelnut–Star Anise Mayonnaise

{ Makes 6 servings }

Many people don't realize how easy it is to grill vegetables. Zucchini, mushrooms, corn, peppers, onions, and tomatoes are all great on the grill. If you don't want to grill the asparagus, steam them. Just be sure not to overcook them—asparagus should be bright green and still slightly *al dente*.

This mayonnaise is also good with steamed artichokes, blanched green beans, grilled zucchini, or grilled fennel, or as a dip for crudités. You can also serve it as a sauce on fish; it would go well with salmon. And it would make a delicious dressing for a chicken salad. If blood oranges are available, wedges make a striking garnish.

FOR THE HAZELNUT–STAR ANISE
   MAYONNAISE
2 large egg yolks (see Note, page 24)
¼ cup sherry vinegar
1 teaspoon orange juice
1 teaspoon fresh lemon juice
1 tablespoon grated orange zest
1½ teaspoons honey
¾ teaspoon kosher salt
Pinch of freshly ground black pepper
2 star anise, ground (about 1 teaspoon, see
   How to Toast and Grind Spices, page 21)
1 cup peanut or vegetable oil
½ cup toasted (page 39), skinned, and finely
   chopped hazelnuts

FOR THE ASPARAGUS
2 pounds asparagus, tough bottoms snapped off
Olive oil for brushing

Kosher salt and freshly ground black pepper
1 orange, sliced or cut into wedges for garnish

I. In a food processor or blender, combine the egg yolks, vinegar, citrus juices and zest, honey, salt, pepper, and star anise. While the machine is running, add the oil in a slow, steady stream until the mixture is emulsified. Reserve 2 tablespoons of the chopped hazelnuts for a garnish and process the rest briefly with the mayonnaise. Remove the mayonnaise to a small bowl.

2. Fire up the grill. Brush the asparagus with olive oil and lay horizontally across the grill grates. This prevents them from falling through the grates. Sprinkle with salt and pepper. Roll the asparagus with tongs to grill them evenly, and don't be afraid to char them a little bit. Cooking time depends on the thickness of the asparagus and the heat of the grill. Medium-thick asparagus takes about 6 minutes.

ON THE PLATE Arrange the asparagus in bundles on plates. Drape some of the mayonnaise over each bundle. Sprinkle the remaining chopped toasted hazelnuts over the mayonnaise and garnish with orange slices or wedges.

A STEP AHEAD The mayonnaise can be made early in the day and stored, covered, in the refrigerator. Use the same day.

Loretta picking wild blackberries

Save Room for Dessert

I'M A SUCKER for sweets. I can never walk past the baking station without grabbing a cookie and slathering it with chocolate butter cream or dredging it through caramel sauce. Make no mistake, though, I'm very democratic; I can enjoy a doughnut as long as there are sprinkles on it as much as I enjoy a fancy Pavlova with three sauces.

We've always put a priority on desserts in our restaurants—you can't say you're serving comfort food without having luscious desserts—and even in the tiniest spaces we dragged a bucket-type ice cream maker into the hallway so we could churn our own ice cream.

Shelley Lance has been our pastry chef for the last ten years, and many of these recipes are her creations. We've always been in sync about what dessert is. It's more about soul-satisfying deliciousness than sugar sculpture and fancy chocolate work. Our desserts are rustic, homey, and simple, like warm raspberries with a crisp cornmeal topping. They come from blissful childhood memories rather than fancy books; we want flavors that go straight to the heart. Dessert should be a fitting end to a grand meal. Dessert should make people happy.

"Tom's World Famous" Crème Caramel

{ Makes 8 servings }

This is called "world famous" crème caramel mostly as a joke—but we really do love it better than any crème caramel we've ever tasted. It's extra rich and luscious because it's made with all egg yolks and heavy cream. This is one of our best-selling desserts and it's always on the menu at Dahlia.

Crème caramels are going to need several hours, or overnight, to chill before you can unmold them, so plan ahead. Because caramelizing sugar can be a bit daunting, read How to Caramelize Sugar Safely (page 195) before starting the recipe.

FOR THE CARAMEL
1 cup sugar
⅓ cup water

FOR THE CUSTARD
4 cups heavy cream
1 cup sugar
1 vanilla bean, cut in half lengthwise
10 large egg yolks

1. Preheat the oven to 300°F. Set out eight 6-ounce ovenproof ramekins near the range where you are planning to caramelize the sugar. In a small heavy-bottomed saucepan, combine the sugar and water. Stir over low heat until the sugar is completely dissolved. Raise the heat to high and cook *without stirring* until the sugar turns dark golden brown. You

may need to gently swirl the pan to distribute the color evenly. Remove the pan from the heat and *carefully* pour a little caramel into each of the ramekins. There should be enough caramel to cover the bottom of each ramekin. Set the ramekins aside to cool while you make the custard.

2. In a large heavy-bottomed saucepan, stir together the heavy cream and sugar. Scrape the seeds from the vanilla bean and add both the seeds and pod to the cream mixture. Place the saucepan over medium-high heat, stirring to dissolve the sugar. In a bowl, lightly beat the egg yolks together. Set a fine-mesh sieve over a large bowl and keep it nearby. When the cream mixture is very hot, but still just below the boiling point, remove the saucepan from the heat. Whisk a small amount of the hot cream mixture into the egg yolks, just to temper them (to keep them from scrambling). Then whisk the warmed yolks into the hot cream mixture and, as soon as the two mixtures are well combined, strain the custard through the sieve, discarding the pod.

3. Place the prepared ramekins in a baking pan and fill each one with custard. Put the baking dish in the oven, then pour hot water around the ramekins, deep enough to come about halfway up the sides. Loosely cover the baking dish with a sheet of aluminum foil (you want steam to be able to escape) and bake until the custard is set, 50 to 60 minutes. You can check this by gently shaking a ramekin, or by making a shallow cut with a

small knife into the center of one of the custards. The custard may look soft, but it shouldn't be liquid inside. Carefully remove the baking pan from the oven and allow it to cool. When the ramekins are cool enough to handle, remove them from the baking pan and set them in the refrigerator for several hours or overnight.

4. To serve, run a small knife around the edge of the custard. Invert a dessert plate over the top of the ramekin and, holding on tight, flip the whole thing over, giving the ramekin a sharp shake. The custard should slide right out onto the plate.

ON THE PLATE   Serve with a few fresh berries and a crisp cookie.

A STEP AHEAD   Put the caramelized sugar in the bottom of the ramekins several hours ahead of time and let them sit at room temperature until you are ready to make the custard. After the crème caramels are baked, you can store them in their ramekins, refrigerated, for 2 or 3 days. When they are completely cold, cover them with plastic wrap. Unmold right before serving.

IN THE GLASS   Demi-sec Champagne

HOW TO CARAMELIZE SUGAR SAFELY

I've always found it easiest to add just enough water to completely dissolve the sugar first. Over low heat, stir the sugar and water until you have a clear solution, then turn the heat up to high to allow the sugar to caramelize. After the heat is turned up, don't disturb the sugar by stirring it or you may cause crystallization. (It's important to prevent crystals from forming. If they do, the sugar syrup will "seize up" into a slushy clump and you'll have to throw it away.)

If a dark brown color develops in one corner of the pan, carefully swirl the pan to distribute the color evenly. When you get the dark golden-brown color you want, immediately remove the pan from the heat. Sugar burns very quickly and it will keep darkening even after you remove it from the heat.

Making caramel is potentially dangerous. Don't ever touch hot sugar with your finger or with any other part of your anatomy. It's not a bad idea to keep a bowl of ice water nearby in case you accidentally get any burning sugar on yourself.

BAKED ALASKA

{ Makes 6 servings }

There is nothing quite like the dramatic effect of a baked Alaska. The results are worth every minute of effort. This is one of my favorite desserts, so I include it here, even though it requires you to purchase a small hand-held propane torch, which is very easy to use. Your guests will love watching you turn the swirls of meringue toasty brown right in front of their eyes.

You can purchase a propane torch at hardware stores, kitchenware stores, or from mail-order catalogs such as Williams-Sonoma or Sur La Table. If you don't have a torch, just follow the instructions at the end of this recipe for browning the meringue in your broiler.

Or you can create ice cream sandwiches. Make 12 chocolate shortbread cookies. Sandwich a scoop of bing cherry ice cream between two cookies, put them in the freezer until firm, then serve the sandwiches with little pitchers of the warm chocolate sauce.

---

6 Chocolate Shortbread cookies (recipe follows)
1 pint Bing Cherry Ice Cream (page 224) or your
　　choice of store-bought ice cream, softened a bit
4 large egg whites (see Note, page 24)
1 cup sugar
Pinch of kosher salt
Chocolate Sauce (page 200), warm

1. Line a baking sheet with parchment or wax paper. Set out the cookies on the sheet. Place a 2-ounce (about ⅓ cup) scoop of ice cream in the center of each cookie. Return the cookies to the freezer to harden for at least half an hour.

2. Set a saucepan of water simmering on the stove. Put the egg whites, sugar, and salt in a metal bowl. By hand, whisk the whites over the saucepan of simmering water until they warm to body temperature (90° to 100°F), about 1 minute. Remove the bowl of egg whites from the stove and whisk the whites with an electric mixer on medium-high speed until they are glossy and form stiff peaks, about 10 minutes.

3. Fit a pastry bag with a medium star tip and fill with the meringue. Remove the ice cream–topped cookies from the freezer and pipe stars of meringue, completely covering each scoop of ice cream.

ON THE PLATE　With a spatula, remove the meringue-topped cookies from the baking sheet and place on dessert plates. Light the propane torch and carefully brown each of the baked Alaskas. (Note that you are not completely browning the meringue; you are just making some attractive patches of color. You should hold the torch so that the flame is just 1 or 2 inches from the surface of the meringue. The flame will brown the meringue within a few seconds.) Ladle some warm chocolate sauce alongside each baked Alaska.

A STEP AHEAD　Prior to browning the baked Alaskas, they can be stored, uncovered, for several hours in the freezer after the meringue is piped over them. Brown the meringue with the torch right before serving.

To brown the Alaskas in your broiler, you will need to chill them, covered with the meringue, in the freezer for a few hours first. Turn the broiler on to high. Position the baking sheet under the broiler so that the tops of the Alaskas are 1½ to 2 inches from the heat source. Broil the Alaskas until they are browned, about 2 minutes, watching them carefully and turning frequently so they brown evenly. Serve immediately with the chocolate sauce.

IN THE GLASS A rich, fruity black Muscat from Washington State

Using a propane torch to brown a baked Alaska

Here are some tips for rolling out cookie dough: Use just enough flour to keep the dough from sticking to your work surface or to the rolling pin, but don't use too much or the cookies will be tough. A metal or plastic board scraper is a helpful and inexpensive tool to use when you are working with dough. I use a board scraper to lift the dough occasionally as I am rolling it to check that the dough is not sticking. If it starts to stick, I add a little more flour. When I'm rolling cookie dough, I reroll the scraps once and cut out more cookies. I don't like to reroll the scraps more than once because the dough has picked up too much flour after that and the cookies may become tough.

Another trick: If the bottoms of the cookies seem to be browning too quickly, "double pan" them by sliding another baking sheet underneath. Also, it's a good idea to turn the pan in the oven once or twice while the cookies are baking so that they cook evenly. If you have more than one baking sheet in the oven, you should switch the top and bottom racks halfway through the baking.

Chocolate Shortbread

{ Makes about 1½ dozen 3-inch cookies }

These tender, rich, buttery shortbreads are melt-in-your-mouth delicious. Use a premium cocoa such as Valrhona (see Sources, page 260) or the best-quality unsweetened cocoa you can find. Cut the dough with a 3-inch round cookie cutter if you plan to use them as a base for baked Alaska. Otherwise, cut them into any size or shape you like.

1 cup (2 sticks) unsalted butter, softened
½ cup sugar
1 teaspoon pure vanilla extract
½ cup unsweetened cocoa powder, preferably a
    premium dark cocoa such as Valrhona
1¾ cups all-purpose flour
½ teaspoon kosher salt

1. Preheat the oven to 325°F. In the bowl of an electric mixer with the paddle attachment, cream the butter and sugar together until light and fluffy. Add the vanilla. Sift the cocoa, flour, and salt together and add to the bowl. Mix just until everything is well combined. Remove the dough to a floured work board.

2. Flour the top of the dough lightly and use a floured rolling pin to roll the dough to a little less than ¼-inch thickness. (Don't roll the dough too thin or you will lose the special texture of the baked cookies.) Cut with a 3-inch round cookie cutter (or other shape) and place the cookies about 1 inch apart on parchment paper–lined baking sheets. Gather the dough scraps together and

roll and cut the cookies again. Bake the cookies, turning the pans around in the oven once or twice until they feel firm and set when you touch them with the tips of your fingers, about 15 minutes. Watch carefully so the bottoms of the cookies don't burn. Remove from the oven, then allow the cookies to cool before you remove them from the baking sheets with a metal spatula. These cookies are fragile; handle them carefully.

ON THE PLATE The cookies are very rich tasting, so you only need one or two per serving. They would make a simple but elegant finish to a dinner party, on their own or served with vanilla ice cream. Also try serving them with Oregon Pinot Noir Raspberry Sorbet (page 226), since red wine and chocolate have a natural affinity.

A STEP AHEAD These cookies will stay fresh in an airtight container at room temperature for up to 3 days. You can also keep the baked and completely cooled cookies in the freezer, tightly wrapped in plastic wrap, for a week or two. The shortbread dough can be made ahead, wrapped, and refrigerated for up to a week, or frozen for even longer.

French bakery Le Panier in the market

CHOCOLATE SAUCE

{ Make about 1½ cups }

This is a great, basic chocolate sauce recipe. Use the best-quality unsweetened cocoa powder you can find, like the Valrhona brand. The best-tasting chocolate sauce can only be made with the best chocolate available.

½ cup heavy cream
3 tablespoons unsalted butter
⅓ cup granulated sugar
⅓ cup firmly packed brown sugar
½ cup unsweetened cocoa powder, sifted
Pinch of kosher salt
¼ cup chopped bittersweet chocolate
   (about 1½ ounces)
¼ cup brewed coffee

In a saucepan over medium-high heat, bring the heavy cream, butter, and both sugars to a boil. Add the cocoa and salt and whisk until smooth. Remove the saucepan from the heat. Add the chopped chocolate and coffee and stir until the chocolate is melted. Serve warm.

A STEP AHEAD   This sauce can be made 2 or 3 days ahead and stored, tightly covered, in the refrigerator. Gently reheat over hot water in the top of a double boiler.

Apple Dumplings with Medjool Dates and Maple Sauce

{ Makes 8 servings }

Some foods just feel like home. My mom never made these apple dumplings, but whenever I eat one, I could almost swear she did. They are familiar, comforting, cheery, and, best of all, delicious.

These apple dumplings are one of the top-selling desserts at Etta's. They are like warm, individual apple pies, filled with date butter and fragrant with cinnamon. You can use any kind of good cooking apple in this recipe. Our favorite is Granny Smith, because its high acidity level complements the sweetness of the dates. Medjool dates are plump, moist, and especially rich in flavor.

FOR THE DATE BUTTER
10 medjool or other dates (about 6 ounces), pitted and chopped
6 tablespoons (¾ stick) unsalted butter, softened
¼ cup firmly packed brown sugar
1 teaspoon ground cinnamon

FOR THE DUMPLINGS
Pastry Dough (page 256)
4 apples (about 7 ounces each), peeled and halved lengthwise
1 large egg yolk
1 tablespoon heavy cream
¼ cup granulated sugar
2 teaspoons ground cinnamon

TO SERVE
Maple Sauce, warm (recipe follows)

1. To make the date butter, combine the chopped dates, butter, brown sugar, and cinnamon in a food processor or in an electric mixer with the paddle. Process until smooth. Remove the date butter to a small bowl and refrigerate until somewhat firm.

2. To make the apple dumplings, preheat the oven to 400°F. Set out a small bowl of water and a pastry brush. Divide the pastry dough in half. On a lightly floured work surface, roll out half the dough about an ⅛ inch thick into a rough square shape. Trim the dough with a knife to make a 12-inch square, saving all the pastry trimmings for decorating the dumplings later. Cut the 12-inch square into quarters. You will have four 6-inch squares of dough. Take each small square and use your knife to make a cut from each corner to about halfway to the center of the square. Repeat with the second half of the dough. You will have eight 6-inch squares of dough.

3. Use a melon baller to remove the core of each apple half and create a little cavity. Fill the cavity of each apple half with a mound of the date butter. Place each apple half, core side down, in the center of a dough square. Brush the corners of the dough lightly with water. Fold the corners of the dough up over each apple in an alternating pinwheel fashion, pressing to seal.

4. Place the dumplings on a parchment paper–lined baking sheet. Reroll the pastry

Fill the cavity of each apple half with a mound of the date butter.

Take a small square of dough and use your knife to make a cut from each corner to about halfway to the center of the square. Place a filled apple half, core side down, in the center. Brush the corners of the dough lightly with water.

Fold the corners of the dough up over each apple in an alternating pinwheel fashion.

Press the dough gently to seal.

Brush each dumpling with egg wash and sprinkle with cinnamon sugar.

trimmings and cut out 8 decorative leaf shapes using a small knife or leaf-shaped cookie cutter. Place one leaf on each dumpling, fixing it on with a pastry brush dipped in a little water.

5. In a small bowl, beat the egg yolk lightly with the heavy cream. Brush each dumpling with the egg wash. In another small bowl, mix the granulated sugar with the cinnamon. Sprinkle 1 or 2 teaspoons of cinnamon sugar on each dumpling. Bake the dumplings in the oven until the pastry is golden and the apples feel tender when pierced with a knife, 20 to 25 minutes. Remove the dumplings from the oven.

ON THE PLATE   Place the hot dumplings on dessert plates and spoon some warm maple sauce over and around them. We like to serve our dumplings with cinnamon ice cream, but good-quality vanilla ice cream would be fine, or a dollop of Sweetened Whipped Cream (page 208).

A STEP AHEAD   The date butter can be made ahead and kept, tightly wrapped, in the refrigerator for several days. The dumplings can be baked early in the day, kept at room temperature, and reheated in a preheated 400°F oven until warmed through, 6 to 8 minutes, before serving.

IN THE GLASS   An aged Muscat liqueur from Australia's Rutherglen region or a Muscat de Beaumes-de-Venise from Provence

APPLES

When is progress not really progress? When they started growing apples that looked better than they tasted, when it became more important to grow apples for color, shape, and shelf life than for flavor. Thankfully, this trend has completely turned in the opposite direction, and today the highest-priced apples are those with the best flavor. New varieties and rediscovered old varieties, like Gala, Braeburn, and Fuji, were created for taste, not appearance, and they now lead the market for eating apples. Even the juice market is going in the direction of "varietals," and some supermarkets carry Granny Smith or Gravenstein apple juice.

Maple Sauce

{ Makes 1½ cups }

This maple sauce and apple dumplings are constant companions on the Etta's dessert menu.

1 cup water
1 cinnamon stick
¾ cup firmly packed brown sugar
2 teaspoons cornstarch
¼ cup pure maple syrup
1 tablespoon unsalted butter

In a small saucepan over high heat, bring the water and cinnamon stick to a boil. In a small bowl, combine the brown sugar and cornstarch. Add the brown sugar–cornstarch mixture to the boiling water, reduce the heat to low, and simmer the mixture for about 5 minutes, whisking occasionally until slightly thickened. Remove from the heat and add the maple syrup and butter, stirring until the butter melts. Remove the cinnamon stick before serving. Serve warm.

A STEP AHEAD The maple sauce can be made ahead and kept, tightly covered and chilled, for about a week. Reheat before serving.

Dahlia Pear Tart
with Caramel Sauce

{ Makes 6 servings }

When we decided to write a cookbook, our customers weighed in with their opinions of just what recipes should be included. Dahlia pear tart and coconut cream pie were at the top of the dessert list. This tart's rich caramel sauce, crisp pastry, and vanilla-scented pears are irresistible.

FOR POACHING THE PEARS

3 pears (about 7 ounces each), ripe but firm,
  such as Bartlett or Bosc
4 cups water
2 cups sugar
1 vanilla bean, sliced in half lengthwise

FOR THE ALMOND CREAM

3 tablespoons almond paste
2 tablespoons sugar
1½ tablespoons unsalted butter, softened
1 large egg yolk

TO FINISH THE TART

1 batch Rough Puff Pastry (page 257) or about
  1 pound store-bought puff pastry
Caramel Sauce (recipe follows), warm
Sweetened Whipped Cream (page 208)

I. To poach the pears, peel the pears and cut them in half lengthwise. Trim out the stem and blossom end and remove the core using a melon baller or paring knife. Combine the water and sugar in a large saucepan. Scrape the seeds from the vanilla bean and add the seeds, pod, and pears. To keep the pears submerged while they poach, put a sheet of parchment or wax paper on the surface and weight it with a plate or small lid. Place the saucepan over high heat. When the liquid comes to a boil, turn the heat down to a simmer. The amount of time it will take to poach the pears depends on their ripeness, probably 15 to 20 minutes after the pears come to a simmer. Test for doneness by poking a pear with the point of a small knife. As soon as the pears are tender but not mushy, remove the saucepan from the heat. Allow them to cool in the liquid.

2. To make the almond cream, cream the almond paste and sugar together in a small mixing bowl with an electric mixer or in a food processor. The mixture will look crumbly. Beat in the butter, bit by bit. Add the egg yolk and mix until creamy and smooth. Set aside.

3. On a lightly floured work surface, roll the rough puff pastry out into a 9 × 15-inch rectangle. Trim the dough with a knife to straighten the edges. The dough should be about ⅜ inch thick. Don't roll it too thin or it won't puff when baked. Cut into 6 squares about 4½ inches on a side, that is, cut the 9-inch length of dough in half to make two 4½-inch strips, then cut the strips 3 times into squares. Place the squares on a parchment paper–lined baking sheet and set it in the freezer. Freeze the puff pastry squares at least 10 to 15 minutes before assembling and baking.

4. Preheat the oven to 425°F. Remove the pastry squares from the freezer and spread about 2 teaspoons of almond cream in the center of each pastry square. Remove the pears from the poaching liquid. (You can save the poaching liquid for poaching other fruit or discard.) Blot-dry the pears on a clean kitchen towel, then slice each pear half lengthwise in ¼-inch-thick slices. Lift each sliced pear half with a spatula and place it over the almond cream, fanning it gently.

5. Set the baking sheet in the oven and bake for 10 minutes. Slip another baking sheet underneath to "double pan" and protect the bottoms of the tarts, then reduce the oven temperature to 375°F and bake until the pear tarts are puffed and golden brown, another 25 minutes. Remove from the oven.

6. Commercial puff pastry needs to be rolled and baked a little differently. Roll out commercial puff pastry ⅛ inch thick and cut it into 4½-inch squares as described above. Assemble the pear tarts according to the directions. Bake at 425°F for 20 minutes.

ON THE PLATE Ladle some warm caramel sauce on each plate. Using a spatula, transfer a warm pear tart to the plate. Garnish with a mound of whipped cream.

A STEP AHEAD The pears can be poached ahead and stored, covered with their poaching liquid, in the refrigerator for a few days. The almond cream can be made a few days ahead and stored, tightly covered, in the refrigerator. You can bake the pear tarts early in the day and leave them at room temperature. Reheat them in a preheated 375°F oven for about 5 minutes before serving.

IN THE GLASS A sweet white Bordeaux like Sauternes or Sainte-Croix-du-Mont

Caramel Sauce

{ Makes 1½ cups }

Everything tastes better with caramel sauce. We always keep a container of it sitting in a hot water bath in the Dahlia kitchen and I often come over and spoon some over a wedge of apple or a piece of cake for a tasty snack. So when we opened Etta's, we put a dessert fondue on the menu: a little fondue pot of warm caramel sauce surrounded by cookies and chunks of fruit for dipping.

Please read How to Caramelize Sugar Safely (page 195) before starting this recipe.

1⅓ cups sugar

⅓ cup water

1 cup heavy cream

2 tablespoons (¼ stick) unsalted butter, softened

Place the sugar and water in a heavy-bottomed saucepan over medium-low heat, whisking occasionally until the sugar is completely dissolved, about 3 minutes. After the sugar is dissolved, raise the heat to high and bring the mixture to a boil, *without stirring*, until the syrup turns a deep golden brown, 15 to 20 minutes. If you see the sugar caramelizing only in one corner, you can gently tilt or rotate the pan to distribute the color evenly, but do not whisk. When the syrup has colored nicely, remove the pan from the heat and immediately add the heavy cream; be careful and stand back because the mixture will sputter. Do not stir until the mixture settles. Return the pan to low heat and stir with a wooden spoon until the strands of caramel melt. Remove from the heat and stir in the butter. Serve warm.

A STEP AHEAD This can be made ahead and stored, covered, in the refrigerator for a few days. Warm it over hot water in a double boiler before serving.

Sweetened Whipped Cream

{ Makes about 3 cups }

It's easiest to whip cream if everything is very cold, including your bowl and whisk.

1½ cups heavy cream
3 tablespoons sugar
1½ teaspoons pure vanilla extract

Place the heavy cream, sugar, and vanilla in the bowl and whip with an electric mixer until soft peaks form. Serve immediately.

Tom and Loretta picking wild blackberries

PEACH CORNMEAL SHORTCAKES WITH CANDIED PECANS

{ Makes 6 servings }

When you come across beautifully ripe and juicy peaches, this summertime dessert is an ideal showcase. You can use nectarines instead, and you won't need to peel them. Cornmeal gives the buttery, tender biscuits a little crunch and a bit of a Southern feel, which is accentuated by the candied pecans. You could also add a little bourbon or Southern Comfort to the whipped cream, if you like. Please read How to Caramelize Sugar Safely (page 195) before starting this recipe.

FOR THE CANDIED PECANS
½ cup sugar
3 tablespoons water
½ cup pecan halves, toasted (page 39)

FOR THE CORNMEAL SHORTCAKES
2 cups all-purpose flour
½ cup medium-ground yellow cornmeal
⅓ cup sugar, plus more for sprinkling
1 tablespoon baking powder
1 teaspoon kosher salt
1 teaspoon pure vanilla extract
9½ tablespoons cold unsalted butter
1 cup heavy cream
1 large egg white, slightly beaten

TO FINISH THE SHORTCAKES
4 peaches
1 to 3 tablespoons sugar, or to taste
Sweetened Whipped Cream (page 208)

1. To make the candied pecans, set up a cooling rack over a baking sheet lined with aluminum foil (for easy cleanup). Spray the rack with vegetable oil spray. Place two forks next to the prepared rack. Combine the sugar and water in a small saucepan over medium heat, stirring occasionally until the sugar is dissolved. Turn the heat up to high and watch carefully until the caramel becomes golden brown in color; *do not stir.* Remove the saucepan from the heat and toss in the toasted pecans. Use the two forks to remove the pecans one at a time to the prepared rack. The caramel coating will harden quickly. Once hard, remove the pecans from the rack and set aside.

2. Preheat the oven to 425°F. In the bowl of an electric mixer with the paddle attachment, combine the flour, cornmeal, sugar, baking powder, and salt. Add the cold butter until crumbly, like a coarse cornmeal. Pour in the cream and mix until just combined. Turn the dough out onto a lightly floured work surface and roll it out to about ¾ inch thick. With a round cutter, cut the dough into shortcakes about 3½ inches in diameter. Place the shortcakes on a parchment paper–lined baking sheet set in another baking sheet. (This double-pan method slows the browning of the bottoms until the shortcakes are cooked through.) Slightly whisk the egg white in a small bowl. Brush each shortcake with egg white and sprinkle with sugar. Bake until golden and cooked through, 15 to 20 minutes.

3. Meanwhile, bring a small pot of water to a boil and fill a bowl with ice water. Cut a small X in the bottom of each peach. Add the peaches to the boiling water until their skins begin to pull away, about 1 minute. Remove the peaches from the boiling water and place in the ice water. Remove the peaches from the ice water, peel them, cut them in half, remove the pits, and slice. In a bowl, toss the sliced peaches with sugar to taste.

ON THE PLATE   Cut the shortcakes in half horizontally. Fill each shortcake with peaches and whipped cream and replace the top. Garnish with the candied pecans.

A STEP AHEAD   The candied pecans can be made a day ahead if stored in an airtight container at room temperature. The shortcakes can be made earlier in the day and stored at room temperature. Reheat in a preheated 400°F oven for 5 minutes before slicing open and serving.

IN THE GLASS   Beaumes-de-Venise, a rich, sweet Muscat from southern France

FIVE-SPICE ANGEL FOOD CAKE

{ Makes one 10-inch cake; 10 to 12 servings }

One year on my birthday, my wife, Jackie, pulled out her beat-up copy of *Joy of Cooking* and made me an angel food cake, jazzing it up with a few random spices from the cabinet. I couldn't stop raving about her creation, so our bakers whipped up their own version using Chinese five-spice powder, and we put it on the menu. This simple, homey dessert doesn't need much besides a shake of powdered sugar, though here we gild the lily by serving it in a pool of orange crème Anglaise accompanied by sweet local strawberries.

We specify cake flour in this recipe because it makes a lighter angel food cake than all-purpose flour. Angel food cake needs to cool upside down in the pan to keep it from collapsing when it's unmolded. It's best to keep the inverted cake pan suspended well above the counter. Placing the hollow center over the neck of a wine bottle works well.

---

1 cup cake flour
1 teaspoon Chinese Five-Spice Powder (page 212)
¼ teaspoon kosher salt
10 large egg whites, at room temperature
1 teaspoon cream of tartar
1 teaspoon pure almond extract
½ teaspoon pure vanilla extract
1¼ cups sugar
Orange Crème Anglaise (page 213)

I. Preheat the oven to 350°F. In a bowl, sift together the flour, five-spice powder, and salt, then sift the mixture again. In the bowl of an electric mixer with the whisk attachment, beat the egg whites, cream of tartar, and extracts together at medium speed. Increase the speed to high and continue to beat until soft peaks form. Gradually add the sugar, beating until just before the peaks are stiff. The egg whites should be glossy and smooth. Be careful not to overbeat. Overbeaten whites will not expand well in the oven and the cake will not be as tall.

2. Fold half the flour mixture into the beaten whites with a rubber spatula. Then fold in the remaining flour mixture, being careful not to overwork the batter. Pour the batter into an ungreased 10-inch tube pan and place on the middle oven rack. Bake until a toothpick inserted in the middle of the cake comes out clean, 45 to 50 minutes. Let the cake sit a few minutes before inverting the pan onto a cake rack or the neck of a wine bottle to let the cake cool in the pan. When completely cool, turn the cake pan back over and gently run a knife around the edges to loosen the cake. Turn the cake out onto a serving plate.

ON THE PLATE Using a serrated knife, cut the cake and serve each piece in a pool of the crème anglaise. Serve with sliced strawberries, if desired.

A STEP AHEAD This cake keeps, well wrapped in plastic wrap, at room temperature for up to 2 days.

IN THE GLASS A late harvest Riesling or Gewürztraminer from Washington State or California

Chinese Five-Spice Powder

You can purchase five-spice powder, but your own freshly ground spices will have better flavor. You can make this spice mix in any quantity you like. (See page 21 for a discussion of toasting and grinding spices.)

---

1 part ground cinnamon
1 part ground cloves
1 part fennel seeds, toasted and ground
1 part ground star anise
1 part Szechuan peppercorns, toasted and ground

Mix the spices together and store in an airtight jar. This powder will keep for several months.

Orange Crème Anglaise

{ Makes 2¼ cups }

I like to serve this creamy sauce with our five-spice angel food cake but it also goes well poured over a bowl of fresh berries or pound cake. Once you learn how to make a crème Anglaise, you can steep anything you like in it: vanilla bean, crushed coffee beans, or any other zest, spice, or herb that appeals to you.

---

2 cups half-and-half
½ cup sugar
Grated zest from 1 orange
6 large egg yolks
1 tablespoon Cointreau or other orange-flavored
*   liqueur*

I. Combine the half-and-half, sugar, and orange zest in a saucepan over medium-high heat. Bring the mixture to a scald (just below the boiling point), then remove from the heat and set the saucepan aside for the flavors to steep for 30 minutes.

2. Return the saucepan to the heat and reheat to the scalding point. In a bowl, whisk the egg yolks. Add a ladle of the scalded cream mixture to the yolks to temper them (to keep them from scrambling). Then add the warmed yolks to the saucepan and cook over medium heat, stirring constantly, until the mixture is thick enough to coat the back of a spoon, about 5 minutes. Do not allow the mixture to come to a boil. Immediately pour through a fine-mesh sieve into a clean bowl. Set the bowl of crème Anglaise into a larger bowl of ice water and allow it to cool, stirring a few times. When cold, stir in the Cointreau.

A STEP AHEAD   This can be made up to 2 days in advance, and stored, tightly covered with plastic wrap, in the refrigerator.

CHÈVRE CHEESECAKE WITH WILD BLACKBERRIES

{ Makes one 8-inch cake; 12 servings }

Don't be afraid to make this cake just because it uses goat cheese. Use a mild, fresh goat cheese, and the cake's flavor will also be mild. I'm not much of a cheesecake fan, but I love this suave and creamy version with its subtle tang of chèvre.

Crumbs made from our homemade gingersnaps add a special twist to the crust. Crush the cookies in a food processor or roll a rolling pin over them until you have fine crumbs.

Fresh berries or figs are the perfect complement to this cake. This is an excellent do-ahead dessert for a party because it is best if chilled overnight before serving.

---

1 cup fine cookie crumbs (made from Gingersnaps,
    page 227, or any cookie you like)
2 tablespoons (¼ stick) unsalted butter, melted
1 pound cream cheese, softened
6 ounces (about 1 cup) soft fresh goat cheese
¾ cup sugar
½ cup sour cream
1 tablespoon fresh lemon juice
1 teaspoon pure vanilla extract
¼ teaspoon kosher salt
1 large egg plus 1 large egg yolk
1 tablespoon all-purpose flour
1 pint fresh blackberries

I. Preheat the oven to 300°F. Spray an 8-inch springform pan with 3-inch-high sides with vegeatble oil spray or lightly butter the pan. Combine the cookie crumbs with the melted butter and press the crumb mixture evenly over the bottom of the pan.

2. In the bowl of an electric mixer with the paddle attachment, beat the cream cheese and chèvre together until very smooth. Scrape down the sides of the bowl with a rubber spatula. Add the sugar, sour cream, lemon juice, vanilla, and salt, beat to combine well, and scrape down again. Add the whole egg and yolk and beat to combine. Use a small sieve to sift the flour into the bowl and mix briefly until just combined.

3. Scrape the mixture into the prepared springform pan and bake for 1 hour. When the cake is done, it will seem set but still slightly jiggly in the center. (Also, the surface will no longer be tacky to the touch.) Remove from the oven and allow the cake to cool in the pan for at least half an hour. Remove the sides of the springform pan, leaving the cake on the springform bottom, and refrigerate for at least 2 hours, or overnight, before serving. The cake may crack while it cools, which is okay.

ON THE PLATE   Slice into 12 wedges, using a knife dipped in hot water and wiped dry between slices. Serve with the blackberries.

A STEP AHEAD   This cake has the best texture if it is refrigerated overnight before serving. When the cake is completely cold, wrap it well in plastic wrap. The cake will keep, wrapped, in the refrigerator for 2 days.

IN THE GLASS   Go for a fine French premier cru Sauternes here.

CHEESE

I was first introduced to farmhouse cheese fifteen years ago when Sally Jackson and her husband drove up to Café Sport in their 1960 gray Volvo station wagon. Sally pulled down the tailgate and showed me the whole back of the car strewn with fragrant hay and eight or ten different homemade cheeses arranged on top. Some were wrapped in grape and chestnut leaves, others in clean dishtowels and cheesecloth; small cheeses floated in buckets of brine, fresh ricotta was in a big crock and you just scooped it out. We even had to bring our own scale out to weigh the cheese.

It was fascinating to listen to Sally talk about how she made the cheese herself. And I mean she really *made* the cheeses (and still does to this day). She didn't buy the milk from somebody else. She grew the hay that fed her goats and cows. She hand-milked them every morning. And then she made the cheese in her barn, fresh every day.

I bought Sally's cheese every chance I could. I couldn't order it though, because Sally didn't have a phone and just made cheese when she had enough milk. When she showed up, I bought as much as she had or as much I could afford because this was strictly cash business. Now we have an abundance of local cheese artisans. Here are some of my favorites:

- Sally Jackson cow cheese wrapped in chestnut leaves: After all these years, I'm still hooked on this fragrant, creamy, buttery cheese.
- Cougar Gold: Oddly enough, a 1930s government-sponsored research project on packaging cheese in cans led to the creation of this cheese. To this day, Cougar Gold is made in Pullman, Washington, on the campus of Washington State University, and it's still packaged in cans. As a matter of fact, people collect and age them all the time for vintage Cougar Gold. This nutty, tangy, Cheddarlike cheese is great crumbled into a newfangled Waldorf salad with slices of Fuji apples.
- Quillisascut Cabernet Crottin: This fresh goat-cheese round is washed in Cabernet lees, which are the dregs left after the fermentation process. You can see and taste the grape skins and seeds on the surface of this earthy, flavorful cheese. It's a wonderful addition to a cheese tray, or try eating a wedge with a slice of rustic bread.
- Oregon blue cheese: For the last fifteen years. I have used this relatively inexpensive and delicious Northwest blue cheese to make a creamy blue cheese dressing, which we serve at Etta's drizzled over wedges of crisp Iceberg lettuce.

TRIPLE COCONUT CREAM PIE

{ Makes one 9-inch pie; 6 to 8 servings }

Who would have thought that this pie would be a best-seller twelve years in a row? We call it triple coconut cream pie because there is coconut in the pastry filling, coconut in the crust, and more coconut on top. To garnish the pie at the restaurant, we toast unsweetened coconut, which is available in very large, attractive "chips," and shave big curls of white chocolate over the top. You may be able to find unsweetened coconut chips or large-shred coconut in a natural foods store or in the bulk section of your supermarket. This recipe is adapted from our friend Jim Dodge's fine book *American Baker* (Simon & Schuster, 1987).

FOR THE COCONUT PASTRY CREAM
2 cups milk
2 cups sweetened shredded coconut
1 vanilla bean, split in half lengthwise
2 large eggs
½ cup plus 2 tablespoons sugar
3 tablespoons all-purpose flour
¼ cup (½ stick) unsalted butter, softened

FOR THE PIE
One 9-inch Coconut Pie Shell (page 218),
*   prebaked and cooled*
2½ cups heavy cream, chilled
⅓ cup sugar
1 teaspoon pure vanilla extract

FOR GARNISH
2 ounces unsweetened "chip" or large-shred coconut
*   (about 1½ cups) or sweetened shredded coconut*
Chunks of white chocolate (4 to 6 ounces, to make
*   2 ounces of curls)*

1. To make the pastry cream, combine the milk and coconut in a medium saucepan. Scrape the seeds from the vanilla bean and add both the seeds and pod to the milk mixture. Place the saucepan over medium-high heat and stir occasionally until the mixture almost comes to a boil.

2. In a bowl, whisk together the eggs, sugar, and flour until well combined. Temper the eggs (to keep them from scrambling) by pouring a small amount (about ⅓ cup) of the scalded milk into the egg mixture while whisking. Then add the warmed egg mixture to the saucepan of milk and coconut. Whisk over medium-high heat until the pastry cream thickens and begins to bubble. Keep whisking until the mixture is very thick, 4 to 5 minutes more. Remove the saucepan from the heat. Add the butter and whisk until it melts. Remove and discard the vanilla pod. Transfer the pastry cream to a bowl and place it over a bowl of ice water. Stir occasionally until it is cool. Place a piece of plastic wrap directly on the surface of the pastry cream to prevent a crust from forming and refrigerate until completely cold. The pastry cream will thicken as it cools.

3. When the pastry cream is cold, fill the prebaked pie shell with it, smoothing the surface. In an electric mixer with the whisk, whip the heavy cream with the sugar and vanilla on medium speed. Gradually increase the speed to high and whip to peaks that are firm enough to hold their shape. Fill a pastry bag fitted with a star tip with the whipped cream and pipe it all over the surface of the pie, or spoon it over.

4. For the garnish, preheat the oven to 350°F. Spread the coconut chips on a baking sheet and toast in the oven, watching carefully and stirring once or twice, since coconut burns easily, until lightly browned, 7 to 8 minutes. Use a vegetable peeler to scrape about 2 ounces of the white chocolate into curls.

ON THE PLATE   Cut the pie into 6 to 8 wedges and place on dessert plates. Decorate each wedge of pie with white chocolate curls and the toasted coconut.

A STEP AHEAD   If not serving immediately, keep the pie refrigerated, covered with plastic wrap. The finished pie should be consumed within a day. Prepare the garnishes just before serving. The coconut pastry cream can be made a day ahead and stored chilled in the refrigerator, covered with plastic wrap as described above. Fill the pie shell and top it with whipped cream and garnishes when you are ready to serve the pie.

IN THE GLASS   Mouscato d'Asti, a delicious sweet sparkling white Muscat from Piedmont

Coconut Pie Shell

In this recipe you need to blind-bake the pie shell: bake an unfilled pastry-lined pan. If you don't have special pie weights, use dried beans to weight the crust to keep it from puffing up during baking. You can store your pie beans in a jar and use them over and over.

Very cold butter will give you a flakier crust. Put the diced butter in the freezer for 10 minutes before making your dough.

---

1 cup plus 2 tablespoons all-purpose flour

½ cup sweetened shredded coconut

½ cup (1 stick) cold unsalted butter, cut into ½-inch dice

2 teaspoons sugar

¼ teaspoon kosher salt

⅓ cup ice water, or more as needed

1. In a food processor, combine the flour, coconut, diced butter, sugar, and salt. Pulse to form coarse crumbs. Gradually add the water, a tablespoon at a time, pulsing each time. Use only as much water as is needed for the dough to hold together when gently pressed between your fingers; don't work the dough with your hands, just test it to see if it is holding. The dough will not form a ball or even clump together in the processor—it will still be quite loose.

2. Place a large sheet of plastic wrap on the counter and dump the coconut dough onto it. Pull the plastic wrap around the dough, forcing it into a rough flattened round with the pressure of the plastic wrap. Chill for 30 minutes to an hour before rolling.

3. To roll out the dough, unwrap the round of coconut dough and put it on a lightly floured work board. Flour the rolling pin and your hands. Roll the dough out into a circle about ⅛ inch thick. Lift the dough with a board scraper occasionally to check that it is not sticking and add more flour if it seems about to stick. Trim to a 12- to 13-inch circle.

4. Transfer the rolled dough to a 9-inch pie pan. Ease the dough loosely and gently into the pan. You don't want to stretch the dough at this point because it will shrink when it is baked. Trim any excess dough to a 1- to 1½-inch overhang. Turn the dough under along the rim of the pie pan and use your finger to flute the edge. Chill the unbaked pie shell at least an hour before

baking. This step prevents the dough from shrinking in the oven.

5. When you are ready to bake the piecrust, preheat the oven to 400°F. Place a sheet of aluminum foil or parchment paper in the pie shell and fill with dried beans. Bake the piecrust until the pastry rim is golden, 20 to 25 minutes. Remove the pie pan from the oven. Remove the foil and beans and return the piecrust to the oven. Bake until the bottom of the crust has golden-brown patches, 10 to 12 minutes.

Remove from the oven and allow to cool before filling.

A STEP AHEAD   The dough can be wrapped in plastic and stored in the refrigerator for a day or two, or frozen for a few weeks. Also the dough can be rolled out and fitted into a pie pan, and the unbaked pie shell can be wrapped in plastic and refrigerated or frozen for the same amounts of time. Frozen pie shells can be baked directly out of the freezer, without thawing; the baking times will be a bit longer.

Peak-of-Summer Berry Crisp

{ Makes 5 to 6 servings }

In the Northwest we're known for our berries—raspberries, strawberries, blueberries, blackberries, marionberries, salmonberries, huckleberries, boysenberries—the list seems endless at the peak of summer. Any combination of berries is fine in this recipe. You can make crisps all year-round, using whatever fruit is in season: rhubarb, apples, peaches . . .

We served this berry crisp one summer at the Bite of Seattle (a very large food event in the Seattle Center, near the Space Needle). It was voted best dessert of the Bite. Who knows how many hotel pans of crisp we made? The number was huge. We scrambled every night of the event to keep up with the demand, begging our produce purveyor for more berries, baking, baking, baking . . . and enjoying every sweet minute.

This very simple dessert, still warm from the oven, cries out for a scoop of homemade ice cream, and may be our favorite dessert of all.

FOR THE CRISP TOPPING
⅔ cup old-fashioned oats
⅔ cup firmly packed brown sugar
⅔ cup all-purpose flour
½ teaspoon ground cinnamon
6 tablespoons (¾ stick) cold unsalted butter,
    cut into dice

FOR THE BERRIES
2 cups fresh raspberries
2 cups fresh blueberries, picked over for stems
½ cup granulated sugar (if berries are very sweet,
    you may want to use less sugar)
2 tablespoons all-purpose flour

FOR GARNISH
*Vanilla ice cream or Sweetened Whipped Cream
(page 208)*

1. Preheat the oven to 350°F. To make the crisp topping, combine the oats, brown sugar, flour, and cinnamon in a bowl. Add the diced butter to the dry ingredients and blend with a pastry blender or the tips of your fingers until crumbly. Set aside.

2. In another bowl, toss the berries with the sugar and flour, using a rubber spatula. Pour the berries into a 9-inch pie pan. Cover the berries with the crisp topping. Set the filled pie pan on a baking sheet to catch any juices, then place in the oven and bake until the topping is golden brown and the juices are bubbling, 40 to 45 minutes.

ON THE PLATE   Spoon generous portions of the warm crisp into wide shallow bowls and top with scoops of ice cream or whipped cream.

A STEP AHEAD   If you enjoy making crisps, make a large batch of crisp topping (double or triple the recipe) and keep it in an airtight container in the freezer.

IN THE GLASS   Try an Auslese (Riesling) from Germany's Rhine or Mosel valleys.

BERRIES

From late summer to the first frost, all of Seattle seems to be out picking wild blackberries. Dark-purple fingers and stained lips are telltale signs of having spent days wrestling sweet treasures from the thorny vines. Some brave souls compete with black bears for huckleberries out in the hills, but if you want my advice, just walk downhill to the Pike Place Market and load up on the abundance of berries that overflow the farmers' tables. In addition to blackberries, blueberries, and raspberries, sometimes there'll be loganberries, marionberries, boysenberries, and black or red currants.

Blueberries are particularly plentiful in this area, coming from large blueberry producers, such as Overlake Blueberry Farm. Blueberries are frequently used in cobblers, cakes, muffins, and the like, but I enjoy their slightly spicy taste in savory dishes, too, such as fresh blueberry-corn relish.

The huckleberry is the blueberry's wild cousin. Not commercially cultivated, huckleberries are picked by recreational or professional foragers. Smaller than a blueberry, the huckleberry is generally less sweet, but full of flavor. I use huckleberries in a sauce for meat or roast duck. If you happen to go to the Huckleberry Festival in Coeur d'Alene, Idaho, be sure to have a huckleberry milk shake. It's out of this world.

Since wild blackberries grow everywhere, including my backyard, we always manage to have a bowl of them with my daughter Loretta's favorite buttermilk pancakes. During the height of the season, in mid- to late August, blackberries are cheap and superabundant. We use them in deep-dish blackberry pies and gorgeous dark purple sorbets, among other dishes.

Washington State is the number two producer of cranberries in the country. You can drive out to Long Beach Peninsula in southwest Washington to see cranberry bogs along the coast. Cranberries are great for their bright color and tart flavor. I like them best in a cranberry-apple crisp; they also make savory jams for serving with pork or venison. At Palace Kitchen, we steep cranberries and vanilla beans in vodka to make cranberry martinis.

Gooseberries are less widely used, but these large, tart, translucent, golden green globes are very appealing. They're easiest made into a pureed and sieved sauce, otherwise you have to "top and tail" (remove the stem and blossom end) each individual berry. The pale green gooseberry jam (and other berry jams) made by Deer Mountain Jam in Granite Falls, Washington, is a particular favorite.

The Washington strawberry season is short and sweet, and I really mean short. Some years, it seems like we get abundant berries from the local crop for only a week or so. They are fragile, spoil quickly, and don't travel well. A whole season's crop can be damaged by too much rain at the wrong time, but their fragrance and sweet taste beat all others, in my humble opinion. Jackie, Loretta, and I try to make at least one trip to a U-Pick strawberry farm each summer. Naturally, most of the berries we pick are eaten on the spot, but if any make it into our pails, I take them home and make a batch of my mom's favorite freezer jam, using the recipe right off the pectin box, just as she always did.

ICE CREAMS AND SORBETS

We started making our own ice cream at Dahlia with a bucket-type ice cream maker that used ice and salt. Every day we made a big mess in the hallway and about two quarts of fantastic ice cream. Now we have a large professional ice cream maker that turns out a couple of gallons in fifteen minutes.

Ice cream makers are now available in all price ranges, from fancy electric ones with a self-enclosed freezer to the type that uses a prefrozen canister to the old-fashioned bucket and churn. An ice cream maker, like a food processor and a rice cooker, has become an essential tool in my home kitchen.

We make the custard bases for our ice creams a day ahead and chill them overnight. You can use the ice cream custard as soon as it is cold, but allowing it to ripen in the refrigerator overnight improves the texture. A sorbet mixture can be run in your ice cream machine as soon as it is well chilled.

STAR ANISE ICE CREAM

{ Makes about 1 quart }

We've experimented with ice creams flavored with almost every spice, herb, fruit, and liquor imaginable. This simple infusion with star anise was a big success. If you love the flavor of star anise, it would be fun to pair this with our Five-Spice Angel Food Cake (page 211). It would also make a good finish for an Asian-influenced dinner, such as Wok-Fried Crab with Ginger and Lemongrass (page 90).

---

12 star anise
2 cups heavy cream
2 cups milk
1 cup sugar
8 large egg yolks

1. Crush the star anise with a rolling pin or the bottom of a heavy pan. In a saucepan, combine the heavy cream, milk, sugar, and crushed star anise over medium-high heat. Bring the mixture to a scald (just below the boiling point), then remove from the heat and set the saucepan aside to allow the flavor to infuse for an hour.

2. When you are ready to proceed, return the saucepan of cream mixture to the heat and reheat to the scalding point. Place the egg yolks in a bowl and whisk until pale yellow. Add a ladle of hot cream to the yolks to temper the eggs (to keep them from scrambling) and whisk briefly. Then pour the warmed yolks into the saucepan and cook over medium-low heat, stirring, until the mixture is thick enough to coat the back of a spoon, about 12 minutes. Immediately pour the custard through a fine-mesh strainer into a bowl. Set the bowl of custard over a larger bowl of ice water. When cool, cover with plastic wrap and refrigerate several hours or overnight.

3. When the ice cream custard is completely cold, pour it into your ice cream maker and freeze according to the manufacturer's instructions. Remove the ice cream to a container. Cover and freeze for a few hours or overnight until completely firm.

ON THE PLATE Serve a few scoops in a pretty bowl with some slices of mango, starfruit, or papaya, and a crisp cookie.

A STEP AHEAD Store in an airtight container in the freezer for a week or more.

IN THE GLASS Try a traditional green tea.

BING CHERRY ICE CREAM

{ Makes 1½ quarts }

Cherries are a major Washington State crop and we look forward to them every year. You can make this ice cream with any kind of sweet cherry. It is delicious eaten plain, or serve scoops of it with our Peak-of-Summer Berry Crisp (page 220) or Peach Cornmeal Shortcakes (page 209), or use it to make Baked Alaska (page 196).

The cherries need to be macerated and the custard must chill a day ahead, so plan accordingly. If you like, you can save the brandy syrup from macerating the cherries and add it to a fruit compote or drizzle over a fresh fruit salad.

FOR THE MACERATED CHERRIES

1 cup sugar

1 cup water

*2 cups stemmed, pitted, and quartered Bing cherries
or other sweet cherries*

3 tablespoons good-quality brandy or Cognac

FOR THE ICE CREAM CUSTARD

2 cups heavy cream

2 cups milk

1 cup sugar

1 vanilla bean, split in half

8 large egg yolks

1. To macerate the cherries, place the sugar and water in a saucepan and bring to a simmer, stirring until the sugar is dissolved. Add the cherries and simmer for 5 minutes. Remove from the heat and pour the cherries and syrup into a bowl. Stir in the brandy. Chill, covered with plastic wrap, in the refrigerator overnight.

2. To make the ice cream custard, place the heavy cream, milk, and sugar in a saucepan. Scrape the seeds from the vanilla bean and add both the seeds and pod to the cream mixture. Place the saucepan over medium-high heat and bring to a scald (just below the boiling point), stirring to dissolve the sugar. Remove the saucepan from the heat. In a bowl, whisk the egg yolks until pale yellow. Add a ladle of scalded cream to the bowl of yolks and whisk to temper them (to keep them from scrambling). Pour the warmed yolks into the saucepan with the cream mixture and return to medium-low heat, stirring until the custard is thick enough to coat the back of a spoon, about 12 minutes. Immediately pour the custard through a fine-mesh strainer into a bowl. Set the bowl of custard over a larger bowl of ice water. When cool, cover with plastic wrap and refrigerate overnight.

3. To finish the ice cream, pour the cherries into a strainer and drain off the syrup. Reserve the syrup for another use, if desired. Set the cherries aside.

4. Freeze the chilled custard in an ice cream maker according to the manufacturer's instructions. Remove the ice cream

from the machine while it is still slightly soft. Fold in the drained cherries with a rubber spatula. Place the ice cream in a container and cover. Freeze for a few hours or overnight until completely firm.

ON THE PLATE   Serve scoops of this in a bowl accompanied by crisp cookies. Since chocolate and cherries are delicious together, you might want to serve it with Chocolate Shortbread (page 198) and Chocolate Sauce (page 200).

A STEP AHEAD   Store in an airtight container in the freezer for a week or more.

IN THE GLASS   A Clear Creek cherry brandy from Oregon or a nice kirschwasser

CLEAR CREEK DISTILLERY

The fragrant, pure fruit brandies that Stephen McCarthy makes at Clear Creek Distillery in Portland, Oregon, are distilled from locally grown pears, apples, plums, and cherries and are dry and clear, like *eaux-de-vie* or *alcools blancs*, French terms for clear distilled spirit. These light brandies are the perfect accompaniment to many of our desserts, especially those made with fruit, like Peak-of-Summer Berry Crisp (page 220). Stephen's family has been growing apples and pears for many years and he still gets much of his ripe fruit from family-owned orchards. His brandies are a good example of the way local artisans are transforming the Northwest's rich agricultural resources into world-class foods and beverages. Stephen also makes grappa and marc from by-products of the wine industry.

OREGON PINOT NOIR
RASPBERRY SORBET

{ Makes 1½ quarts }

We were inspired by Michele Scicolone's wonderful Italian dessert cookbook *La Dolce Vita* (William Morrow, 1993) to make this sorbet. We like to use a good Pinot Noir from Oregon, preferably from the Willamette Valley. And, of course, Washington produces copious amounts of berries every summer, so we're always looking for ways of using the bounty. The wine gives this sorbet a lovely pink-red color and (because the alcohol lowers the freezing point) a smooth, creamy texture. It is equally delicious made with blackberries.

---

2 pints fresh raspberries
1½ cups sugar
1 cup Oregon Pinot Noir (Adelsheim is one of my favorites)
2 cups water

Combine the berries, sugar, wine, and water in a saucepan over medium-high heat. Bring to a boil, stirring occasionally to dissolve the sugar, then reduce the heat to medium-low and simmer for 15 minutes. Remove the pan from the heat and pass the mixture through a food mill, using the fine plate. Or, with a rubber spatula, force the mixture through a sieve. Chill the mixture completely, then freeze in an ice cream machine following the manufacturer's directions. Transfer the sorbet to a container, cover, and freeze for several hours or overnight until firm.

ON THE PLATE Serve this with a few fresh berries and some cookies for a nice light ending to a rich meal.

A STEP AHEAD Store the sorbet in an airtight container in the freezer. The wine flavor begins to fade after a few days.

IN THE GLASS Whidbey Island Loganberry liqueur

GINGERSNAPS

A simple, homey cookie, but one of our favorites. Grated fresh ginger, instead of powdered ginger, gives these cookies the snap the name promises. We serve gingersnaps with creamy desserts, such as ice creams, sorbets, or custards. These flavor-filled cookies are best when they are still very slightly warm from the oven.

---

1 cup sugar, plus ½ cup more for rolling

¾ cup (1½ sticks) unsalted butter, softened

1 large egg

¼ cup molasses

2 teaspoons peeled and grated fresh ginger

2 cups all-purpose flour

2 teaspoons baking soda

½ teaspoon kosher salt

½ teaspoon ground cinnamon

1. Preheat the oven to 350°F. In a large bowl with an electric mixer or with a wooden spoon, cream the butter and 1 cup of the sugar until light and fluffy. Add the egg, molasses, and ginger and mix to combine. In a small bowl, combine the flour, baking soda, salt, and cinnamon. Add the dry ingredients to the wet ingredients and mix to combine. Refrigerate the dough, covered with plastic wrap, for at least an hour before shaping the cookies.

2. Sprinkle the remaining ½ cup sugar on a plate. Form ¾-inch balls of the dough and roll the balls in the sugar before placing them on parchment paper–lined baking sheets. Press the balls of dough flat with the palm of your hand. The cookies should be spaced 2 or 3 inches apart after they are flattened. Bake until golden brown and set around the edges but still slightly soft in the center, 7 to 8 minutes, turning the baking sheet around in the oven halfway through the baking time. Remove from the oven and allow the cookies to cool on the baking sheet before removing them with a metal spatula. The gingersnaps will firm up as they cool.

A STEP AHEAD Gingersnaps will stay fresh for a few days in an airtight container at room temperature. You can also keep the baked and completely cooled cookies in the freezer, tightly wrapped in plastic wrap, for a week or two. The cookie dough can be made ahead, tightly wrapped, and refrigerated for up to a week, or frozen for even longer.

Seattle in the palm of your hand

Breakfast: Wake Up and Smell the Coffee

IN SEATTLE YOU could make an argument that the most important moment of the day is when you have your first cup of coffee or espresso (or your second or your third or your fourth). Since you probably need to eat something with your coffee, a breakfast chapter is essential for this book. At Etta's the line forms early for brunch every weekend, so we've included some of our most popular dishes, like corned beef hash with habañero ketchup and huevos rancheros with black beans.

Some folks feel really strongly about what they eat for breakfast. It's where they have the most established rituals, when they know exactly what they want before they walk in the door. For this reason, I'm very careful when I try to introduce new breakfast dishes at Etta's. One customer exclaimed when he couldn't find corned beef hash on the menu (it was temporarily sold out), "You've ruined my life!" A bit extreme, but typical of a breakfast eater. While I could (and do) change the dinner menu seven nights a week, God forbid I touch breakfast!

BREAKFAST IN SEATTLE

If you're going to be "sleepless in Seattle," you might as well have breakfast. The best place to do that is the Pike Place Market. If you want the whole nine yards and then some—a plate full of fried eggs, hash browns, sausage, bacon, and toast—try the Athenian. It's one of the last untouched Seattle joints with a great view of the Sound. You'll share the premises with a colorful mix—guys in T-shirts having a beer and a shot for breakfast, workers waiting for the market to open, and tourists looking for adventure and Tom Hanks.

If you want a more genteel breakfast in gentrified surroundings—truffled eggs and golden brioche—try Café Campagne in Post Alley. For a quick croissant and a shot of espresso, go to Le Panier. And for a kick-ass Saturday or Sunday brunch of homemade corned beef hash or huevos rancheros with a great Bloody Mary there is, of course, our very own Etta's.

ATHENIAN INN
1517 Pike Place
(206) 624-7166

CAFÉ CAMPAGNE
1600 Post Alley
(206) 728-2233

LE PANIER
1902 Pike Place
(206) 441-3669

ETTA'S SEAFOOD
2020 Western Avenue
(206) 443-6000

Corned Beef Hash with Yukon Gold Potatoes

{ Makes 4 servings }

There is only one place to get good corned beef in Seattle—The Market House. For years we've been serving their succulent briskets, made into hash at Etta's for brunch. You can see by the recipe that I go heavy on the beef. You can make your own adjustments to the meat-and-potato mix, if you prefer. Cook the eggs any way you like. I love the flavor and color of Yukon Gold potatoes in this hash, but you can use any kind of potato.

Note that it takes three hours to cook the corned beef, so you probably should do this the day before you want to make the hash. Or you could use 3 cups of cooked and chopped leftover corned beef for the hash.

---

2 pounds uncooked corned beef

½ pound Yukon Gold potatoes or other smooth-skinned potatoes

5 tablespoons unsalted butter or a combination of butter and bacon fat

⅔ cup diced onions

1 poblano chile, seeded and minced (about ⅔ cup)

1 carrot, diced (about ⅓ cup diced)

2 tablespoons plus 1 teaspoon bottled chili sauce (such as Heinz)

Kosher salt

8 large eggs

Habanero Ketchup (recipe follows)

1. Place the corned beef (and any spices that were in the bag) in a large pot and cover with water. Bring to a boil, then reduce the heat to a simmer and cook until very tender, about 3 hours, adding more water as needed to keep the meat covered. Remove the corned beef from the pot and allow to cool. Remove and discard the fat from the corned beef and shred the meat by pulling it apart with your fingers. Roughly chop the shredded meat and set it aside.

2. Peel the potatoes, then cut into ½-inch dice. Place the potatoes in a pot of cold salted water and bring to a boil. Reduce the heat to a simmer and cook just until the potatoes are tender, about 15 minutes total cooking time. Drain the potatoes and set aside.

3. Preheat the oven to 200°F. Melt 3 tablespoons of the butter in a 12-inch sauté pan over high heat. Add the potatoes, onions, poblano, and carrot and fry, stirring occasionally, until the potatoes begin to brown and the vegetables are soft. Add the corned beef and stir in the chili sauce. Season to taste with salt. Add the remaining 2 tablespoons butter to the pan and continue to cook over high heat, tossing or turning the hash with a spatula, until it starts to get crisp and brown. Set the pan in the oven to keep the hash warm while you prepare the eggs any way you like them: poached, scrambled, over easy, or sunny side up.

ON THE PLATE   Divide the hash among 4 plates and top each with 2 cooked eggs. If desired, serve with habañero ketchup.

A STEP AHEAD   You can cook the corned beef a day ahead. Shred and chop it and store it, covered, in the refrigerator. Or you can freeze the chopped corned beef for several weeks.

IN THE GLASS   Black coffee

Habanero Ketchup

Habanero chiles are hot, hot, hot. Be sure to wash your hands with soap and water after handling them or wear gloves. Dried habaneros are easier to find than fresh ones. For this recipe use a whole dried habanero or a fresh one cut in half. Or substitute a few dashes of a habanero-based hot sauce to taste. If all else fails, use a sliced fresh jalapeño.

½ cup ketchup
⅓ cup orange juice
1 dried habanero chile
1 tablespoon molasses
½ teaspoon Worcestershire sauce
2 cloves

In a small saucepan over medium-high heat, combine the ketchup, orange juice, habanero, molasses, Worcestershire, and cloves. Simmer for 5 minutes and strain; discard the habanero and cloves. Let cool and serve. This keeps, refrigerated, for a week or more.

PASTRAMI

You don't generally hear pastrami and Seattle mentioned in the same sentence. You're more likely to find out about Dungeness crab or salmon or Willapa Bay oysters. But I'm here to tell you that some of the best pastrami outside of New York or L.A.'s west side is made by a local butcher who can't keep up with the crowds clamoring for his spicy pastrami sandwiches.

He's even got a local Seattle twist: All the leftover ends are chopped up and wrapped in a yeasty dough and *voilà*—pastrami humbow.

Roxy's Deli
1909 First Avenue
(206) 441-6768

ESPRESSO CHILE GLAZED HAM

{ Makes 16 or more servings }

Every Easter I get my favorite apple-wood–smoked ham from eastern Washington and add a little Seattle magic to it: some Starbucks espresso, a touch of hot chile paste, and a bit of aromatic orange zest and—bingo—my version of red-eye gravy. Add scalloped potatoes and hot-cross buns and call it brunch.

For this recipe use a fully cooked smoked ham preferably wood smoked with no water added. Trim the outside layer of fat and skin all the way back to the pink meat, so when you're ready to carve you don't cut away all the flavorful glaze.

Half a fully cooked ham (about 8 pounds)
1 quart fresh orange juice
1 tablespoon grated orange zest
1 cup firmly packed brown sugar
1 cup Kahlúa or other coffee-flavored liqueur
1 tablespoon Chinese chile paste with garlic or sambal olek (page 15)
½ teaspoon freshly ground black pepper
2 shots (about ¼ cup total) brewed espresso or 1 tablespoon instant espresso powder, like Medaglio d'Oro

1. Preheat the oven to 325°F. Cut the thick layer of fat and the skin from the ham and discard. Place the ham in a roasting pan. For easier cleanup, line the pan with aluminum foil, because the glaze will drip off and burn on the bottom of the pan. Roast the ham for 1 hour.

2. While the ham is roasting, make the glaze. Combine the orange juice and zest, brown sugar, Kahlúa, chile paste, and pepper in a large saucepan. Bring to a boil over high heat, then reduce the heat to medium and simmer the mixture until it is reduced by about half and is as thick as maple syrup, about 35 minutes. Whisk in the espresso or espresso powder. You should have almost 2 cups of glaze. You are going to use half of this glaze to brush the ham while it is roasting and reserve the other half for brushing on the ham after it is sliced.

3. After the first hour of cooking, brush the ham with the glaze. Roast for another hour, brushing with the glaze every 15 minutes. Since the ham is already cooked, you just need to warm it all the way through. Check for an internal temperature of 130° to 140°F using an instant-read meat thermometer. Remove the ham from the oven when it is nicely browned and warmed through.

ON THE PLATE We like to serve this with warm cornbread (page 156). For a lovely presentation, slice half the ham and arrange the slices up against the unsliced part on a big platter. Brush the slices with the remaining glaze.

A STEP AHEAD The glaze can be made a few days ahead and stored, tightly covered, in the refrigerator.

IN THE GLASS A sparkling Prosecco from Italy's Veneto is the perfect brunch wine.

Black Bean Huevos Rancheros

I can't help but think of my old friend and co-worker Francisco Fornes every time I make this dish. Francisco was a beloved friend of ours who worked with us at Dahlia for some years. He was tragically killed in a car accident. Francisco made the greatest huevos rancheros I ever ate, and his secret was frying the tortillas in duck fat. I always save the fat from roast duck, and whenever I fry up a batch of tortillas for this dish I remember Francisco. If you don't have duck fat on hand, vegetable oil will do.

---

1 cup dried black beans, picked over and rinsed

1 recipe Pico de Gallo (page 132)

5 tablespoons fresh orange juice

½ teaspoon cumin seeds, toasted and ground (page 21)

Kosher salt and freshly ground black pepper

¼ cup vegetable oil or rendered duck fat

4 flour tortillas

8 large eggs

½ pound pepper Jack cheese, grated (about 2 cups)

1 ripe avocado, pitted, peeled, and sliced

1. Put the beans in a pot and cover generously with water. Bring to a boil, then turn the heat down to a simmer and cook until the beans are tender, 1½ to 2 hours. Drain. Return the beans to a medium saucepan with 1 cup of the pico de gallo (save the rest for garnish), the orange juice, and cumin. Heat the beans until warm. Season to taste with salt and pepper.

2. Heat the oil or duck fat in a medium sauté pan over medium-high heat. Fry the tortillas in the hot fat until golden brown and crispy, about 1 minute per side. Cook the eggs to your liking: poached, scrambled, over easy, or sunny side up.

ON THE PLATE Placed a fried tortilla on each plate. Spoon a mound of warm black beans onto the center of each tortilla. Sprinkle generously with grated cheese. Top with 2 eggs. Garnish with slices of avocado and a spoonful of pico de gallo.

A STEP AHEAD You can cook the beans a day ahead and refrigerate them, or soak them a day ahead and they will cook faster. The tortillas can be cooked ahead and warmed in a preheated 400°F oven for 5 minutes.

IN THE GLASS Ice-cold Corona beer with lime

GRAVLAX

{ Makes 1 pound }

Most of the twenty-five or so years that I have lived in Seattle have been spent in the Norwegian enclave of Ballard. It is such a treat to stroll through Olsen's Scandinavian Foods and pick up foods like potato *lefsa*; air-dried lamb legs (somewhat like prosciutto); herring, herring, and more herring; potato sausage, *lütefisk,* and gravlax. While the tradition in Ballard is to cure salmon with dill, experiment with your own flavor preferences.

It's best to use a piece of salmon that is no more than an inch or two thick. A thicker piece will take longer to cure. A salmon fillet with the skin on will help you slice the gravlax paper thin after it is cured.

FOR THE GRAVLAX CURE

⅔ *cup kosher salt*

⅔ *cup granulated sugar*

¼ *cup firmly packed brown sugar*

1½ teaspoons paprika

1 teaspoon ground juniper berries

1 teaspoon fennel seeds, ground

¼ *teaspoon cayenne*

FOR THE SALMON

1¼ pounds salmon fillet, preferably skin on, pin bones removed (see How to Pin-Bone Salmon, below)

1. Combine the gravlax cure ingredients in a small bowl. Sprinkle the bottom of a non-reactive baking pan with about ½ inch of the cure and place the fish in the pan, skin side down. Blanket the fish with the remaining cure, which should form a layer about 1½ inches thick.

2. Cover the salmon with a piece of wax paper and another smaller pan, then weight it down with a few cans. Store in the refrigerator for 2 to 3 days until the salmon is quite firm to the touch; the exact amount of time will depend on how thick your piece of salmon is. Remove the wax paper and the cans, and then use a rubber spatula to scrape the cure from the salmon. Remove the salmon from the pan and briefly rinse it, then pat it dry with paper towels. Slice the gravlax very thinly on the bias.

A STEP AHEAD   Gravlax will keep for a week, covered in plastic wrap, in the refrigerator.

IN THE GLASS   Ice-cold vodka—straight

HOW TO PIN-BONE SALMON

Salmon has rows of pin bones in its flesh. Run your fingers along the surface of the fillet to locate them. Then pull them out one by one with a tweezers or needle-nose pliers.

WILD RICE WAFFLES WITH SALMON GRAVLAX AND CHIVE CRÈME FRAÎCHE

{ Makes 8 servings }

These would be great for breakfast or brunch, or as an appetizer or first course: Cut each waffle into quarters and serve a quarter of a waffle with a slice of gravlax and a small dollop of crème fraîche on top. If you don't want to make your own gravlax, you can substitute thinly sliced smoked salmon.

⅔ cup raw wild rice
2 cups all-purpose flour
1½ teaspoons baking powder
½ teaspoon baking soda
1 teaspoon kosher salt
1¾ cups buttermilk
4 large eggs, separated
10 tablespoons (1¼ sticks) unsalted butter, melted
1 pound thinly sliced gravlax (page 235)
1 cup Chive Crème Fraîche (recipe follows)
8 fresh chive stems or 8 chive blossoms

1. Bring a large pot of salted water to a boil. Add the wild rice and cook, stirring occasionally, until tender, 25 to 30 minutes. Drain and set aside to cool. You should have about 2 cups cooked wild rice.

2. Combine the flour, baking powder, baking soda, and salt in a bowl. In another bowl, mix together the buttermilk, egg yolks, melted butter, and wild rice. Add the dry ingredients to the wet ingredients. In an electric mixer with the whisk attachment, whip the whites to soft peaks. Fold the whites into the batter half at a time.

3. Preheat the oven to 400°F and heat your waffle iron. Cook the waffles until golden brown according to the manufacturer's instructions. Spray the waffle iron with vegetable oil spray to keep the waffles from sticking. Use about ½ cup to ⅔ cup batter per waffle. You should have 8 waffles. When all the waffles are cooked, place them on a baking sheet and warm them in the oven for 5 minutes.

ON THE PLATE Place a waffle on each plate. Lay slices of gravlax over each waffle and dollop with crème fraîche. Garnish with chives or with chive blossoms, or for a real splurge, some delicious caviar.

A STEP AHEAD You can make the waffles a few hours ahead and leave them at room temperature. When you are ready to serve, reheat them in the oven as directed in the recipe.

IN THE GLASS Aquavit is a Dutch caraway liqueur—it makes a fabulous Bloody Mary.

Chive Crème Fraîche

{ Makes 1½ cups }

This is also delicious on poached or grilled fish.

1 cup crème fraîche (page 255)
¼ cup thinly sliced fresh chives
Kosher salt and freshly ground black pepper

In a small bowl, combine the crème fraîche and chives and season to taste with salt and pepper. This keeps, refrigerated, for 3 days.

ORANGE CINNAMON FRENCH TOAST

{ Makes 4 servings }

There's not an ounce of France in me that I know of, but my daughter, Loretta, thinks I make the best French toast. The key is getting nice, crusty, golden-brown slices, and giving them enough time in the oven to cook the center all the way through. No slimy, mushy centers in this house!

6 large eggs
2 cups half-and-half
⅔ cup fresh orange juice
Grated zest from 1 orange
⅓ cup pure maple syrup, plus more for serving
1 teaspoon ground cinnamon
¼ teaspoon freshly grated nutmeg
8 slices hearty bread, 1 inch thick
¼ cup (½ stick) unsalted butter, plus more for serving

1. Preheat the oven to 375°F. Combine the eggs, half-and-half, orange juice and zest, maple syrup, cinnamon, and nutmeg in a bowl. Soak the bread thoroughly in the custard mixture.

2. Heat a large sauté pan over medium-high heat and add 2 tablespoons of the butter. Once the butter is melted and beginning to foam, place 4 slices of the soaked bread in the pan. Fry the bread until golden brown, about 3 minutes, then flip and brown the other side. Remove the French toast to a baking pan and brown the remaining 4 slices in the remaining 2 tablespoons butter. When all the bread is in the baking pan, put the pan in the oven for 5 to 10 minutes, until the French toast is hot and cooked through.

ON THE PLATE Serve with lots of butter and warm maple syrup and garnish with fresh berries or sliced banana, if you like.

A STEP AHEAD The custard can be made a day ahead and stored, covered tightly with plastic wrap, in the refrigerator.

IN THE GLASS It has to be a French 75. In a cocktail shaker filled with ice, combine 1 ounce gin and 1 ounce Sweet & Sour. Shake. Strain into a martini glass and top with 2 ounces Champagne.

LORETTA'S BUTTERMILK PANCAKES
WITH WILD BLACKBERRIES

{ Makes 6 servings }

In Seattle blackberries grow like ferocious weeds in everybody's backyard. When I get tired of whacking them down, sometimes I stop and pick a few to have with these pancakes. My daughter, Loretta, likes silver dollar–sized pancakes, but you can make them larger if you like.

Pure maple syrup is best, and if you can find grade B maple syrup, buy it. It's slightly less expensive, but darker and even more flavorful than grade A.

---

3 cups all-purpose flour

1 tablespoon sugar

1½ teaspoons baking soda

1½ teaspoons kosher salt

1 teaspoon baking powder

2 large eggs

3½ cups buttermilk

¼ cup (½ stick) unsalted butter, melted, plus more
    for serving

Pure maple syrup

1 pint fresh blackberries

In a bowl, sift together the flour, sugar, baking soda, salt, and baking powder. In another bowl, combine the eggs and buttermilk, then add the melted butter. Gradually add the wet mixture to the dry mixture, stirring with a wooden spoon until just smooth. Heat a nonstick griddle over medium-high heat. Drop the batter by the ¼ cupful (or, if you want to make the tiny silver dollar pancakes Loretta likes, drop the batter by the tablespoonful) into the hot pan and cook until full of bubbles and the bottom side is golden (lift the pancake with a spatula to check the bottom), 2 to 3 minutes. Flip and cook the other side, about 1 more minute.

ON THE PLATE Serve these pancakes drenched with melted butter and maple syrup along with a bowl of the blackberries.

IN THE GLASS Fresh-squeezed grapefruit juice

GRANDMA DOUGLAS' SCHNECKEN

{ Makes 12 to 14 schnecken }

As long as I can remember, and long before that, my family has made these rolls (similar to cinnamon rolls) for most every holiday. My brother and sisters always fought for the gooey middle rolls, but I love the ultracaramelized golden-brown corners.

FOR THE DOUGH
½ cup (1 stick) unsalted butter, plus more to butter
   bowl and pans, as needed
1 cup milk
5 tablespoons granulated sugar
1 tablespoon active dry yeast
1½ teaspoons kosher salt
1 large egg plus 1 large yolk
3 to 3½ cups all-purpose flour, as needed

FOR THE SUGAR-PECAN TOPPING
¾ cup (1½ sticks) unsalted butter
¾ cup firmly packed brown sugar
¼ cup light corn syrup
¾ cup chopped pecans

FOR THE CINNAMON SUGAR FILLING
¼ cup (½ stick) unsalted butter
1 cup granulated sugar
1 tablespoon ground cinnamon

1. To make the dough, melt the ½ cup butter in a small saucepan over medium-low heat. Add the milk and granulated sugar and heat just to lukewarm (about 110°F), stirring to dissolve the sugar. Pour the warm milk mixture into a bowl. Stir in the yeast. Allow the mixture to sit for 10 minutes. Stir in the salt. Beat the whole egg and yolk together and add to the yeast mixture. Stir in the flour 1 cup at a time until you have a sticky dough. Scrape the dough out onto a floured work surface and knead, about 5 minutes, adding a little more flour as necessary, until you have a nice smooth dough. Butter a large bowl. Place the dough in the prepared bowl and cover with plastic wrap. Put the bowl in a warm place and allow the dough to rise for 2 hours until tripled in volume.

2. Meanwhile, prepare the pan. Spray a 9 × 13-inch baking pan with vegetable oil spray or brush it with butter. To prepare the sugar-pecan topping, melt the butter with the brown sugar and corn syrup in a small saucepan over medium-low heat, stirring to combine. Remove from the heat and spread the mixture over the bottom of the pan. Sprinkle with the chopped pecans.

3. Punch down the dough and turn it out of the bowl onto a lightly floured work surface. Knead for a minute, then use a lightly floured rolling pin to roll the dough into a rectangle about 15 × 12 inches and ⅛ inch thick. To make the cinnamon sugar filling, melt the butter in a small saucepan over medium-low heat and allow it to cool. Brush the butter thoroughly over the surface of the

dough. In a bowl, mix together the granulated sugar and cinnamon. Sprinkle the cinnamon sugar evenly over the melted butter. Roll the rectangle up, like a jelly roll, along one long edge.

4. Slice the log of rolled dough into 1-inch-thick slices and arrange the slices, cut side up, in the prepared pan. Cover the pan with a piece of plastic wrap (you can spray the wrap with vegetable oil spray to be sure it doesn't stick to the dough) and allow it to rise in a warm place for about 40 minutes.

5. Preheat the oven to 350°F. Bake the schnecken until golden brown, 35 to 40 minutes. Check them occasionally during the baking time and, if they seem to be browning too quickly, cover them with a sheet of aluminum foil.

6. Remove the pan from the oven. Allow the schnecken to cool for 5 to 10 minutes, then turn them out of the pan while still warm by inverting the pan over a large platter or a baking sheet. Serve warm.

A STEP AHEAD You can prepare the schnecken a day ahead up to the point of forming the rolls and setting them in the prepared pan. Cover the pan with plastic wrap and store them, unbaked, in the refrigerator overnight. When you are ready to bake the schnecken, remove the pan from the refrigerator and set it in a warm place for about an hour. Then bake as directed in the recipe.

IN THE GLASS Café latte, of course

CHERRY ALMOND SCONES

{ Makes 8 scones }

We serve these scrumptious scones during brunch at Etta's where they disappear quickly. We've made lots of different flavors through the years, but my all-time favorite is the cherry almond.

FOR THE SCONES
2½ cups all-purpose flour
¼ cup sugar
1 teaspoon baking powder
1 teaspoon grated lemon zest
¾ teaspoon kosher salt
¼ teaspoon baking soda
*10 tablespoons (1¼ sticks) cold unsalted butter, cut
    into dice*
½ cup dried cherries, coarsely chopped
*½ cup sliced blanched almonds, toasted (page 39)
    and cooled*
¾ cup buttermilk
¼ teaspoon pure vanilla extract
¼ teaspoon pure almond extract

FOR BRUSHING THE SCONES
¼ cup heavy cream
¼ cup sugar

1. Preheat the oven to 425°F. In a large bowl, combine the flour, sugar, baking powder, lemon zest, salt, and baking soda. Cut the butter into the dry mixture, using a pastry blender or two knives, until the mixture looks like coarse cornmeal. Mix in the cherries and almonds.

2. Gradually pour in the buttermilk and extracts and mix with a wooden spoon or rubber spatula until the dough just comes together. Do not overmix. Turn out the dough onto a lightly floured work surface and pat it with your hands into a 9-inch round about 1 inch thick. Cut the dough into 8 wedges with a floured knife or metal board scraper. Place the scones on a parchment paper–lined baking sheet. Brush them with the heavy cream and generously sprinkle them with the sugar. Bake for 10 minutes, then reduce the oven temperature to 350°F and finish baking until golden brown and cooked through, about 15 minutes.

ON THE PLATE   Serve warm with butter and honey or jam, if desired.

A STEP AHEAD   These are best eaten right away, preferably while they're still warm from the oven.

IN THE GLASS   Steamed almond milk

SOUR CREAM BLUEBERRY COFFEE CAKE

{ Makes 12 servings }

This simple, moist, old-fashioned coffee cake makes an absolutely delightful treat for breakfast, and it's another way to use local berries in the summer. You can substitute any other kinds of berries for the blueberries or even use frozen berries if they're IQF—individually quick frozen—not in syrup. If you like nuts, add a cup of chopped walnuts, pecans, or hazelnuts to the streusel mixture.

FOR THE STREUSEL
½ cup all-purpose flour
½ cup firmly packed brown sugar
1 teaspoon ground cinnamon
6 tablespoons (¾ stick) cold unsalted butter, cut into dice

FOR THE COFFEE CAKE
2½ cups all-purpose flour
2 teaspoons baking powder
1 teaspoon baking soda
1 teaspoon salt
1 cup (2 sticks) unsalted butter, softened, plus a little more for buttering the pan
1 cup granulated sugar
3 large eggs
1 cup sour cream
1 tablespoon pure vanilla extract
2 cups blueberries, raspberries, or blackberries, picked over

TO SERVE
Fresh berries and mint leaves for garnish

1. To make the streusel, combine the flour, brown sugar, and cinnamon in a bowl. Add the diced butter and blend with a pastry blender or the tips of your fingers until crumbly. Set aside.

2. To make the coffee cake, preheat the oven to 350°F. Spray a 9 × 13-inch baking pan with vegetable oil spray or butter the pan. In a bowl, sift together the flour, baking powder, baking soda, and salt and set aside. In an electric mixer with the paddle attachment or with a wooden spoon in a large bowl, cream the butter and granulated sugar together until light and fluffy. Add the eggs one at a time, beating well after each addition. Mix in the sour cream and vanilla. Add the sifted dry ingredients, a third at a time, and mix just until everything is blended together. Fold in the berries gently with a rubber spatula. The batter will be very thick.

3. Scrape the batter into the prepared pan and spread it evenly with the spatula. Sprinkle the streusel over the surface of the cake. Bake until the top of the cake is golden brown and a toothpick inserted into the center comes out clean, 45 to 50 minutes. Allow the cake to cool in the pan 10 to 15 minutes before serving.

ON THE PLATE Cut the cake into 12 squares and serve while still warm. Garnish with berries and mint leaves.

IN THE GLASS Pike Place Market Mocha (page 248)

Pepper-Vodka Bloody Mary

{ Makes 1 serving }

I never liked tomato juice until somebody gave me a glass of some with vodka and a pickled asparagus spear in it. What a revelation! Now I often serve Bloody Marys with gin or aquavit, but this pepper-vodka version is my favorite for brunch.

1 cup tomato juice
1¼ ounces pepper vodka
¼ teaspoon peeled and freshly grated horseradish
¼ teaspoon Worcestershire sauce
Dash of Tabasco sauce
Pinch of celery salt
Freshly ground black pepper
1 lemon wedge
1 spear Pickled Asparagus (recipe follows)

Half fill a cocktail shaker with small ice cubes. Add the tomato juice, vodka, horse-radish, Worcestershire, Tabasco, celery, salt, and pepper. Put the top on and shake. Pour into a large glass. Squeeze in the lemon wedge, garnish with the pickled asparagus, and serve.

Pickled Asparagus

During asparagus season we pickle thousands of spears just for pepper-vodka, Bloody Marys. Local Yakima Valley asparagus comes in three different sizes. The field-cut kind contain all three: fatties, medium, and pencil. I love fatties on the grill, mediums for salad or pickling, and pencils for someone who doesn't know better.

½ pound medium-thin asparagus
1 cup Champagne vinegar or other white wine
    vinegar
¼ cup sugar
½ teaspoon kosher salt
¼ teaspoon coriander seeds
¼ teaspoon fennel seeds
¼ teaspoon mustard seeds
¼ teaspoon ground allspice
¼ teaspoon black peppercorns
3 cloves
1 bay leaf

I. Trim the asparagus by snapping off the tough bottoms. Combine the vinegar, sugar, salt, and spices in a small saucepan. Bring to a boil, stirring to dissolve the sugar. Place the asparagus in a small nonreactive dish. Pour the hot pickling liquid over the asparagus.

2. Allow the asparagus to cool, then cover with plastic wrap and refrigerate overnight.

A STEP AHEAD   Pickled asparagus will keep, covered, for up to 2 weeks in the refrigerator.

Outsiders probably know Seattle for coffee, software, and planes, or maybe the goofy Space Needle or awesome Mount Rainier. Oh, and then there's the rain. But *coffee* is a huge part of our culture. Coffee has poured its way through our way of life, and coffee houses have become local institutions. Describing our love for the beverage as a mania is no understatement. You can't walk a half block in Seattle without passing an espresso stand. Inside every kind of store imaginable, including my local hardware store, the muffler shop, the car-wash place, there are *baristas* pulling shots of espresso. No top restaurant can get away with serving drip coffee alone. Seattleites can't go a minute without a sip of java. Everyone on the street seems to be grasping a steaming travel mug or an insulated paper cup. Even the kayaks on sale at REI, the sporting goods store, have a mug holder inside them.

We are serious about our coffee. Starbucks is responsible for raising the bar in Seattle, then across the country, and now throughout the world. These days, however, our town is home to countless independent roasters, and we have become steadfastly loyal to our favorites: Torrefazzione, Lighthouse, Café Vita, Vivace, Café Ladro, the list goes on. There's even a nonprofit coffee house, set up by one of the many young Microsoft millionaires, that donates all its profits to local charities.

Coffee is a perfect solution to the rain. It's gray here a lot of the time, so it's either coffee addiction or trips to the full-spectrum lighting salon. Coffee is warm and soothing going down, not to mention giving you that caffeine buzz that makes you miss the sun a little less. The sound of milk whirling around the steaming wand of the mixer and the scent of coffee brewing are comforts like the aroma of Grandma's strawberry jam or Mom's good ole apple pie in the oven. The espresso stand or coffee shop becomes a third place in your daily routine (to home and work). Seattle is a small town that way. You'll run into a half-dozen friends while standing in line for your double tall skinny mocha or your doppio espresso macchiato. The barista gets to know your favorite drink and starts to make it when you walk in the door, just like a bartender.

Great coffee has to do with the quality of the beans, the way they are roasted, and the way the coffee is brewed. But, like everything, you don't get quality until you have an educated consumer willing to pay for it and seek it out.

Roasting coffee is an art and has everything to do with the flavor in the cup. There are several styles of roasting: light roast, medium roast, and dark roast. A lighter roast can accentuate the acidity and subtle flavor notes of some beans, while a dark roast can bring intense, caramelized, and pungent flavors to the cup. There are so many types of beans from around the world; you just have to taste them to decide what you like best. My own preferences tend toward Indonesian and African coffees, as well as Guatemalan and Costa Rican.

To make great coffee, buy quality beans and grind them just before brewing. Don't let coffee sit around on a burner, which will quickly give it a burned "off" flavor. Put your freshly made coffee in a Thermos to keep it hot; drink your coffee within fifteen minutes of making it. The beautiful aromatics, even in the Thermos, fade with time.

Because of our addiction to great coffee, it's hard for us Seattleites to leave our damp but caffeine-laced paradise. Whenever I travel more than a few miles from home, I bring my own special Sumatran beans, a little mini-grinder, a drip pot, and a Thermos jug. The Seattle coffee kit fits in my suitcase right next to my traveling martini pack, the two essentials for survival.

A COFFEE GLOSSARY

Barista: the soda jerk of the coffee world

Espresso: finely ground dark roast coffee extracted with pressurized hot water

Café latte: Seattle's most popular coffee drink, espresso and steamed milk

Cappuccino: similar to a latte, but with half steamed milk and half foamed milk

Caffe mocha: a combination of espresso, chocolate, and steamed milk

Espresso macchiato: a shot of espresso in a demitasse, "marked" with a bit of foamed milk

Caffe Americano: a shot of espresso with hot water added

Short: an 8-ounce cup

Tall: a 12-ounce cup

Grande: a 16-ounce cup

Single: one shot of espresso

Double: two shots of espresso

Skinny: made with skim milk

PIKE PLACE MARKET MOCHA

The original Starbucks store is just half a block down the street from Etta's in the Pike Place Market. I particularly like the Italian roast in this drink. The strong coffee complements the sweetness of the liqueurs and the Mexican chocolate. Mexican chocolate is sweetened with sugar and flavored with cinnamon. It is used in Mexico to make hot chocolate drinks. It has a grainy texture and is easy to grate.

---

2 teaspoons Frangelico (hazelnut liqueur)
2 teaspoons dark rum
2 teaspoons Tía Maria or other coffee-flavored liqueur
½ cup freshly brewed coffee
2 tablespoons heavy cream
½ teaspoon confectioners' sugar
Mexican chocolate for grating, such as Ibarra

Fill a heatproof glass mug with boiling water, then pour the water out. Pour the Frangelico, rum, and Tía Maria into the warmed mug. Add the hot coffee. In a small bowl, using a whisk, briefly whip the cream with the confectioners' sugar until the cream thickens slightly. Spoon the cream over the top of the coffee. Use a small hand grater to grate the chocolate over the cream. Serve immediately.

Basic Recipes

B ASIC RECIPES ARE the building blocks of a kitchen. Without a good stock, you have a lifeless soup, a thin gravy, a watery consomme. Without careful attention, you have slack and tough pie dough, puff pastry that doesn't puff, and soufflés that are more scrambled than sophisticated. And eventually, without enough care given to the foundations of a recipe, you have a menu that can't stand on its own two feet.

If you cook frequently at home, you can do some "basic prep." Plan ahead a little. When you've committed to making dinner at home, think about setting yourself up for the next time. Make life a little easier. Let's say you'll be hanging around the kitchen because you put a prime rib roast in the oven. This would be a great time to pick up some chicken bones and make a stock on the back burner for another day. Same amount of time, very little extra work, and you've got a freezer full of delicious stock.

Let's say you've committed to an apple pie. Double the recipe for the pie dough and keep the extra in the freezer. The next time you make a lemon-curd tart, you just have to make the lemon curd, and the task won't seem so daunting.

There is an old axiom: "When you throw a party, you should throw two or three so you only have to clean house once." Well, the same goes for cooking. Set yourself up a little, so when the time comes for the big show, you're not a wilted mess for the main event.

Pasta Dough

{ Makes 1 pound }

For years I struggled to find a pasta product, especially a stuffed pasta, that I could use in my restaurants. I was never happy until we started making our own. Now that we have three restaurants, I have the luxury of being able to afford to pay someone full time to make pasta for me. A pasta machine with an electric motor helps when making large quantities of fresh pasta, but what is key is finding a patient, painstaking cook who really loves making pasta.

I don't use semolina flour in fresh pasta dough because it makes the dough sticky and gummy. Regular all-purpose flour gives your pasta a nice, soft quality. I loved the pastas I tasted in Italy that were bright yellow with egg yolks. We buy organic free-range eggs for our pasta dough because you can taste the difference.

If you go to all the trouble of making your own pasta, treat it simply and let the flavors shine through. I usually like to toss ravioli or fresh-cut noodles in a little herb butter and shave some Parmigiano-Reggiano over the top.

I love to show off the ravioli station in our prep kitchen. Day after day, little hand-stuffed flavor nuggets roll off the fingertips of our dedicated pasta prepsters. This recipe requires purchasing a pasta machine (see Equipment, page 258). If you love to make pasta, it's a good investment. Tagliarini are long, thin ribbon noodles, similar to linguine.

2 cups all-purpose flour
½ teaspoon kosher salt
3 large eggs
1 tablespoon olive oil

Making the dough: In a bowl with a wooden spoon or in the bowl of an electric mixer fitted with the paddle attachment, combine the flour and salt. In a bowl, combine the eggs and oil. Add the eggs to the flour and mix until the dough forms a ball. Turn the dough out onto a lightly floured work surface and knead until smooth, about 5 minutes. Wrap the dough in plastic and let rest for half an hour at room temperature.

Rolling the dough: Cut the dough in half. With your hands, press each half into a rectangular piece that will fit through the pasta machine at its widest setting. Roll each piece through the widest setting. Fold each piece into thirds and pass it through the machine again on the widest setting. Repeat this folding and passing two more times. Now pass the pieces through the machine, reducing the setting each time. As necessary, cut the pieces into more manageable lengths (see Pasta Tips, page 252). Proceed with either cutting the pasta or forming ravioli.

Cutting the pasta: Using your pasta machine, roll the pasta sheets to the thinness you want, usually two notches wider than the thinnest setting. Roll the pasta through the desired setting twice, to prevent the dough from shrinking back up and thickening. Cut each of the sheets to the length you like for noodles. Then roll it through your pasta machine's cutter attachment for tagliarini or linguine.

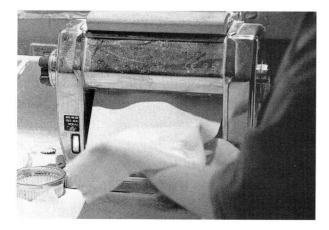

Roll out your sheets of pasta dough using a pasta machine. It's important to support each sheet as it passes through the rollers, but don't pull on the dough or stretch it.

Place mounds of filling on the bottom half of the sheet of pasta dough.

After lightly brushing the pasta dough with water, fold the top half of the sheet of dough over the filling.

Seal the ravioli by pressing the pasta together with your fingertips, pushing out all the air.

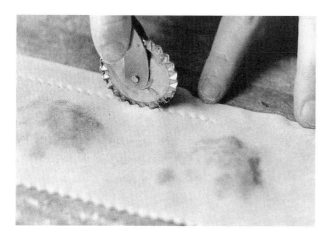

Using a wheel-shaped pastry cutter, trim away the top edge and the bottom of the strip of filled dough. Then cut between the mounds of dough to form square-shaped ravioli.

Place the pasta on a baking sheet lined with parchment or wax paper and sprinkled with flour or on a dry pasta rack.

Forming ravioli: Roll the pasta sheets to the thinness you want, usually one notch from the thinnest setting. Roll the pasta through the desired setting twice, to prevent the dough from shrinking back up and thickening. Have handy a small dish of water with a pastry brush or a spray bottle filled with water. Place mounds of filling on the bottom half of a sheet of pasta and fold the top half over them. The mounds should be about 1 teaspoon each, about 2 inches apart, and about ¾ inch in from the bottom edge. Lightly brush or spray the top edge with water and fold it down over the balls of filling. Lightly press each ball of filling flat with the palm of your hand. Seal the ravioli by pressing the pasta together with your fingertips, pushing out all the air. Using a wheel-shaped pastry cutter, trim away a strip from the top edge and the bottom edge of the length of filled dough, then cut between the mounds of dough to form square-shaped ravioli. Place the ravioli on a baking sheet lined with parchment or wax paper and sprinkled with flour.

Cooking dried pasta: To properly cook dried pasta, bring a large pot of heavily salted water to a rolling boil. After adding the pasta, stir to prevent sticking until the water returns to a boil. Taste the pasta to test for doneness; don't rely on time alone. Consider the time given on a package merely a guideline. Bite into a piece of pasta to make sure that it is cooked through and that the white center is gone.

Cooking fresh pasta: Fresh pasta cooks faster than dried pasta. Still, it is important to taste the pasta to be sure it is cooked through. Fresh pasta actually changes color from yellow to white when it is ready. Cut noodles take about 2 minutes. Ravioli takes a bit longer because the edges are a double thickness of pasta. Test a piece of ravioli for tenderness by feeling the edge.

A STEP AHEAD   Fresh pasta is best used the same day. If not using immediately, store for a few hours in the refrigerator.

PASTA TIPS

- You want to gently support the dough as it goes through the rollers, but don't pull it through. Pulling stretches the dough and toughens your pasta.
- You need a lot of space to make pasta because the dough pieces grow longer and longer as they go through the thinner settings. At some point in the process, it will be necessary to cut the pieces down into a more manageable size.
- Different pasta machines have different numbers representing the thickness settings. The pasta for noodles like tagliarini is rolled slightly thicker than the pasta for ravioli.
- Use flour as necessary on your work surface and on the pasta dough to prevent sticking, but remember that too much flour toughens your pasta.

CHICKEN STOCK

{ Makes 1 gallon }

Homemade chicken stock will give your cooking a depth of flavor that you can't get from canned stock or broth. If you must use canned broth, buy the low-sodium version. Regular canned chicken broth is usually too salty.

To get a nice clear stock, always start with cold water. Never let stock boil hard; it should just simmer. The easiest way to skim the fat from a stock is to chill it overnight. All the fat will rise to the top in a solid layer that you can lift off with a spoon.

Be sure you allow hot stock to cool completely before you cover it. You can chill a container of stock more quickly by placing it in a larger bowl of ice water. Stir occasionally until it is cool, then cover and refrigerate.

I like to roast the bones and vegetables for more flavor, but if you'd like to make your stock more quickly, skip this step and simply combine the bones and vegetables with the water in a large pot.

Some people save chicken bones in their freezer or some butchers may give you bones. Otherwise, you can buy packages of chicken wings or chicken backs at the supermarket.

Stock freezes well, so if you need a project for a rainy day, this is a good one. I store stock in conveniently sized, sealable freezer bags. Even if you only need a few cups of chicken stock for a recipe, make this whole recipe and freeze the rest for another use.

4 pounds chicken bones (or wings, backs, and necks)
2 onions, roughly chopped
2 carrots, roughly chopped
2 ribs celery, roughly chopped
1 tablespoon olive oil
6 quarts cold water
½ bunch flat-leaf parsley
2 bay leaves
1 teaspoon black peppercorns

Preheat the oven to 450°F. Roast the chicken bones on a baking sheet until browned, about an hour. In a bowl, toss the onions, carrots, and celery with the oil. Spread the vegetables on another baking sheet and roast until browned, about 40 minutes. In a large pot over high heat, combine the roasted bones and vegetables, cold water, parsley, bay leaves, and peppercorns. Bring to a boil, then reduce the heat to a gentle simmer. Let the stock simmer for 2 hours, skimming occasionally to remove any foam from the surface. Strain the stock into a large bowl and discard the solids. Let the stock sit for 5 to 10 minutes so the fat floats to the surface, then skim off the fat or refrigerate the stock overnight and remove the fat the next day.

A STEP AHEAD   Chicken stock can be stored, covered, in the refrigerator for a few days, or for several weeks in the freezer. Bring to a boil before using.

DUCK-ENRICHED CHICKEN STOCK

{ Makes about 1 quart }

Use this enriched chicken stock to make Roast Duck with Huckleberry Sauce (page 145). The flavor of the red wine is an important element, so pick a wine that you like. I generally use the same wine I plan to drink with the duck.

Hearts, gizzards, and wing tips from 2 ducks
1 tablespoon olive oil
2 carrots, roughly chopped
2 ribs celery, roughly chopped
1 large onion, quartered
1 leek, greens trimmed away, split in half, rinsed
  well, and roughly chopped
2 shallots, quartered
1 head garlic, unpeeled and cut in half crosswise
2 cups dry red wine
6 cups chicken stock (page 253)
½ teaspoon black peppercorns
1 bay leaf

In a large, heavy-bottomed saucepan, brown the duck parts over high heat, about 10 minutes. Add the olive oil, carrots, celery, onion, leek, shallots, and garlic and brown, about 10 more minutes. Add the wine. Boil for a few minutes, scraping the bottom of the pan to dissolve any caramelized bits. Add the stock, peppercorns, and bay leaf and simmer for about an hour, adding more water or stock if necessary to keep the vegetables and duck parts covered. Don't let the stock boil vigorously, or it will become cloudy and greasy. Strain the stock though a fine-mesh strainer. Let it sit for 5 to 10 minutes, so the fat floats to the top, and then skim off the fat or refrigerate overnight and skim the next day.

A STEP AHEAD   This stock can be made a few days ahead and stored, covered, in the refrigerator, or can be frozen for several weeks. Bring to a boil before using.

CRÈME FRAÎCHE

Use crème fraîche as you would use sour cream or heavy cream. Spoon sweetened crème fraîche over a bowl of fresh berries. Or stir chopped fresh dill, grated lemon zest, and ground black pepper into crème fraîche and serve it with smoked salmon or smoked trout. This recipe easily doubles or triples.

1 cup heavy cream
2 tablespoons buttermilk

Combine the heavy cream and buttermilk. Place in a container, cover, and leave out at room temperature for 2 to 3 days until thickened.

A STEP AHEAD   Crème fraîche will keep, covered, in the refrigerator for a few weeks.

✳

DRIED BREAD CRUMBS

{ A half loaf of European-style white bread, 12 ounces or about 8 slices, yields 2½ cups bread crumbs }

1. Preheat the oven to 325°F. We use European-style white bread to make our bread crumbs. We don't remove the crusts, since we sieve the crumbs if we need them to be fine. Slice the bread (½-inch-thick slices). Place them in a single layer on an ungreased baking sheet. Put the baking sheet in the oven and bake until the bread feels dried out in the center, about 40 minutes. Turn the bread over from time to time so it dries out evenly. Remove the bread from the oven and allow to cool. Tear the bread into pieces and place in a food processor.

2. To make coarse bread crumbs, pulse until the bread is in coarse crumbs.

3. To make fine bread crumbs, continue pulsing until the crumbs are very fine. Then sieve the crumbs to remove any large pieces.

A STEP AHEAD   Dried bread crumbs will keep a couple of weeks in a closed jar.

PASTRY DOUGH

{ Makes 8 pastry squares for Apple Dumplings }

Making pastry dough in the food processor is fast and easy. Since you don't handle the dough much with your hands, it doesn't heat up and the pastry will be light and flaky. I turn the dough out onto a sheet of plastic wrap so I can use the plastic to gather it up instead of my hands. If you want to make more than one batch of this dough, don't double the recipe. Instead, make a series of batches, one at a time, in the food processor. You don't need to wash out the bowl between batches.

To ensure that the pastry is flaky, the butter needs to be very cold. A good trick is to cut the butter into small pieces, then put it in the freezer for about 10 minutes before making the dough. The amount of water you need varies with the humidity in the air, the moisture in the flour, etc., so add the water carefully, using only as much as you need to.

Some more tips for working with pastry dough: Keep the dough chilled and handle it as little as possible. When you're rolling the dough, use enough flour to keep things from sticking, but no more. I always lightly flour my work surface, rolling pin, and my hands. When I'm rolling the dough, I lift the dough occasionally to make sure it is not sticking, adding more flour if needed.

Place the flour, sugar, and salt in a food processor. Pulse to mix. Add the cold butter all at once and pulse a few times until the butter and flour form crumbs. Start adding the ice water, I tablespoon at a time, pulsing each time. Use as much ice water as needed for the dough to hold together when a clump is gently pressed between your fingers. The dough will not form a ball in the processor; it will be quite loose. Dump the dough out onto a large piece of plastic wrap. Use the plastic wrap to gather the dough together and force it into a flattened round. Chill the plastic-wrapped dough about an hour or longer before rolling it out.

A STEP AHEAD You can make the pastry dough ahead and keep it wrapped and refrigerated for a day or two, or the dough can be kept frozen for a few weeks.

2½ cups all-purpose flour
1 tablespoon sugar
1 teaspoon kosher salt
1 cup (2 sticks) cold unsalted butter, cut into pieces
6 to 8 tablespoons ice water, as needed

ROUGH PUFF PASTRY

{ Makes 6 squares for Pear Tarts }

Rough puff pastry is a quick or simplified version of classic puff pastry. It needs to be made, shaped, and baked carefully to get the maximum puff. You don't want to incorporate too much flour into the finished dough or it will be tough. So, as you roll, use enough flour to keep the dough from sticking to the work surface, but before you finish folding and rolling the dough, use a clean, dry pastry brush to brush off any excess flour.

1 cup plus 6 tablespoons (2¾ sticks) cold unsalted butter, cut into ½-inch dice

2 cups all-purpose flour

1 teaspoon kosher salt

½ cup plus 2 tablespoons ice water, plus up to 1 tablespoon more if necessary

I. Place the diced butter in the freezer for 10 minutes before making the dough. Put the flour and the salt in a food processor. Pulse a few times to mix in the salt. Add about one third of the very cold diced butter. Pulse until the butter is in small crumbs. Add the remaining cold diced butter. Pulse 3 or 4 times to distribute the butter. There should still be visible clumps of butter. Add the ice water. Pulse until the dough just starts to clump. If the mixture is very dry, add more water, 1 teaspoon at a time, and pulse again. Do not overprocess. The dough will look a bit lumpy and uneven with butter, but it will smooth out during the rolling and folding process.

2. Turn the dough onto a lightly floured work surface and shape into a rough rectangle. You can use a board scraper to keep the edges more or less square. At this point, the dough will be crumbly and fragile, but don't worry, it will come together as you work with it. Lightly flour the surface of the rectangle, press the dough with a lightly floured rolling pin to flatten it, then roll back and forth several times to make a 12 × 18-inch rectangle of dough.

3. With a long side of the dough facing you, fold the top third of the dough down and the bottom third of the dough up to make a 4 × 18-inch rectangle. Then use your hands to roll the dough up from one short end, like a jelly roll. Next, use the rolling pin to roll this "jelly roll" out into a 4 × 18-inch rectangle. Once again, use your hands to roll the dough up from one short end, like a jelly roll. Wrap the dough in plastic wrap and refrigerate for 1 hour until firm.

A STEP AHEAD Refrigerate the dough for up to a day. It can be stored in the freezer, well wrapped in plastic, for a few weeks.

Equipment

ALL YOU REALLY need in your kitchen is one sharp knife and a good heavy pan, but there's plenty of kitchen equipment out there to make things more fun, from a $2 swivel vegetable peeler to a $500 ice cream machine. I'm a bit of a sucker for gadgets. I love to watch the hucksters pitching their products at the Puyallup Fair and I often end up buying something, like a V-slicer with all the attachments. My favorite piece of equipment is a heavy-duty sausage stuffer—though you have to make a monster batch of sausage to really need it.

Simple, well-made tools are the best. Every December I stop by a restaurant supply store and stock up on restaurant-quality tongs, spatulas, whisks, and slotted spoons. I've discovered that they make the most appreciated Christmas gifts for friends. Don't forget to check out the kitchenware departments of Japanese or other Asian food stores that are in your town. You can pick up a variety of slicers that are fun to use, including spiral slicers that produce beautiful long threads of carrots or beets for garnishes, as well as woks, cleavers, and rice cookers.

Board scraper: From appetizer to dessert, this simple tool is useful.

Burr mixer: This small, hand-held food processor is great for pureeing soups and sauces right in the pan.

Electric deep-fat fryer: Probably the least necessary kitchen tool that I have. Instead, I keep one deep, heavy, straight-sided pot specifically for frying.

Electric mixer: Even after all these years, there is still none better than the KitchenAid. In addition to mixing bat- ters, whipping egg whites, and whipping cream, it's a great machine for making bread dough, and the paddle is handy for mixing things like sausage forcemeat and mashed potatoes.

Grills: Only charcoal grills need apply to be in my backyard. I prefer a kettle-style grill with:

- dampers, top and bottom
- thermometer attached
- baskets for charcoal for easy indirect cooking
- grills with an opening for access to charcoal
- rotisserie attachment
- place for the lid to hang so it's not always in the way

For a home smoker, I like a fisherman's-style smoker such as Little Chief.

Ice cream machine: There are several kinds of ice cream machines available to the home cook. The old-fashioned kind has a churn mechanism and uses ice and salt for cooling. Some ice cream machines have a self-enclosed freezer. These are by far the most expensive, but they turn out a great product and they're a pleasure to use. There are also well-priced ice cream makers that operate by putting the machine's canister in the freezer overnight or longer before churning the ice cream. Ice cream machines are available in kitchenware stores and by mail order (see Sources, page 260).

Instant-read meat thermometer: I prefer an instant-read meat thermometer to check the internal temperature of meats or poultry. Don't keep this kind of thermometer in the meat while it is cooking. Insert the metal stem into the meat and you'll get an immediate reading, either on a dial or a digital display.

Pasta machine: If you like to make pasta, an Italian hand-cranked pasta machine (such as Atlas) is a good investment. It's not too expensive (about $40) and will probably last forever. Dust excess flour off the machine with a dry rag or a dry pastry brush. Don't use water on your machine or you will gum up the works.

Propane torch: Restaurant cooks often use a small hand-held propane torch to do last-minute browning and caramelizing of various dishes. It's perfect for crème brûlée, baked Alaska, and sugar work. These torches are fairly inexpensive and available at many hardware stores. They're becoming more popular at home and have been showing up in kitchenware stores and catalogs such as Williams-Sonoma or Sur La Table.

Rice cookers: I love these! They cook rice perfectly and hold it warm for quite a while. See if you can find one with a nonstick bowl for easy cleanup.

FAVORITE HAND TOOLS AND PANS

Tongs: Professional cooking tongs are a gift from the chef gods. They are about the only gift that I've given my mother, a notorious cookware packrat, that actually made her throw away her old ones.

Measuring spoons and cups: The new solid stainless steel ones are great and worth the extra expense.

Flexible nonstick baking sheet (such as Silpat): If you do a lot of baking, you may want to invest in one of these. Though pricey (about $25), one of these sheets will replace the need for buying parchment paper and can be used over and over again. Available by mail order from Williams-Sonoma or Sur La Table.

Cleaver: Chinese hardware stores have a good selection of cleavers or they can be ordered (see Sources, page 260). I like a heavy cleaver for smashing and cleaving poultry and meat and the thinner slicer-cleaver for slicing vegetables and fruits.

Nonstick pans: These are especially good frying pans. Get the chef's style that has a metal handle with a removable rubber sheath. This style of pan can go into the oven and is very handy. Get at least three sizes of nonstick pans: 7-inch, 10-inch, and 12-inch.

Woks: Get a big one for stir-frying. If you have an electric stove, you are better off using a flat-bottomed frying pan rather than a wok.

Sources

UWAJIMAYA MARKET
519 6th Avenue
Seattle, WA 98104
(206) 624-6248
www.uwajimaya.com

> Asian ingredients of all kinds, especially Japanese, such as nori, rices, noodles, wasabi, etc.

SOSIO'S FRUIT AND PRODUCE
1527 Pike Place
Seattle, WA 98101
(206) 622-1370

> Local mushrooms and peppers

WALLA WALLA GARDENER'S ASSOCIATION
210 N. 11th Street
Walla Walla, WA 99362
(800) 553-5014

> Walla Walla sweet onions

ANTIQUE APPLE ORCHARD
28095 Santiam Highway
Sweet Home, OR 97386
(541) 367-4840

> Organic and hard-to-find apples, 150 varieties, tree ripened; they do not ship, but are worth the visit

OAKRIDGE ORGANIC ORCHARDS
367 Oakridge Road
White Salmon, WA 98672
(509) 493-3891

> Organic apples and pears

KRUEGER FAMILY PEPPERS AND PRODUCE
462 Knight Lane
Wapato, WA 98951
(509) 877-3677

> U-Pick pepper farm

EL MERCADO LATINO
1514 Pike Place
Seattle, WA 98101
(206) 623-3240

> Dried chiles and other South and Central American products

CHUKAR CHERRY COMPANY
P.O. Box 510, 320 Wine Country Road
Prosser, WA 99350
(800) 624-9544
chukar@chukar.com

> Dried cherries

HOLMQUIST HAZELNUT ORCHARD
9821 Holmquist Road
Lynden, WA 98264
(360) 988-9240

> Hazelnuts

WORLD MERCHANTS—SPICE, HERB, & TEA HOUSE
1509 Western Avenue
Seattle, WA 98101
(206) 682-7274
www.worldspice.com

> Spices of all kinds

TO ORDER RUB WITH LOVE:
www.tomdouglas.com

> Tom Douglas's spice rubs for meat, poultry, and fish

HOPPIN' JOHN'S
(800) 828-4412
www.hoppinjohns.com

> Stone-ground slow-cooking grits

DEER MOUNTAIN JAM
P.O. Box 257
Granite Falls, WA 98252
(360) 691-7586

Raspberry, blackberry, strawberry, gooseberry, and other jams

Deer Mountain Jam does not do mail order from their own phone number. Their jams are available by mail order through: Made in Washington (888) 838-1517

MUTUAL FISH
2335 Rainier Avenue South
Seattle, WA 98144
(206) 322-4368

Smoked salmon, local oysters and mussels, kasu marinade, tobiko, ocean salad

BAVARIAN MEAT PRODUCTS
1920 Pike Place
Seattle, WA 98101
(206) 441-0942

Bacon, ham hocks, and other smoked meats

JON ROWLEY
3916 15th Place West
Seattle, WA 98119
(206) 283-7566
rowley@nwlink.com

For composting information

QUILLISASCUT CHEESE
(509) 738-2011
Artisan goat and cow cheeses

VELLA CHEESE COMPANY OF CALIFORNIA
315 Second Street East
P.O. Box 191
Sonoma, CA
(800) 848-0505

Vella Dry Jack

ROGUE RIVER VALLEY CREAMERY
311 North Front Street
P.O. Box 3606
Central Point, OR 97502
(541) 664-2233

Oregon blue cheese

WSU CREAMERY
101 Food Quality Building
P.O. Box 641122
Pullman, WA 99161-1122
(800) 457-5442

Cougar Gold cheese

REDHOOK ALE BREWERY
14300 N.E. 145th Street
Woodinville, WA 98072
(425) 483-3232
www.redhook.com

For information on finding Redhook in your area

PIKE AND WESTERN WINE SHOP
1934 Pike Place
Seattle, WA 98101
(206) 441-1307

Northwest wines

CHINOOK WINERY
(509) 786-2725

WASHINGTON WINE COMMISSION
(206) 667-9463
www.washingtonwine.org

Winery tour information

CLEAR CREEK DISTILLERY
1430 NW 23rd Avenue
Portland, OR 97210
(503) 248-9470
www.clearcreekdistillery.com

Fruit-based brandies and grappas

STARBUCKS COFFEE COMPANY
2401 Utah Avenue South
Seattle, WA 98134-1431
800-starbuc
www.starbucks.com

SCHARFFEN-BERGER CHOCOLATE MAKER
(800) 930-4528
www.scharffen-berger.com

For Scharffen-Berger chocolate

VALRHONA
(310) 277-0401

For Valrhona chocolate

FRAN'S CHOCOLATES (Seattle's Queen of
Chocolate)
1300 East Pike
Seattle, WA 98122
(800) 422-FRAN
www.franschocolates.com

SUR LA TABLE
84 Pine Street
Seattle, WA 98101
(800) 243-0852
Catalog available

Kitchen equipment such as: pudding molds;
pastry bags; flexible nonstick baking sheets;
ice cream machines; thermometers; pasta
machines; quality pots, pans, and knives. Also
Asian-inspired plates, bowls, ramekins,
chopsticks, and serving dishes for bento.

WILLIAMS-SONOMA
(800) 541-2233
www.williams-sonoma.com
Catalog available

Kitchen equipment such as: pudding
molds; pastry bags; ice cream machines;
thermometers; quality pots, pans, and
knives; propane torches; and pasta
machines; and food such as: quality
chocolates; sometimes cheese such as Vella
Dry Jack, especially around Christmas

Index